In Memory of Bernie —
an exceptional, fascinating, brilliant
man whom I wish I'd known.
His kids turned out great, though...

Love,
Victoria 2017

# The Vanishing Stepwells of India

Victoria Lautman

The Vanishing Stepwells of India

Foreword by Divay Gupta, INTACH

MERRELL
LONDON · NEW YORK

For my son, Finnian

First published 2017 by
Merrell Publishers, London and New York

Merrell Publishers Limited
70 Cowcross Street
London EC1M 6EJ

merrellpublishers.com

Text copyright © 2017 Victoria Lautman
Foreword copyright © 2017 Divay Gupta
Illustrations copyright © 2017 Victoria Lautman, with the exception of pp. 18, 21, 22 bottom (see right)
Design and layout copyright © 2017 Merrell Publishers Limited

All rights reserved. No part of this publication may be reproduced, stored in a retrieval system or transmitted, in any form or by any means, electronic, mechanical, photocopying, recording or otherwise, without the prior written permission of the publisher.

British Library Cataloguing in Publication Data.
A catalogue record for this book is available from the British Library.

ISBN 978-1-8589-4658-0

Produced by Merrell Publishers Limited
Designed by Nicola Bailey
Project-managed by Claire Chandler
Proofread by Rosanna Fairhead
Indexed by Hilary Bird

Printed and bound in China

ILLUSTRATION CREDITS
Page 18: Stepwell diagram from *Stepwells of Ahmedabad: A Conversation on Water and Heritage*, exhibition by Anthill Design, Ahmedabad, 2016; drawn by Aashini Sheth, Priyanka Sheth, Rony Payuva, Juneza Niyazi and Purva Bhende.
Page 21: Photographs of Toorji ka Jhalra, Jodhpur, by K. Noor-Priya, in support of JDH Urban Regeneration Project.
Page 22 bottom: Photograph of Charles Correa stairway by Shashank Tarphe, Inter-University Centre for Astronomy and Astrophysics.
Photograph of Victoria Lautman on inside jacket: David Salkin.

Jacket, front: Mahila Baag Jhalra; see pp. 194–97.
Jacket, back: Batris Kotha Vav; see pp. 58–59.
Page 2: Maa Jee Shah ki Bawari, Lavera, Rajasthan, *c.* 17th century.
Page 6: Rani ki Vav; see pp. 52–55.
Page 8: Rudabai Vav; see pp. 103–105.
Pages 10–11: Sai Nath ji ki Baoli, Jodhpur, Rajasthan, *c.* 16th century.
Pages 24–25: Panna Meena ka Kund; see pp. 114–17.
Pages 216–17: Mata Bhavani ni Vav; see pp. 48–49.
Page 219: Women create *rangoli* to mark the festival of Mahashivratri at Harbola ki Baori; see pp. 126–27.
Page 220: Sai Nath ji ki Baoli, Jodhpur, Rajasthan, *c.* 16th century.
Page 224: Mahila Baag Jhalra; see pp. 194–97.

CONTENTS

7   Foreword by Divay Gupta, INTACH
9   Preface
13 Introduction

25 The Vanishing Stepwells of India

218 Bibliography
221 Acknowledgements
222 Index

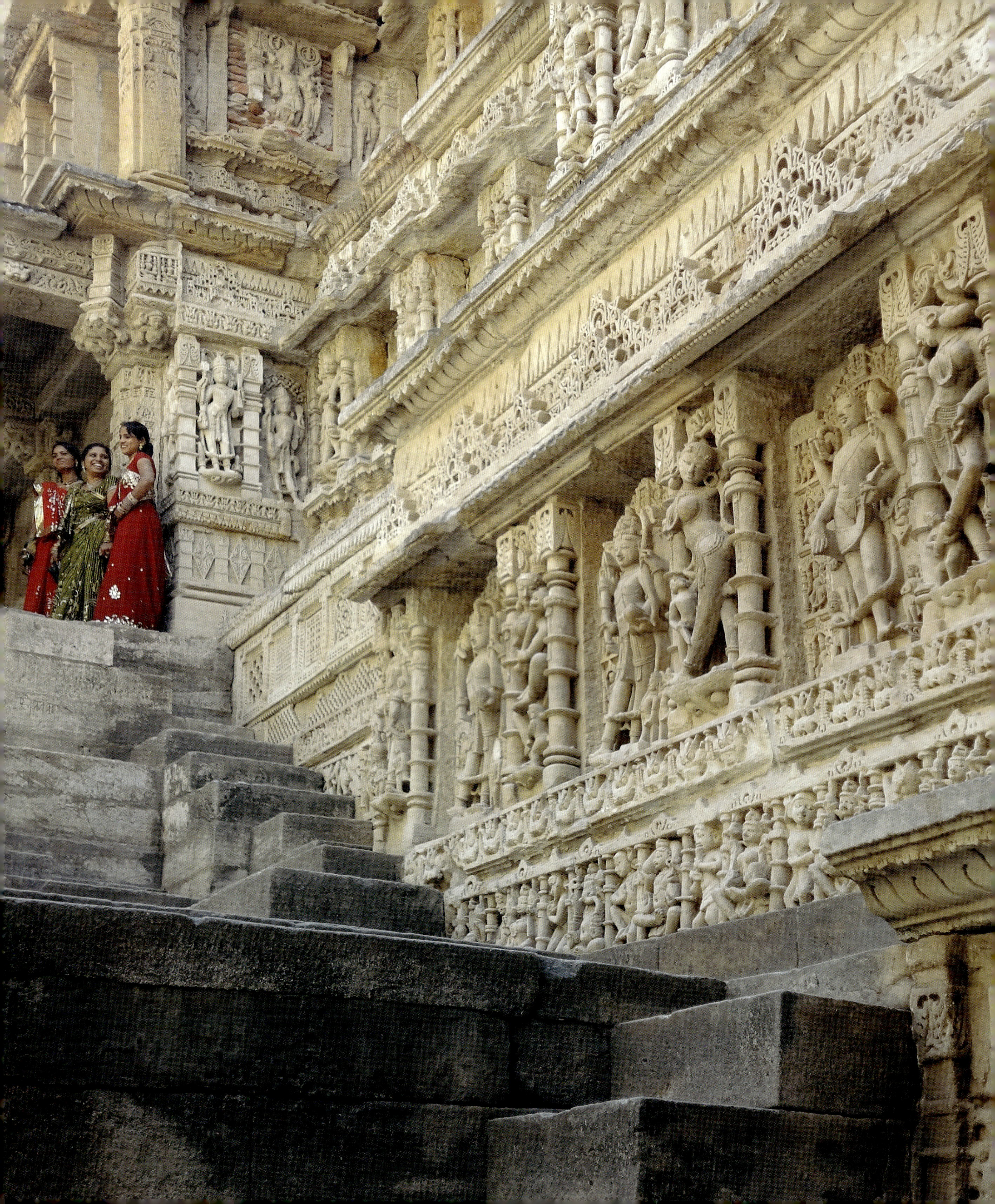

FOREWORD

In India, water has always played an integral part in architecture and city planning. The subcontinent has a long tradition of buildings connected with water: for example, the Harappan civilization's Great Bath of Mohenjo Daro, the seashore temples of Tamil Nadu, the lake palaces of Rajputana, and such riverfront cities as Varanasi and Delhi. The connection between architecture and water is generally regarded as a connection between the secular and the sacred, between earth and heaven. Among the finest examples of such architecture are stepwells. Baolis, vavs or bawadis, as they are called in various parts of the country, are a building typology unique to the Indian subcontinent. They are testimony to the traditional water-harvesting systems developed in ancient times, and to the engineering and construction skills and the craftsmanship of those who built them.

Stepwells were no less magnificent in their conception, architecture and ornamentation than the temples and palaces of their times. They were sacred sites and places of worship, but secular in their function; they also fulfilled various civic and socio-economic needs of local communities. The inscriptions we find on them suggest that they were built by generous patrons for the benefit of the community – and perhaps with a view to showing off their wealth, too. While temples may soar high in the sky to declare their glory and grandeur, stepwells were dug deep into the ground. At ground level, they may be almost invisible. They can be fully appreciated only by descending into their depths.

Stepwells come in a variety of sizes and styles, and the level of ornamentation varies from well to well. The first engineered stepwells, built in about 600 CE in Gujarat, were of Hindu origin. Hindu stepwells reached their zenith between the eleventh and thirteenth centuries, but the construction of wells continued under Islamic patronage between the fifteenth and eighteenth centuries. The tradition persisted until the twentieth century, but today, with technological advances and modern plumbing, stepwells have lost their original significance as both sources of water and social spaces. Unfortunately, the communities that once made use of and celebrated the water in stepwells sometimes abuse these structures by treating them as rubbish dumps, throwing waste into the water they no longer drink. Even the flowers and fruits offered to gods enshrined within wells are sometimes dumped into the water, which for centuries had been considered sacred. Now, with rapidly receding water tables, the wells are drying up, which makes them prey to land grabs and encroachment. Their disappearance is being hastened by a general disregard for their plight.

Although they were built primarily in northern, western and central India, stepwells also existed in the southern Indian states of Andhra Pradesh, Telangana and Karnataka. Rani ki Vav in Patan, Gujarat, is now a UNESCO World Heritage Site, but there are many more stepwells across the country that lie abandoned, awaiting designation as sites of historical significance; being cared for by their communities is of utmost importance before they disappear. Many such stepwells are featured in this beautiful publication.

India's temple architecture is well documented and much studied. In contrast, stepwells have never received the attention they deserve. They are rarely mentioned in any history of architecture, nor are they included in any school curriculum. Along with other recent efforts to document and restore these structures, this book is a vital, timely step in the right direction, helping to raise awareness of stepwells. I sincerely hope that the book will stimulate interest in these architectural gems and lead to increased protection and conservation. The survival of stepwells will be assured only when we recognize their place in Indian history.

Divay Gupta
*Principal Director, Architectural Heritage Division,
Indian National Trust for Art and Cultural Heritage
(INTACH), New Delhi*

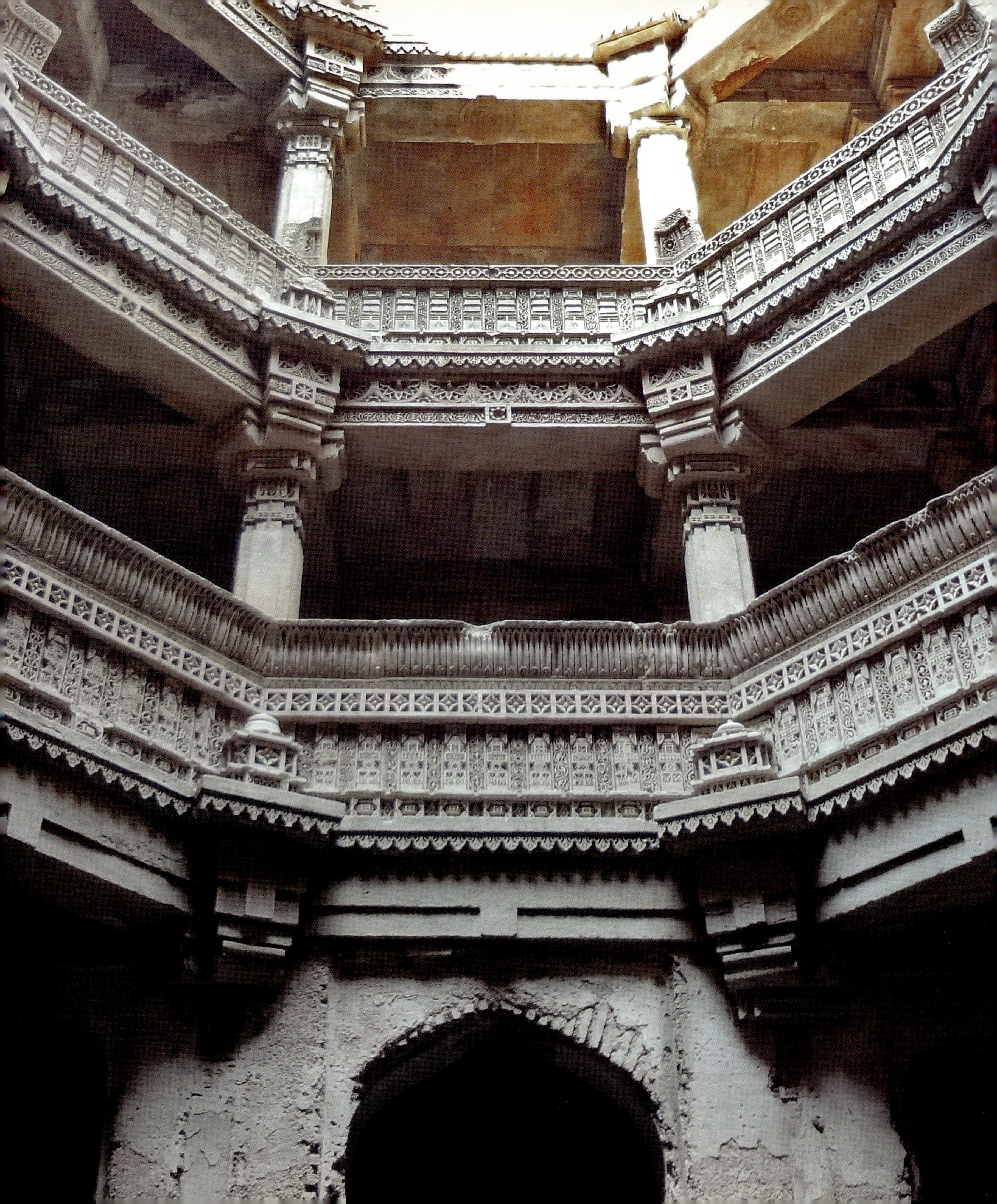

PREFACE

We do not choose our obsessions; they choose us, and I could never have predicted that stepwells would commandeer such a large slice of my life. All it took was one look over a modest stone wall on my first trip to India more than thirty years ago, and the ground disappeared. In its place was a man-made canyon with a complex parade of steps, columns and platforms leading into the earth to an unfathomable depth. It was utterly disorientating. I had no idea what I was seeing, but it subverted the experience of architecture as something we look *up* at, not *down* into. It was exciting and transgressive, and ultimately catapulted me into an unplanned trajectory across India in search of the most fascinating and mysterious structures I have ever seen but had never heard of.

Every form of architecture has an immediate, physical impact as we move through it, but descending into the earth is a particularly powerful, even profound experience. At that first stepwell, Rudabai Vav in Gujarat (pp. 103-105), the extreme contrasts that exist in so many stepwells heightened my senses the further I descended. Sweltering heat turned to an enveloping cool, and the din above ground became hushed. The glaring sunlight dimmed with each step, but where those steps led was not discernible. Views telescoped into indefinite space, constantly shifting, and I could tell neither the depth nor the length of the structure. Towers of ornately sculpted columns loomed over me, sunlight filtered in, a pool of water appeared, and it all seemed like an enchanted alternative reality. And that is exactly how a stepwell would have been experienced a thousand years ago.

By now I have visited more than two hundred of these incomparable subterranean structures – many breathtaking, many heartbreaking, most often both. But these are just a small fraction of the existing wells. There are hundreds more throughout India, many others I could have included here, and it is to be hoped that the groundswell of stepwell hunters will eventually become a deluge. It can be a challenging pursuit, not ideal for anyone with a phobia of heights, confined spaces, bats, bees, snakes, mongooses or just general filth. It is easy to fall and injure yourself, or to wonder how the twists and turns in your life brought you to the bottom of an ancient, decrepit and remote Indian pit.

I am neither a professional photographer nor an academic, just a curious journalist following a passion and snapping pictures along the way – that is the easy part. The hard work was done by the sources I synthesized, especially the indispensable research of the genuine scholars Jutta Jain-Neubauer, Julia Hegewald and Morna Livingston. No serious stepwell enthusiast can survive without their books, and I owe them each a great deal. But as you will discover in the entries here, basic, reliable information, such as dates, names and even spellings, is hard to pin down, or may be contradictory or simply non-existent. Consequently, my decisions have been fluid – a combination of cross referencing, triangulation, intuition and then hoping for the best. The entries are arranged in chronological order, as far as possible (for lack of a more rational system), and I have had valuable input from restoration architects, tourism websites, local historians, conservators, neighbourhood residents, structural engineers, water-management specialists, architectural historians, tea-sellers and, in one important case, a knowledgeable cowherd. My motivation was not just to produce a book that is beautiful, readable and informative, but also to raise awareness about something that desperately deserves attention. This is a framework, not a treatise.

The GPS coordinates (occasionally approximate) are included in each entry because they would have saved a lot of time and anguish if they had been available to me, and they will be useful to anyone who wants to see as many stepwells as possible. That is the only way these architectural wonders will survive.

Happy hunting,

Victoria Lautman
August 2016

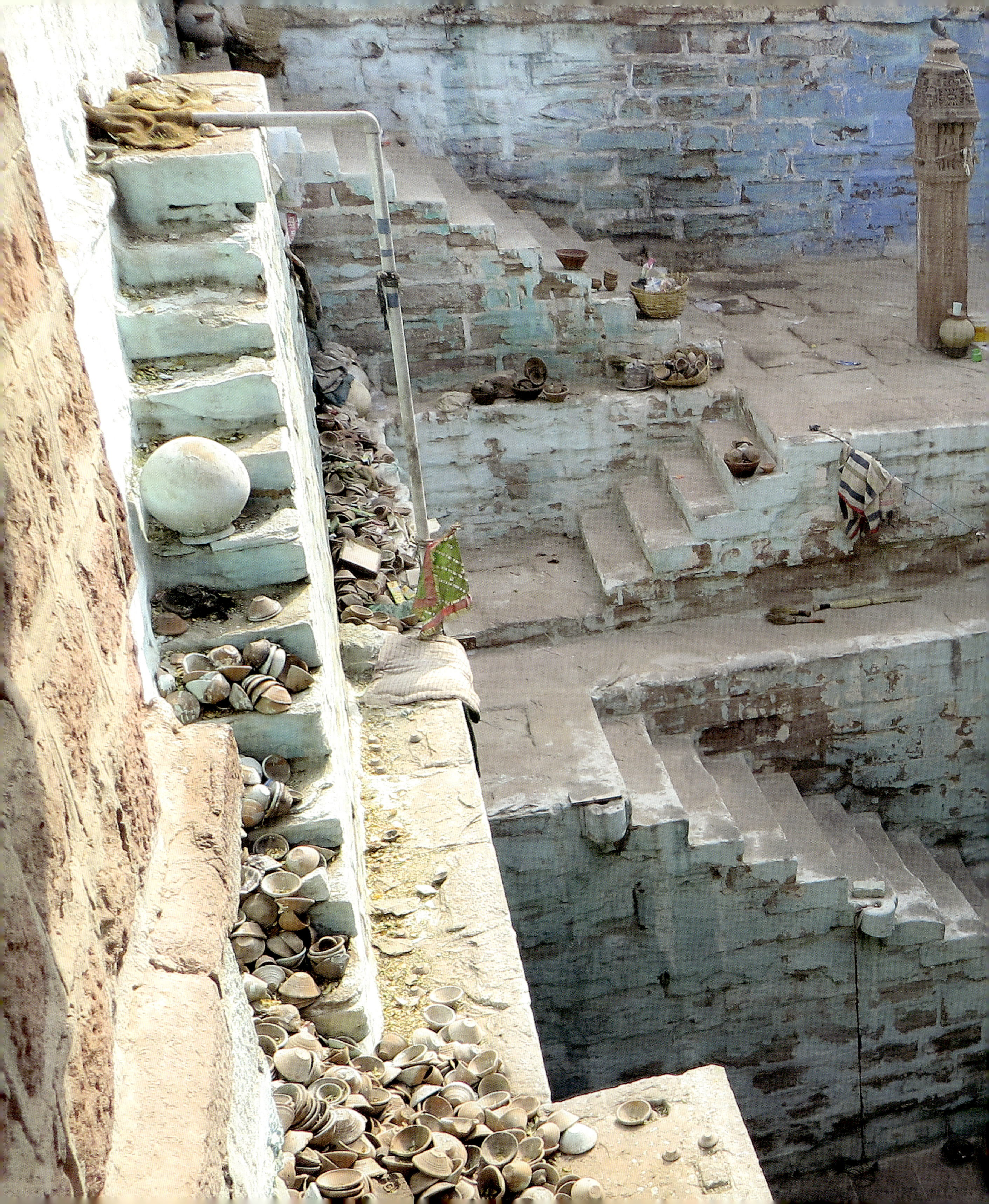

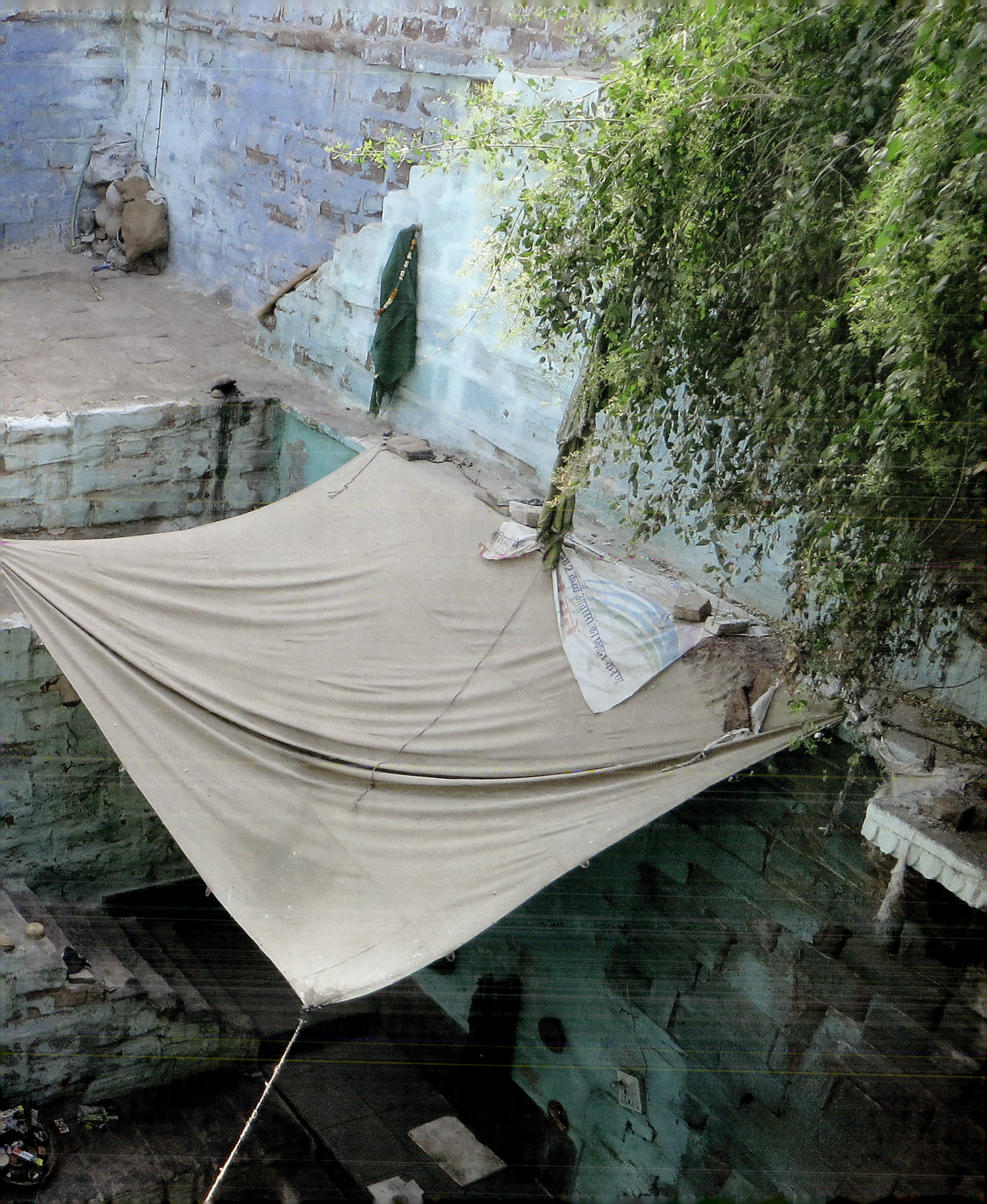

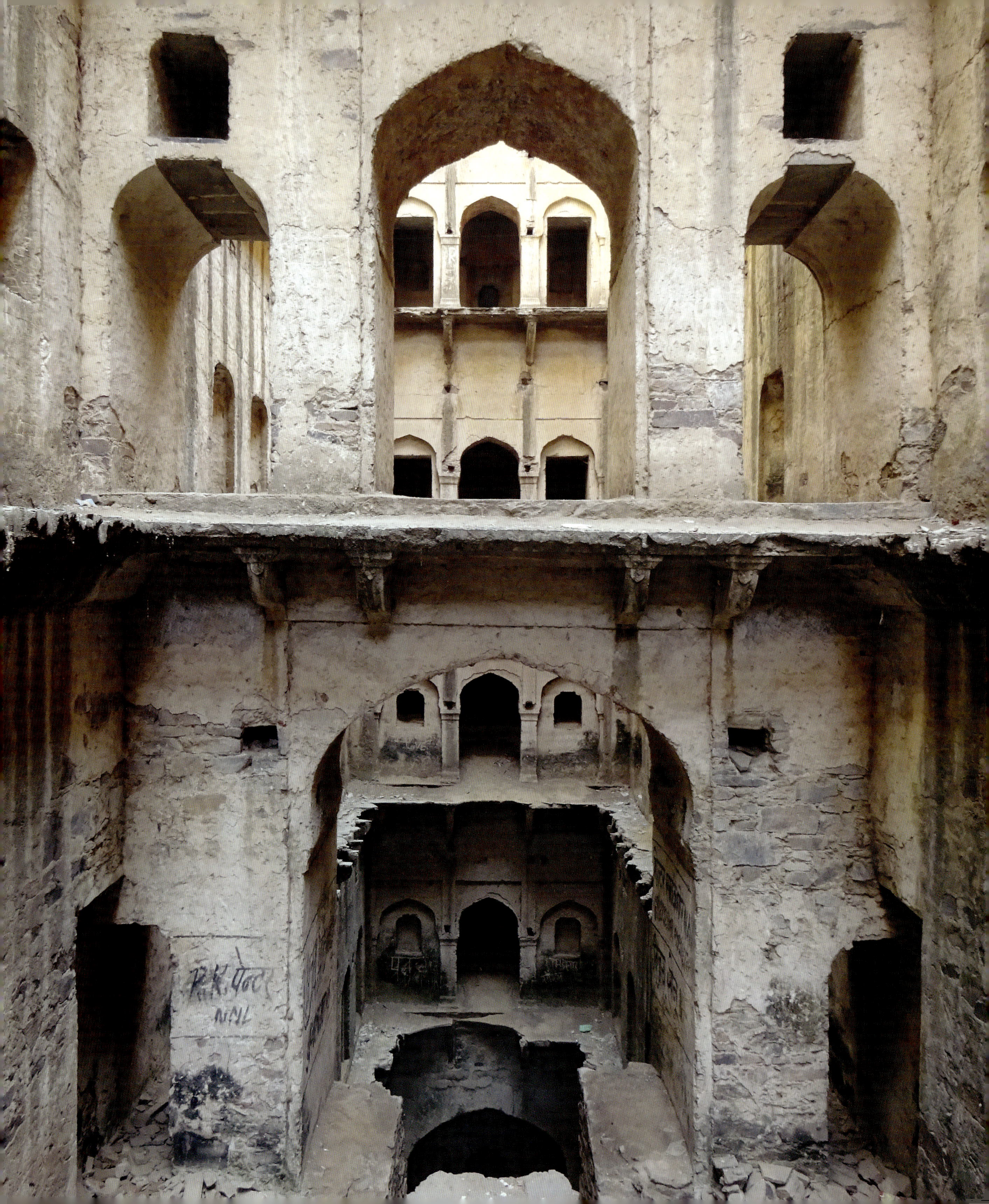

INTRODUCTION

How does an entire category of architecture slip off the grid of history? Few people have heard of these ingenious and beautiful subterranean marvels, let alone seen one, yet a stepwell would have been arguably the most significant structure in any community that it served. In a tradition that stretches back thousands of years, stepwells were among India's most efficient water-harvesting systems. It is believed that by the eighteenth century there were more than 3000 such wells throughout the subcontinent. Built by benevolent patrons and patronesses, they served as refuges, gathering places and spiritual centres. Their water was used for drinking, irrigation and religious ablutions. Some were commissioned to offset the economic devastation of an extreme famine. Stepwells for public use proliferated in cities and villages, along isolated trade routes and adjacent to temples and mosques; those for private use were constructed in compounds for the wealthy. They could be almost unimaginably huge or intimately scaled; some were encrusted with ornament, while others were modest and utilitarian. A shallow stepwell might have had two or three levels, while others plunged a vertiginous nine storeys.

The prominence of stepwells in the past did not guarantee a reliable future. Today there are a number of magnificent restored and protected stepwells in India, but they are almost always unknown to tourists. Many continue to function as temples and shrines, but even more have had their formerly profound connection to the local community severed, and they are no longer valued after centuries of disuse. However, even the most dilapidated or abandoned stepwells retain the essence of their former glory, the sublime engineering, craftsmanship and masonry that kept them at the forefront of social and religious life in India for many centuries. This makes the fact that they are so little known all the more puzzling.

Each year, millions of tourists throng India's palaces, forts, temples, mosques and tombs, sites of such historical and cultural significance that a vast number of studies and guidebooks are devoted to them. Just one book focuses on the stepwells in a particular city (Bundi; see p. 148), and it was published only in 2015. A fourteenth-century stepwell lies just a few yards from the photo opportunities at the world-famous Red Fort in Delhi (pp. 74–75), and one of India's most astounding subterranean structures can be found fifteen minutes off the busy highway between Jaipur and Agra (Chand Baori, pp. 40–43), but ask any India lover if they have visited these sites and they will nearly always say no. As subterranean structures with little above-ground presence, stepwells often hide in plain sight, lying undetected behind walls or amid skyscrapers, or obscured by newer buildings that crowd around – or even on to – their edges. Certainly, some are off the well-worn tourist track, but, by venturing away from their strict itineraries just a little, visitors may be rewarded with an authentic welcome from helpful, albeit slightly mystified locals. The search for stepwells can be part of the allure – or it can be maddeningly frustrating (I have provided GPS coordinates in this book, if you want to locate a well speedily). Wherever they are found, be it in a city, village or remote desert, every stepwell is individual (but see the twin kunds on pp. 162–63), and I would argue that there is no such thing as a bad stepwell.

Stepwells are considered to be unique to the subcontinent. They were built as a response to India's dramatic but predictable climate, which, especially in the arid western states, guarantees a bone dry environment for most of the year, followed by weeks of monsoon rains. It was imperative to establish a reliable, year-round water supply, and this required direct access to the water table. While such access was a simple proposition in areas where water was relatively close to the surface, in certain areas of India – modern-day Gujarat, Rajasthan and Haryana, in particular – the water could be as much as 60 metres (200 ft) underground, necessitating extraordinarily deep well shafts. The extreme weather cycle in India generates equally extreme fluctuations in the water table, akin to a dripping tap in the desert that suddenly gushes, then slowly returns to a steady dribble. Thus, stepwells were designed for a secondary, equally valuable purpose: to act as cisterns that could retain as much of the precious resource for as long as possible. A flight of steps adjacent to the well cylinder ensured that groundwater could be accessed even when it retreated to the lowest trickle. As the flow increased, the steps became submerged, and any descent was significantly

The spectacular but disintegrating stepwell at Neemrana (pp. 140–41) is one of the largest and deepest in India. Nine storeys of steps descend to the bottom of the baoli, which has silted up over the centuries.

At right, a small shrine to Bahuchara Mata at Sampa Vav (pp. 94-94) is decorated with brightly coloured garlands, silks and banners. Below, a stone tower within the cylinder at Indaravali Baoli (pp. 136-39) is filled with floral offerings.

shortened. As the water receded once again, more steps reappeared.

The most common stepwell design is a straight, stepped corridor that leads to the well cylinder. But stepwells can also be square, L-shaped or round, and may incorporate two, three or occasionally four entrances. One stylistic variation is known as a *kund*. Kunds are easily recognized by their deep funnel shape, which resembles an inverted pyramid, and their steps are arranged in mesmerizing triangular patterns that cascade down to the water. It is virtually impossible to take a bad photograph of a kund.

The terminology of stepwells can be daunting, because people in every region and state refer to them by different names. In Gujarat, for example, a stepwell is most commonly referred to as a *vav*, while in Rajasthan a well may be called, among other names, *baoli*, *baori* or *bawadi*. In this book, for the sake of consistency, I have used the terms *vav* and *baoli* for the appropriate states.

Any study of stepwells that focused on only their architecture would be superficial. As I mentioned in my opening paragraph, stepwells served other purposes than the provision of water alone. Indeed, the characterization of stepwells as 'advanced water-harvesting systems' is wildly simplistic - even if many of their other functions were largely intangible. In fact, stepwells performed more functions than any other public buildings of their time; they were civic centres that contributed to the quality of life of the communities around them. One critically important function was as a place of devotion, where ritual purification and prayer were performed. Baolis and vavs were commissioned predominantly by Hindu and Muslim patrons, whose faiths required the daily use of water in their ceremonies and rituals. Consequently, many stepwells were built near temples and mosques. Hinduism equates the life-giving properties of water with fertility and the mother goddess (Devi, often referred to simply as 'the Goddess'). This connection is reflected in the names of many stepwells and temples across India, such as Mata Bhavani ni Vav and Gelmata ni Vav (pp. 48-49, 62-63), since the meaning of *mata* is 'mother'. The Goddess is manifested in all revered female deities - some of which are local and unrecognized outside a specific town - and many of the rituals devoted to them are performed by women in order to ensure marriage or children. In some cases, baolis named 'Ma' or 'Maaji' (for example, Maaji ki Bawadi; pp. 190-93) may refer to the woman, most probably royal, who commissioned the well, rather than to a goddess. Stepwells were - and still are, when they are active - also inhabited by male deities, among

The modest Vijay Bagh ki Bawadi adjoins a neighbourhood park in Amer, just outside Jaipur, Rajasthan. It is believed to date from the eighteenth century, but there is no information about its origin.

A relief of the deity Ganesh can be seen between brackets supporting a platform at the graceful baoli in the small Rajasthani village of Ghanerao. This stepwell was constructed in the late eighteenth or early nineteenth century.

them Shiva, Ganesh, the sun god Surya and especially Vishnu, whose reposing figure can often be seen within a well cylinder on account of his association with cosmic waters at the beginning of creation. Several particularly beautiful examples of the deity are visible at Rani ki Vav in Gujarat (pp. 52–55).

Beyond the spiritual, there was an important social and communal aspect of stepwells, which would have been especially vital for women. The daily fetching of water has always been the work of women, and their constrained lives undoubtedly benefited from the protected confines of a vav or baoli close to them. Inside, they would also have found refuge from the overpowering summer heat. With each subterranean step inside a well, the temperature can be felt to drop. Men, too, would have found respite from the sun, but away from the women, perhaps beneath the pavilions. Under Muslim rule, stepwell designs often included shady loggias and small chambers for rest. Thus, along trade routes, any stepwell was also an essential lifeline for caravanserais and travellers.

While we know why stepwells were built, in some instances, in the absence of written records, we do not fully understand how they were constructed. The humble tools of the time were not remarkably different from those seen in many parts of India today. For a glimpse of a medieval Indian building site, see the *Akbarnama*, a sumptuously illustrated chronicle of the reign of Emperor Akbar (1556–1605). Wonderfully detailed paintings of the construction of the city of Fatehpur Sikri depict the oxen, ramps, baskets and sheer manpower that were required to build above-ground structures. But the forces above ground are easier to contend with than those below. For the builders of stepwells, it must have been a constant struggle to hold back many tons of earth relentlessly thrusting in from all sides, and the construction of the well cylinder would have been the most dangerous aspect.

In *The Queen's Stepwell at Patan* (1991), the author Kirit Mankodi describes a system in which masons were lowered in stages on wooden support rings, facing the walls with stone as they descended to the water table. When each level was complete and stabilized, soil was excavated from beneath the rings, which were then lowered to the next level, until the masons reached the groundwater. The final stage of construction would have been possible only during the driest season, since, at that point in the process, water was the enemy and had to be bailed out quickly. Logs were packed around the walls and on the floor to prevent seepage while the facing was completed, but the builders would have had sufficient knowledge to anticipate the depth of the water table. The hydrological systems of the early Harappan civilization of the Indus Valley (c. 3300–c. 1700 BCE) were among the oldest and most sophisticated on Earth. At the ancient settlements of Dholavira and Mohenjo Daro, there is evidence of drains and wells dating back to around 2600 BCE. Shikha Jain, a director at the Development and Research Organisation for Nature, Arts and Heritage (DRONAH), believes that dowsers were also consulted on the critical issue of the siting of stepwells. (As late as the 1920s, the British colonial government in India employed an official water diviner, Major C.A. Pogson, for five years.)

It was not the availability of water that dictated the design of a stepwell; it was the geology, and initial engineering decisions depended on the specifics of each region. For instance, much of Gujarat's soil is soft, loamy clay, which required a significant shoring-up of

Towering rock walls at Adi Kadi Vav (pp. 78–81) form a man-made chasm that ends abruptly at the water's edge.

Stepwells accessed groundwater year-round by means of a deep cylinder reached via a subterranean stepped corridor, as seen in the section and plan below. As the water level in the cylinder rose, the storeys would become submerged. This basic plan was employed at both small stepwells and enormous ones, such as Rani ki Vav (opposite; pp. 52–55).

walls. Characteristic of Gujarati vavs are the 'pavilion towers' known as *kuta*. Comprising platforms supported by columns, these may look purely decorative, but were necessary to hold the walls in place. Sandstone blocks, sometimes massive, were hewn to a perfect, mortar-free fit, reinforcing the structure to such a degree that it was capable of withstanding numerous earthquakes. The effectiveness of this method is more than evident in the number of 1000-year-old vavs still standing. In a rockier area, such as Delhi, the harder, quartzite-rich terrain made these elaborate interventions superfluous. The most common construction material seen in surviving baolis there is rough-surfaced rubble masonry, which, in some cases, would receive a coat of plaster.

It took centuries to perfect this technology. Early stepwell precursors – shallower and less sophisticated than even the oldest wells featured in this book – appeared around the fourth century CE, cut into solid rock without any separate structural components. The first examples of engineered stepwells were built around 600 CE in the town of Dhank, Gujarat (pp. 30–35), establishing the common stepwell configuration of a stepped corridor leading to a well cylinder that accessed groundwater. This was the basic blueprint that evolved over the centuries into increasingly complex, ornamental subterranean structures.

The plethora of baolis and vavs that exist today attests to the success of the building methods, and any structural failures will never be known – with one catastrophic exception. It occurred at the grandest stepwell of all, the eleventh-century Rani ki Vav (opposite). It is believed that the well took some fifteen to twenty years to build on a site near the Saraswati River. Not long after the completion of the vav, the river changed course. A devastating flood of mud ensued, followed by an accumulation of silt that eventually buried the well. It was not until the Archaeological Survey of India (ASI) began serious restoration in the 1980s that – like the ash-entombed ancient Roman cities of Pompeii and Herculaneum, discovered by archaeologists in the eighteenth century – Rani ki Vav revealed its jaw-dropping splendour. It became a UNESCO World Heritage Site in 2014.

In the vast majority of cases, the only name associated with any stepwell, other than that of a deity, is that of the person who held the purse strings.

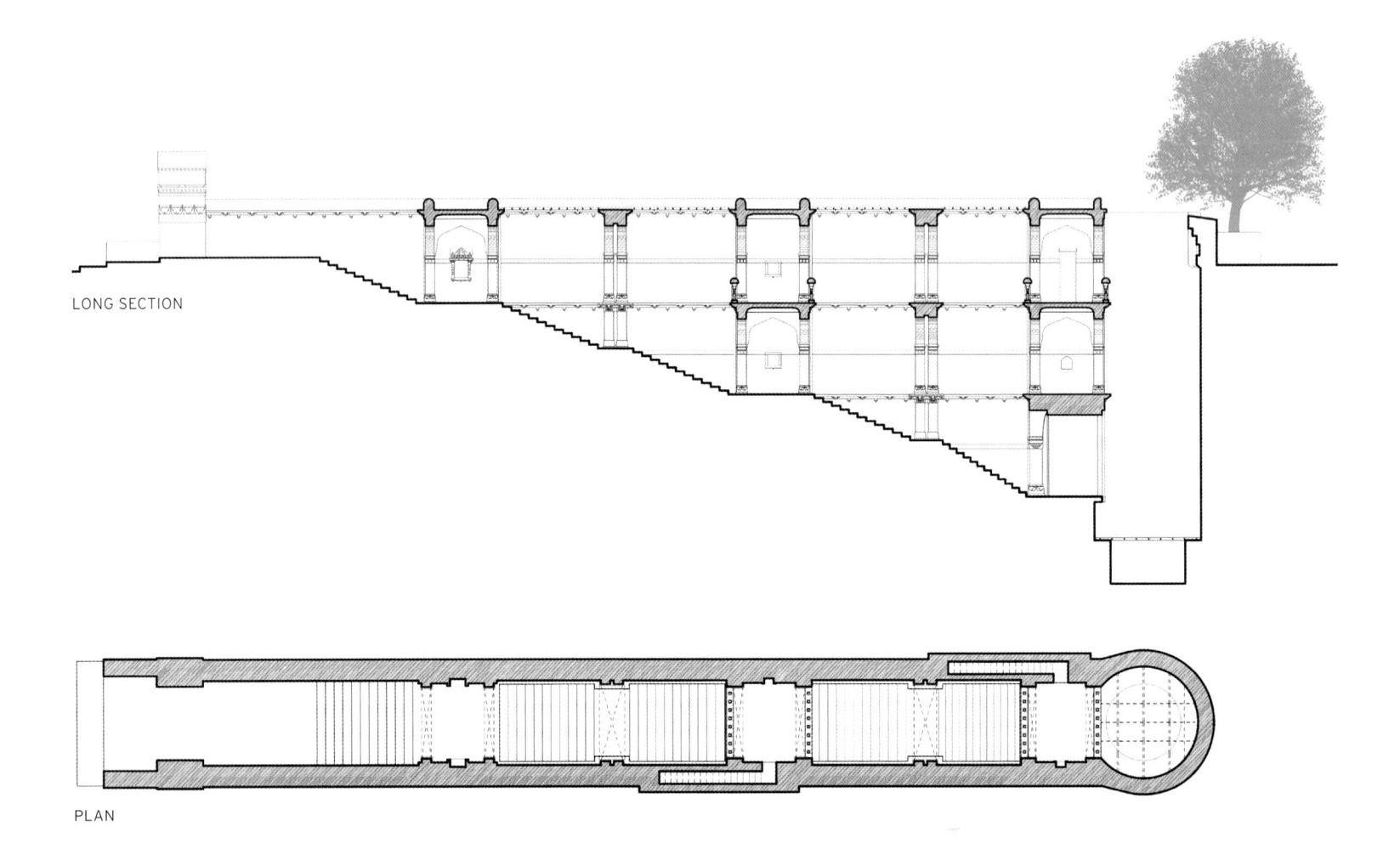

LONG SECTION

PLAN

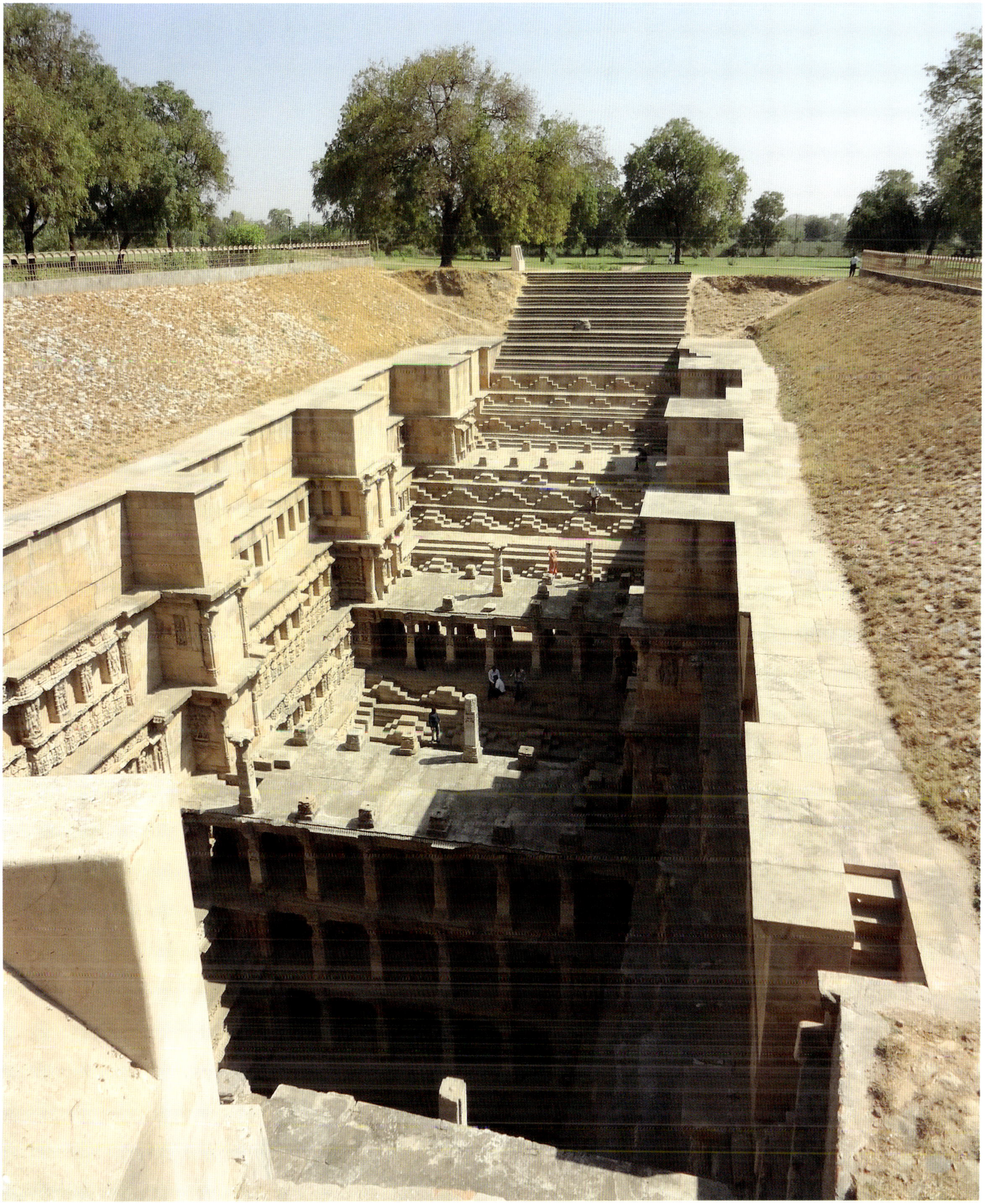

That name may be known only if a dedication panel exists. Using this information, we may be able to discover the date of construction, the ruler then in power, and sometimes the profession of the donor. It is possible that a quarter of all stepwells built in India were commissioned by women, royal or otherwise. The building of public works was a civic responsibility, particularly for queens, as reflected in the fact that many stepwells are named after a rani, or queen. Rani ki Vav was commissioned by Queen Udayamati, Raniji ki Baori by Queen Nathawati-ji (pp. 152–53) and Mertaniji ki Bawari by Queen Mertani (pp. 198–201). It is rare indeed to find a woman whose name lives on in Indian history, and even though the stepwells that these women built were often honouring dead husbands and sons, they were extremely expensive, visible acts of charity. Charitable giving was a tenet of many religions, and, for Hindus, commissioning a stepwell was the equivalent of endowing a temple.

The offering of water – whether to travellers, passers-by or animals – was a teaching observed by the followers of several faiths, particularly Jains, who were also patrons of stepwells. Even today, it is not unusual in some parts of India to see shelves of water pots by the side of the road or in front of houses – a benevolent act on a smaller but still meaningful scale. Charity is one of the Five Pillars of Islam, and the construction of stepwells thrived during Muslim rule in India. Stepwells were previously unknown in the Muslim world, even though there was a long tradition of sublime water buildings in Islamic architecture. The elaborate subterranean structures so captivated the Muslim invaders that they not only protected any in their otherwise destructive path, but also adopted the typology themselves, adding specifically Islamic flourishes. Beginning in about 1500, octagons – an important Islamic symbol – began to feature in stepwell design (for example, the octagonal open-air shafts that terminate in square pools at Rudabai and Dada Harir vavs; pp. 103–107), as did 'true' domes and arches; hitherto, Indian architecture had relied on a trabeated (post-and-lintel) system of construction, with simple corbelled domes. On account of figurative representation being prohibited in Islamic art and architecture, ornamentation began to move away from the sculpted deities and creatures that had been common in Hindu stepwells; they were replaced by geometric and floral motifs that had significance for both faiths. During this period, many luxurious private wells were built for royal or wealthy Muslim families. Set in lush, secluded gardens or within the walls of a fort, these were true pleasure retreats for bathing and lounging.

The building of stepwells throughout India continued for another 400 years, into the twentieth century. A mysterious, anonymous stepwell not far from Delhi was, according to a local authority, built around 1903, and what is thought to be the last well was constructed in about 1930. It was a private 'folly', within what is now a palace hotel at Wankaner, Gujarat. But the long heritage of traditional baolis had begun to taper off around the late eighteenth century, hastened by the disintegration of the Mughal Empire and the ascendancy of the British East India Company. The British did not approve of the use of stepwells for bathing and drinking, and, not understanding their many other functions, considered them to be merely dirty incubators of various diseases. Many stepwells were filled in or closed. One British official reputedly wrote that the water in Mertaniji ki Bawari was so poisonous that anyone who drank it would die within two hours. The locals, meanwhile, valued the water for its power to cure skin diseases.

It was not just a clash of cultures that precipitated the demise of stepwells, but also the march of progress. With the British came alternative methods of procuring water that were clearly preferable to walking up and down a hundred steps a day. There were, for instance, hand pumps and eventually, for the lucky few, indoor plumbing. When stepwells were no longer necessary for the provision of water, their use as temples and shrines also declined – but fortunately did not stop completely. Stepwells across India are still used as venues for rituals and festivals. A prime example is Mata Bhavani ni Vav in Asarwa, a suburb of Ahmedabad, Gujarat, where the activity, sounds and smells transport visitors back to the eleventh century. No matter that it lacks water; as an important temple and part of the community, it is lovingly cared for. Mata Bhavani is not alone in continuing ancient traditions or repurposing centuries-old structures, but the vast majority of baolis are frequently too dilapidated, and even those with shrines intact harbour abundant rubbish, their once-venerated water left to stagnate.

When you are visiting a stepwell today, it may be difficult to imagine its original context. The small village it served may have been absorbed into a huge metropolis, where it is now surrounded by shops and homes. A stepwell that was once used as a rest stop for travellers may no longer be situated on a remote frontier. New construction may encroach so much that it stands on the walls of an ancient baoli, or the well may be hemmed in to the extent that it is completely inaccessible. Essentially trapped, like a fly in amber, such stepwells are generally filled with litter.

A dramatic 'before' (right) and 'after' comparison, the images taken two years apart, shows Toorji ka Jhalra in Jodhpur. The restored eighteenth-century stepwell is now a destination for the community, and guests at an adjacent hotel dine overlooking the fascinating structure.

The architect Charles Correa's elegant spiral stairway at the Inter-University Centre for Astronomy and Astrophysics in Pune (above) shares an affinity with the sixteenth-century Helical Vav in Champaner, Gujarat (top; pp. 118–19).

Visitors, particularly those from outside the subcontinent, may be quick to make judgements about the often deplorable state of stepwells. But in cities with rapidly growing populations, any bit of land is a coveted commodity, and the empty space around an unused stepwell may look appealing. Likewise, in a country that lacks a reliable refuse collection, a big old pit is surely fair game. Comparing contemporary photographs to the rich resources of the American Institute of Indian Studies or the Indira Gandhi National Centre for the Arts can be a means by which to demonstrate clearly a stepwell's decline.

Successful stepwells continue to harvest water uninterrupted, thanks to the annual recharging of groundwater, the most important source of which is rainfall percolating into the soil. Today the water crisis in India makes the daily news, and images taken in 2015 as part of NASA's Gravity Recovery and Climate Experiment (GRACE) showed that the country has the second-worst depletion of groundwater on the planet. Among farmers, industries and homeowners there is prevalent use of motorized pumps, which are removing more water than can be replaced. Moreover, rainwater is not able to percolate through tarmac and cement. Run-off is of no use to anyone. The crisis has led to an upsurge in efforts to reinvigorate – and in many cases, save – baolis. Initiatives at the local, private level have had the most impact, since these involve people who are displaying their commitment by funnelling their own time, money and other resources directly into their communities, without the participation of any outsiders. Two such projects may be found, coincidentally, within a few blocks of each other in Jodhpur, Rajasthan, and each has brought an outstanding eighteenth-century stepwell back to life.

In 2014 the Toorji ka Jhalra, a kund, had water, but it was filled with trash, the depth was unclear, sections of the structure were crumbling away, and the community took no interest (p. 21). The JDH Urban Regeneration Project for Jodhpur was established and, in collaboration with the adjacent RAAS hotel, it drained the toxic water and removed 300 truckloads of rubbish. An astonishing stepwell with many unusual features was revealed, and fish, birds and frogs quickly took up residence. Today the kund is a popular tourist destination, and the hotel guests can dine overlooking it. Toorji ka Jhalra has come full circle, having begun as a charitable public gift and then, some 300 years later, being resurrected as one.

The other project is Mahila Baag Jhalra (pp. 194–97). It was the first project undertaken by the local environmentalist Rajesh Joshi, who became motivated after noticing a dead fish in the well, caught in a plastic bag. Joshi embarked on a one-man campaign – although he occasionally had help from volunteers – to remove centuries of muck and clean the water. His hard work resulted in a doubling of the well's storage capacity. Joshi has gone on to restore five more wells in Jodhpur, a city that was once renowned for its effective water engineering, and children are now happily swimming in the replenished water. Grassroots interventions such as these, if adopted in other cities, could help to turn things around for not only the stepwells, but also the local communities and the tourist industry.

There have been inroads, too, at the international level. The Aga Khan Trust for Culture recently restored an important baoli in Delhi's ancient Nizamuddin neighbourhood, and the Indian NGO Gram Bharati Samiti (Society for Rural Development) partnered with both the Global Heritage Fund in the United States and the Prince Claus Fund in The Netherlands to clean and restore village stepwells in Rajasthan. Now actively participating in the upkeep of these wells, the communities have a renewed sense of ownership.

Over the decades, government agencies such as the Archaeological Survey of India and the monuments departments of individual states have repaired and restored a number of significant stepwells. The ASI has been tackling the recharging of several baolis in Delhi, and has plans to do more. Its work should raise the profile of these city-wide structures, which are unknown to nearly all tourists and most inhabitants. Finally, since its foundation in 1984, the architectural heritage arm of the NGO the Indian National Trust for Art and Cultural Heritage (INTACH) has been documenting and restoring a wide range of historic structures, including stepwells, thanks to its dozens of branches throughout the country.

Despite these efforts, it would be almost impossible in a country as large and with as rich a cultural history as India to restore or even protect all the significant historical sites. There will never be sufficient money or manpower to tackle even a fraction of the projects, and then there is the question of who should decide where to direct the efforts. If there is a choice between two equally important structures, one accessible, the other less so, which should command the limited funds and available time?

There needs to be more creative, out-of-the-box approaches. Sanjay Puri and the late Charles Correa are only two architects who have used stepwells as inspiration. Another architect, Anu Mridul, designed the award-winning Birkha Bawari rainwater-harvesting system, based on traditional baolis and kunds, for a recent development in Jodhpur. Local red sandstone was used throughout the project, and the masons applied skills passed down from generation to generation. Artists have repurposed stepwells for installations and concerts, and the Rawla Narlai hotel in Rajasthan offers romantic, candlelit dinners in the ancient stepwell on its property. The social media presence of stepwells is burgeoning, with a crop of websites devoted to individual wells. Rani ki Vav even has its own Facebook page.

However, it takes time to nurture respect and pride for historically significant structures that have lost their value or purpose, and without more awareness the task is unachievable. For every architect, artist and educator who has ever heard of a stepwell, there are many more, including in India, who have no knowledge of them whatsoever. It is difficult to formulate a reason for this, other than the fact that stepwells were under the architectural radar for so long that they just never made it into the accepted canon. Many aspects of non-Western culture have been overlooked until relatively recently, but stepwells have not managed even to penetrate guidebooks.

The few books that exist on stepwells are essential reading, but many more are required, along with study courses and specialized tours across India. I look forward to the moment when tour buses start pulling up in the baoli-rich villages and towns, and these extraordinary structures – such vital components of India's architectural, cultural and social history – finally have their day once more.

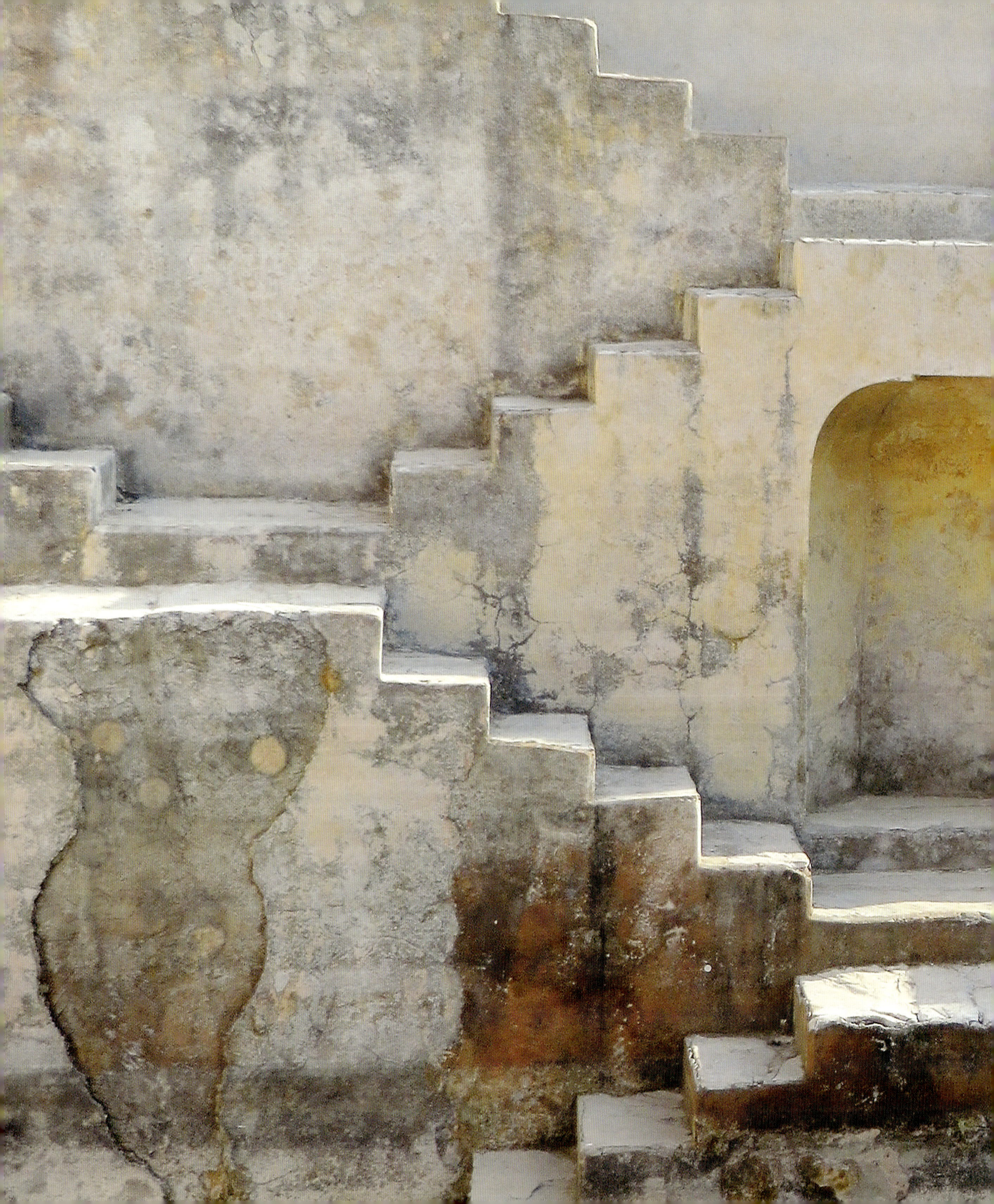

The Vanishing Stepwells of India

NAVGHAN KUVO
JUNAGADH, GUJARAT
4th/6th/MID-11th CENTURY
21°31'26.21" N
70°28'16.79" E

As in the case of the nearby Adi Kadi stepwell (pp. 78–81), the date range of this curious rock-cut well is difficult to pin down. Rock-cut stepwells generally pre-date those built with cut blocks (such as at Dhank; pp. 30–35), but neither Navghan Kuvo nor Adi Kadi Vav has distinguishing architectural or sculptural detail to help locate it in time. Many scholars consider Adi Kadi, also rock-cut, to be a later construction than Navghan. Government signage, which often conflicts with other sources, does not offer much help at the latter, explaining that the forecourt might be earlier than the actual well, and that some people believe Navghan Kuvo to be the earliest of all stepwells.

Compared to other early rock-cut wells, Navghan has an eccentric, complex layout. To enter the forecourt is to feel as if one is in a quarry, a deep, carved pit with sheer rock on all sides. There is a small shrine adorned with devotional offerings of bangles and garlands, and chiselled alcoves are piled with stacked stones, as seen at many sacred spaces. An adjacent wall is studded with further niches, too high to reach but serving as homes for the pigeons that are omnipresent at stepwells. Birds without their own apartments cling to the walls.

The descent underground is always an affecting experience and one of the most memorable aspects of stepwells. At Navghan Kuvo this experience is amplified, and the cave-like entrance deters some visitors from stepping inside. Stairs between the walls wind around the square well shaft, in a similar fashion to the steps inside a tower or battlement. Small openings in the walls let in rays of light, but these barely penetrate the gloom. The ceiling is low in places, and the eroded steps (thankfully supplemented by modern concrete) end very abruptly at the water's edge. Navghan Kuvo is not conducive to photography, but that is just fine. Preserving its aura of mystery is preferable to unmasking and illuminating it.

Prayers take the form of stone piles around a shrine outside the well (right, top), while birds nest in small alcoves.

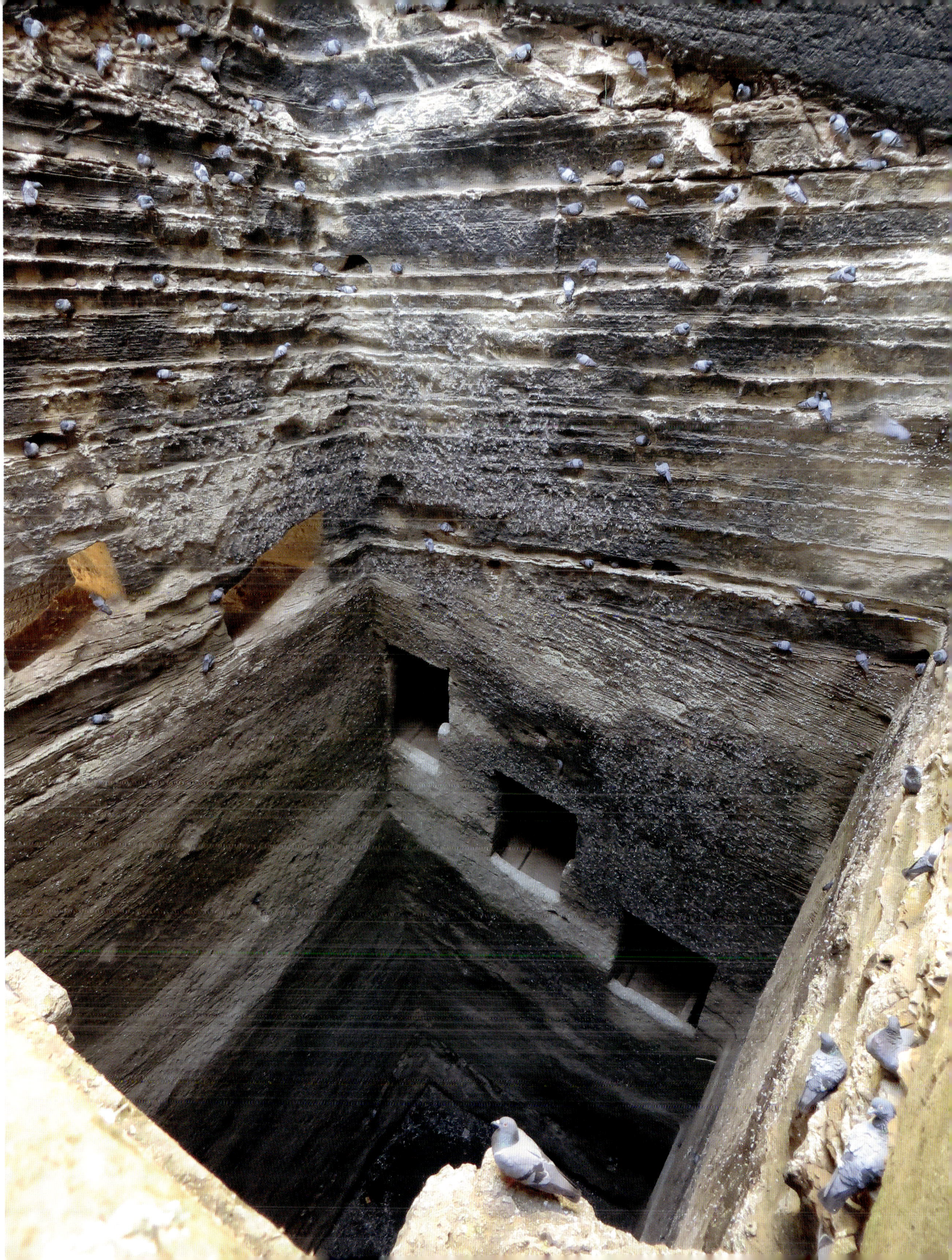

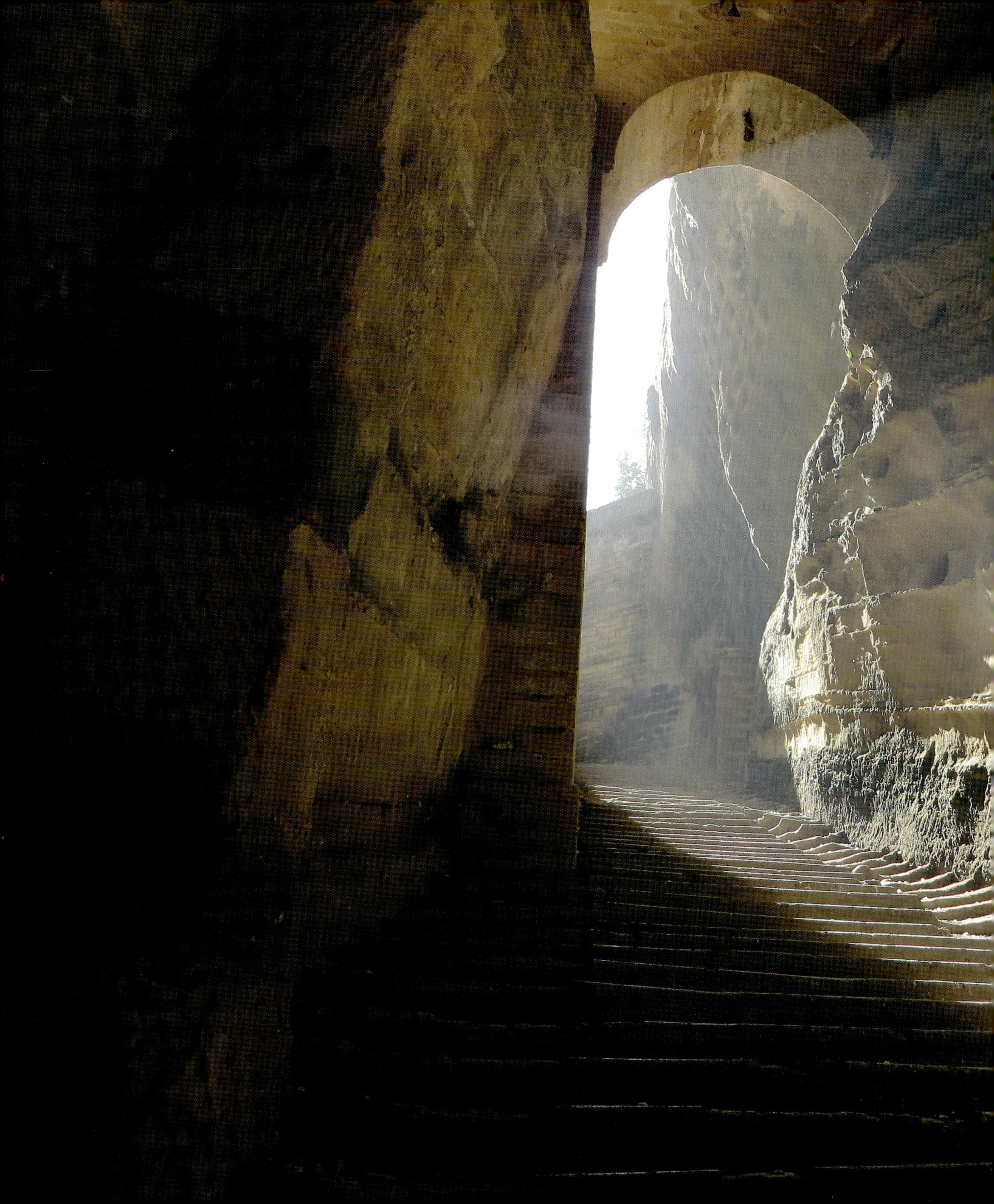

Stark contrasts of light and dark heighten an already powerful environment; some visitors find Navghan Kuvo claustrophobic.

THE STEPWELLS OF DHANK, GUJARAT

MANJUSHRI VAV
c. 600 CE
21°46'53.93" N
70°7'51.87" E

Gujarat state seems to be home to the most difficult-to-reach stepwells, with many built along desert trade routes. They can be profoundly vexing to locate, even within small towns (I was very grateful to be accompanied by my guide Nirav throughout this excursion), though all the more rewarding once found. The vavs in and around the remote town of Dhank are considered to be India's oldest engineered stepwells, meaning that their walls were constructed from masonry blocks rather than chiselled from stone. While the cylinder itself was still hewn out of the rock, small, mortarless stone blocks – precursors of the monoliths later employed to span huge spaces – were used in the main areas of the well. The walls of the wells at Dhank are narrow, and construction must have been a nerve-racking process. The arches shoring up the walls in all three wells are almost certainly subsequent additions, perhaps built to stabilize the structures centuries later.

Inconsistencies in the dates of construction are minor compared to the many stepwells that have a much wider range of dates assigned to them. These three were probably built within a few decades of one another, and they are most frequently dated to around the late sixth or early seventh century. Two are L-shaped, with only Jhilani, usually considered the earliest of this trio, having a straight corridor that leads directly to water.

This vav is located on the northernmost edge of Dhank, where the town ends and the scrubland begins, in a small walled enclosure invisible from the lane. The narrow entrance is marked by a pair of simple pillars.

Manjushri is frightening to explore, in spite of its small scale. As one descends, the steps become increasingly filthy, unstable and dangerous, courtesy of what must be centuries of nasty trash and muck. Many stepwells have dicey stairs, but a downwards slide on one's backside is required here in places where the steps have been obscured. At the end of the corridor, the forbidding rock wall looms, with an open well pit below, and the thought of slipping into the pit is hard to avoid.

Even these earliest stepwells, simple as they may be, display their fundamental function as sacred spaces. A pair of substantial, ornamented niches mark the corner before the descent into Manjushri's maw, and there are two more on the way to the well pit. The narrow, confined space, open to the sky and narrowing visibly, could only have heightened the spiritual connection to water and earth. It is apparent that, at some point, Manjushri was tampered with; mortar, invisible in earlier photographs, has now been applied between the masonry blocks. Perhaps the vav was falling down at last.

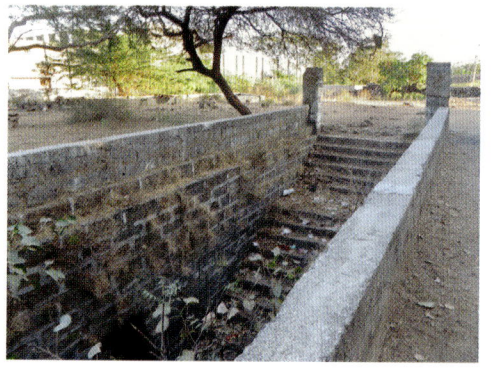

Unobtrusive pillars mark the entrance to one of India's earliest stepwells. The narrow corridor ends abruptly (opposite).

31

JHILANI VAV

c. 600 CE
21°46'38.87" N
70°6'57.27" E

Jhilani Vav is 2 kilometres (1½ miles) outside town in the underbrush, accessible by cow path. If it were not for an amiable herder, Khimabai, we could not have found the way, especially in the setting sun. Khimabai, who hailed from the ancient, pastoral Rabari community, knew every track and bush in the vicinity. He explained that there were originally four vavs in Dhank – the fourth being unceremoniously filled in decades back – and they were named after a quartet of local sisters.

This vav is in somewhat better shape than its urban sibling, the distance from town keeping it free of ancient, compacted garbage. It is cared for to some extent by others like Khimabai, who come to drink the plentiful water. Jhilani Vav is still performing efficiently, some 1400 years after it was built.

A valuable oasis in an arid landscape, the ancient Jhilani Vav is weakened by the roots of nearby trees, but still offers respite from the heat when required.

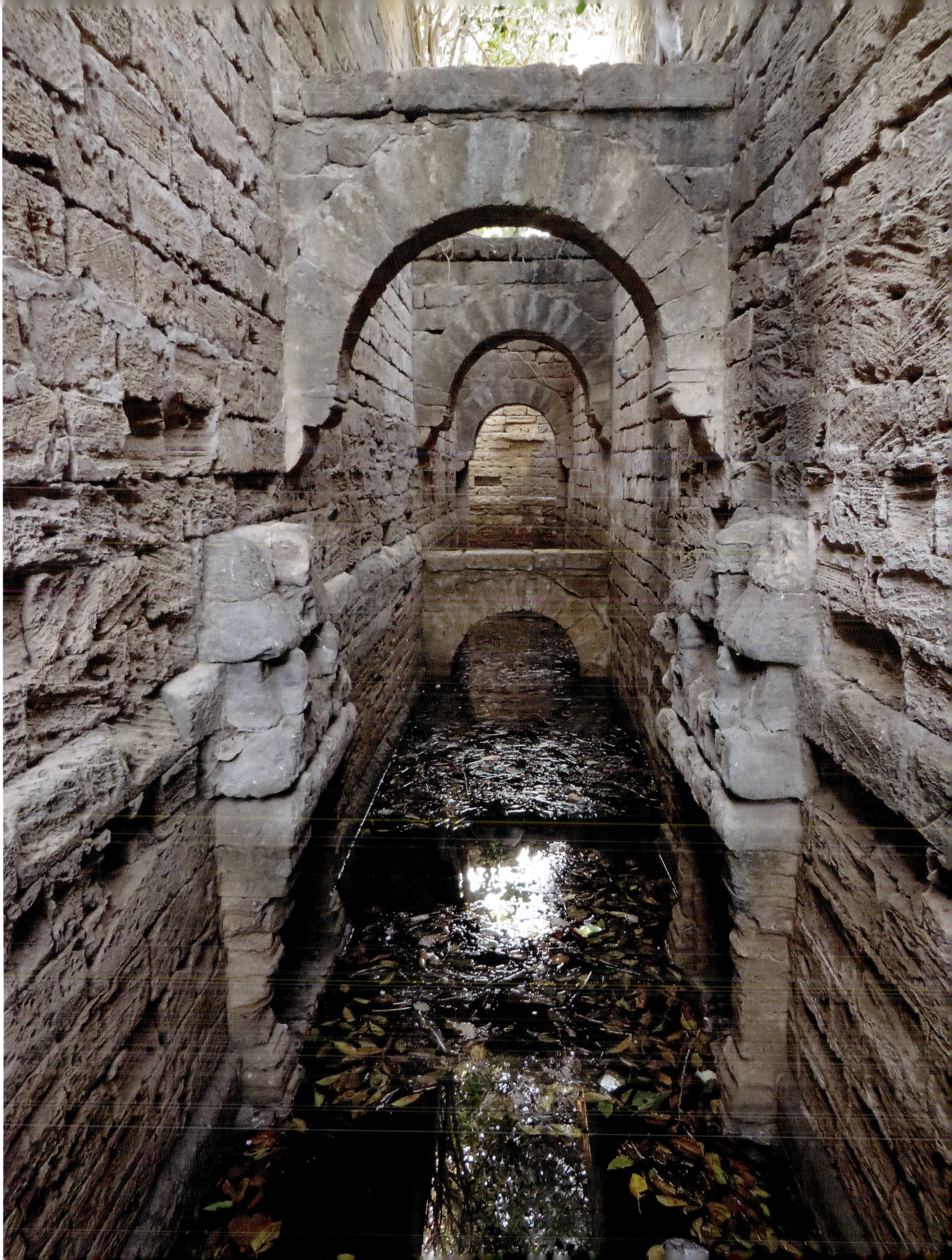

VAYADI NI VAV
(possibly BOCHAVDI VAV)
c. 600 CE
21°48'42.76" N
70°8'5.50" E

Stumbling across a completely unanticipated stepwell is a joy. Even if it is in terrible condition, to encounter it out of the blue is like sighting an elusive bird: unlikely but welcome.

Khimabai led us to his village, more than 4 kilometres (2½ miles) away, just a small collection of houses on agricultural land. A community of Patels, known to be wealthier than the Rabaris, tend the tidy green fields, and it was there, tucked among the tractors and bedecked with hoses and electrical wires, that the third sister-well appeared. Vayadi ni Vav, as the locals call it, is privately owned and still in use as a shrine. Arched as in the case of the other two existing wells, it is L-shaped and essentially a smaller version of Manjushri, but with the blockier, less sophisticated niches of Jhilani.

Regardless of the dates ascribed to this mysterious trio, each well has a distinct personality. Manjushri has become a dumping ground, while Jhilani continues as a welcome oasis. Vayadi adapted to the modern world, still managing to nurture crops and support livelihoods.

L-shaped and sturdy, the surprise backyard Vayadi ni Vav displays structural similarities to the other two remaining stepwells in Dhank. The lineage, in various forms, continued for more than a thousand years.

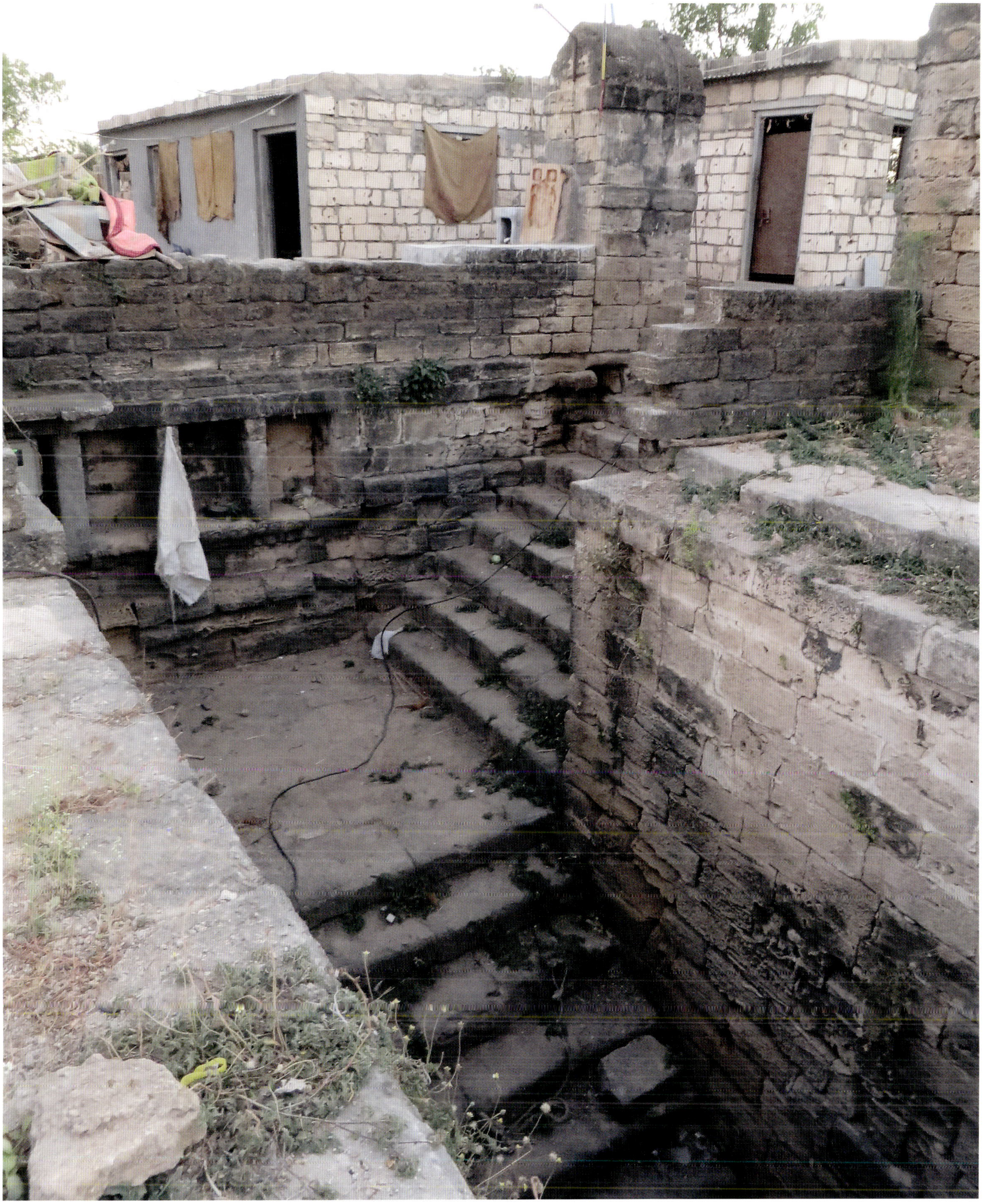

KATAN BAOLI

OSIAN, RAJASTHAN
c. 800 CE
26°43'24.8" N
72°54'40.6" E

Between the eighth and eleventh centuries, Osian, which lies just over 110 kilometres (70 miles) from Jodhpur, was a prominent trading centre on the Silk Route. During this time an important group of Hindu and Jain temples was built. Although some temples are in ruins today, Osian is still a significant and fascinating pilgrimage site, as well as a haven for tourists craving camel rides and accommodation in tented camps. However, the extraordinary Katan Baoli, a square kund of rich red sandstone, attracts little attention.

As in the case of Chand Baori in Abhaneri (pp. 40-43), Katan dates from around the turn of the ninth century; they are thus two of Rajasthan's oldest stepwells. Although Chand is far larger and deeper, both have a similar design, one seen in many kunds: a wall of 'apartments' and the well cylinder on one side, with tiers of pyramidal steps on the other three sides. At Osian, these run nine storeys deep.

Unfortunately, the public and governmental spotlight that was shone on Chand never turned to Katan, nor do the scores of pilgrims visiting the temple complex wander over. Houses are built up to the edge of one wall, so they have a great view of the massive, ruined main entrance. As is made clear by the rebuilt steps, a degree of restoration was undertaken here, but evidently the work stopped at some point.

Pavilions on either side of the huge cylinder have exceptionally beautiful carving inside, on columns, pilasters and ornamental niches, where sculpted deities can still be seen. With deep overhanging eaves offering shelter from the hot sun, the pavilions would have been delightful viewing platforms when the now dry pool was sparkling with water.

As with nearly every kund, the geometric pattern of the steps at Katan Baoli is hypnotic. Unfortunately, partial restoration has not stabilized the important but badly eroded structure.

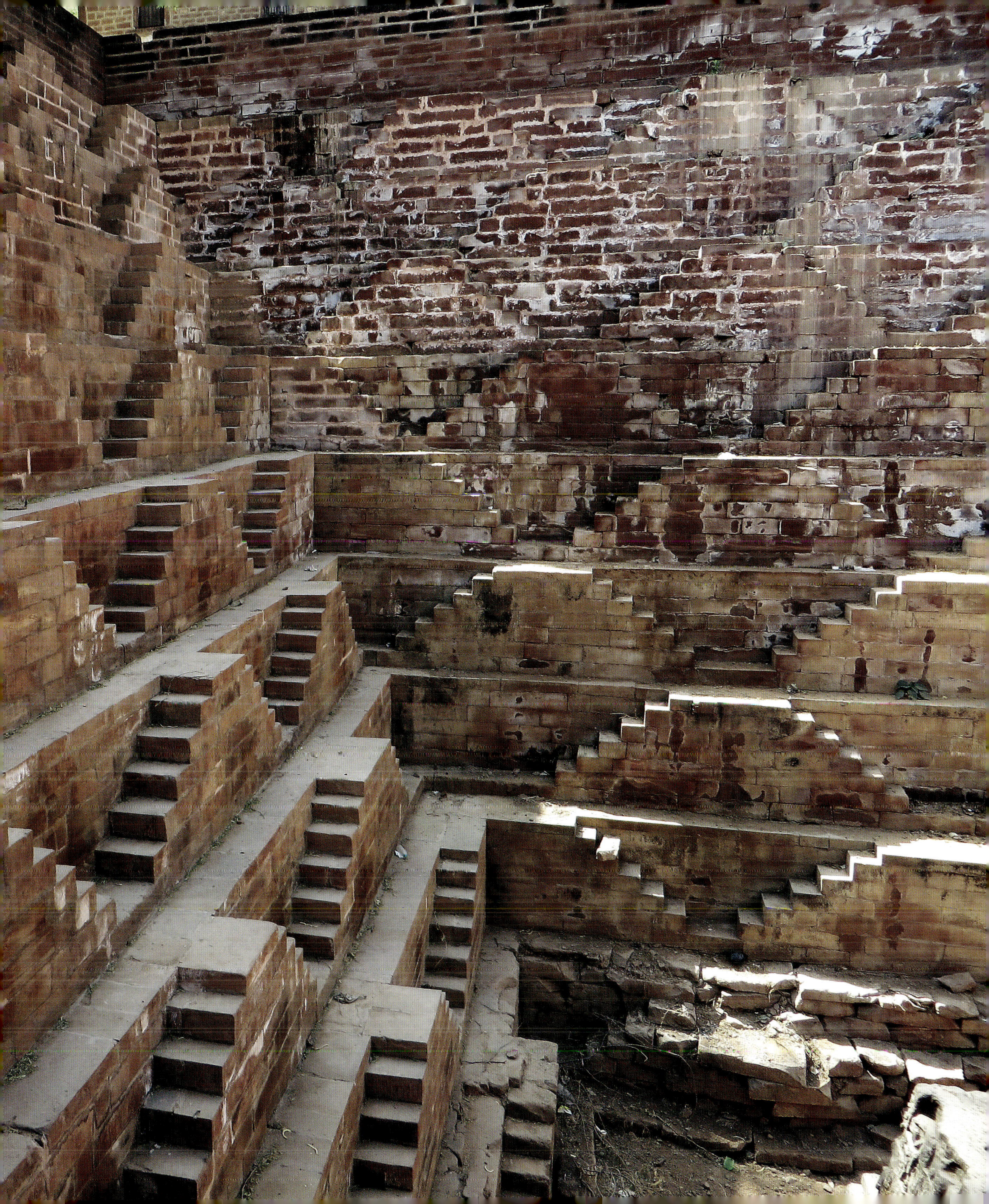

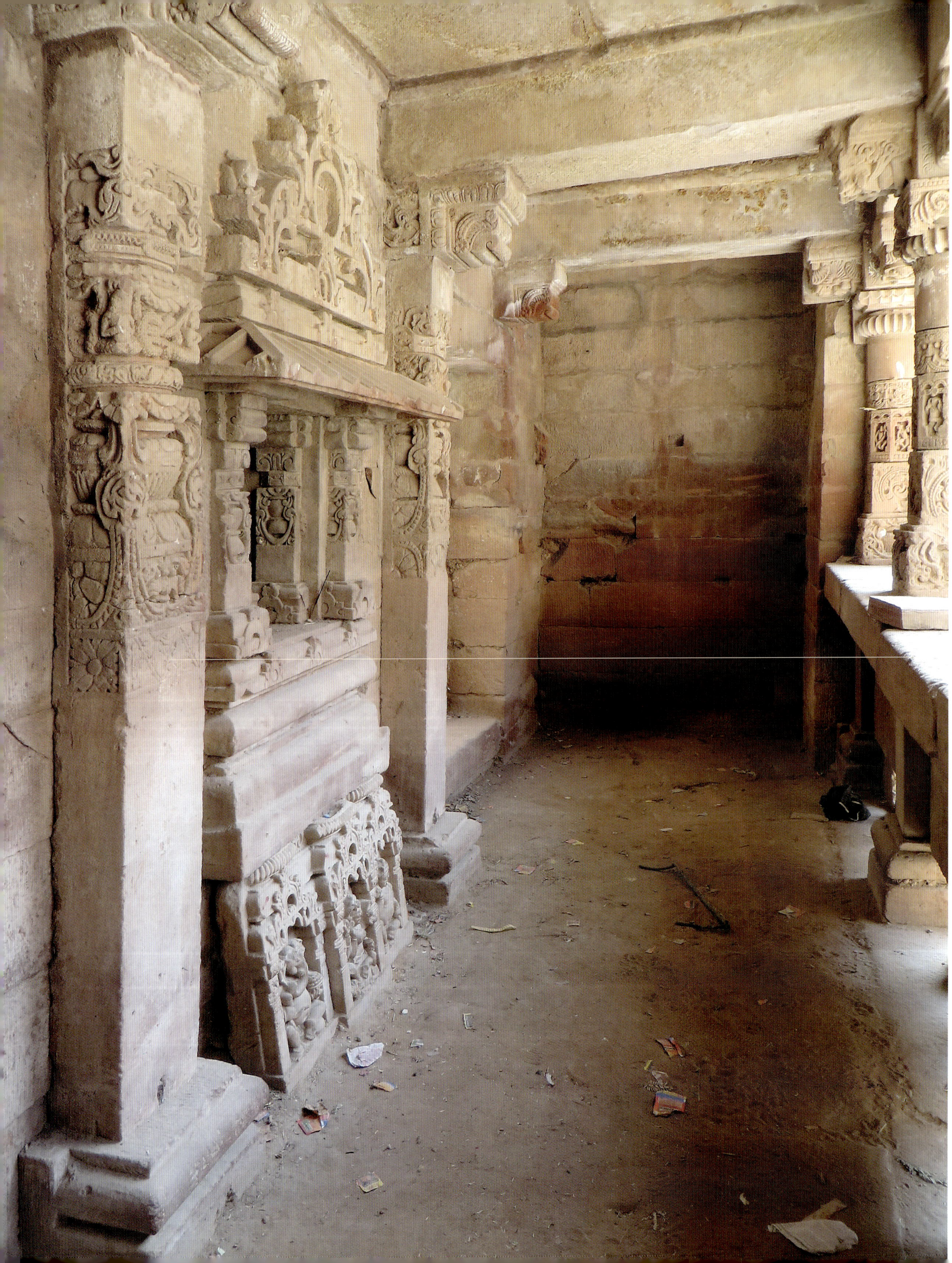

A gigantic well shaft bisects the kund's fourth side, which resembles a fortification. Badly in need of repair, the structure houses within its pavilions extraordinary columns, pilasters and sculptural reliefs (opposite).

CHAND BAORI

ABHANERI, RAJASTHAN
c. 800 CE/18th CENTURY
27°0'26.37" N
76°36'23.92" E

Chand Baori is perhaps the most recognizable of all stepwells, even though most people do not realize that they have seen it. It has featured in several movies, including the beloved Hindi romance *Paheli* (2005) and the English-language films *The Fall* (2006) and *The Dark Knight Rises* (2012). However, few tourists are aware of this marvel or have any idea how close it is to the Jaipur-Agra highway; most tours zoom past.

Alongside Rani ki Vav in Gujarat (pp. 52-55), Chand Baori is undoubtedly the most impressive stepwell in India by virtue of its immense scale, vertiginous depth, dazzling steps and the chambers that cascade down to the water on one side. It is this last feature that accounts for a complex pedigree and range of dates, since the stepwell has been revamped through the centuries by numerous rulers practising various faiths. The first iteration was Hindu, built around 800 CE by Raja Chand (*chand* means 'moon'), possibly in conjunction with the nearby Harshat Mata Temple. At the twelfth level down, the remains of Chand's structure are remarkably well preserved, with shrines retaining the deities who overlook the sacred water. As the water level rises, the deities become submerged.

Considering the lavish, eighteenth-century Mughal addition atop this original structure, it is rather surprising that the deities survived intact. It is unusual to see these different styles of architecture in such close proximity, since the Islamic faith forbade any figuration; but it is certainly fortunate that much of the ninth-century edifice was left in place close to the water's edge, its shaded balconies reminiscent of those at Katan Baoli (pp. 36-39), which dates from the same period. The Mughal structure is a fascinating complex of rooms, galleries, graceful arches and flat terraces.

As is the case at nearly every kund, it is impossible to take a bad picture at Chand. The rhythm of the steps - all 3500 of them - is hypnotic. Like Rani ki Vav and Agrasen ki Baoli (pp. 84-85), Chand Baori now has its own website; most stepwells will never have a social media presence. Today the baori is maintained by the Archaeological Survey of India (ASI), which has erected fences on two levels to prevent any tumbling, intentional or otherwise, into the water.

The scale of Chand Baori is both unexpected and overwhelming, and the thousands of steps never fail to mesmerize. The dark chambers that spill down from ground level heighten the well's enigmatic aura (below).

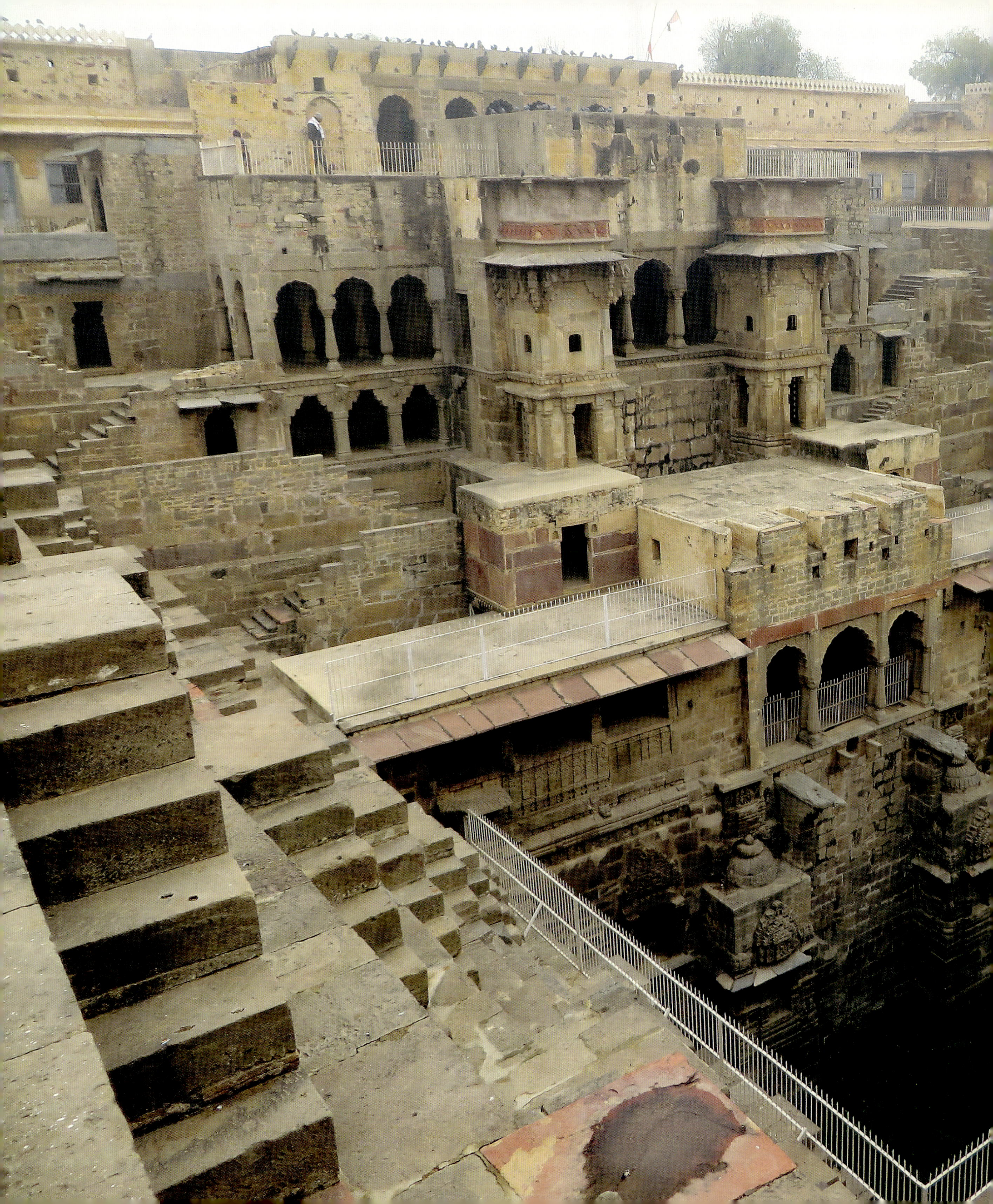

Hindu shrines still sheltering deities are visible near the water. They date from the kund's oldest period of construction.

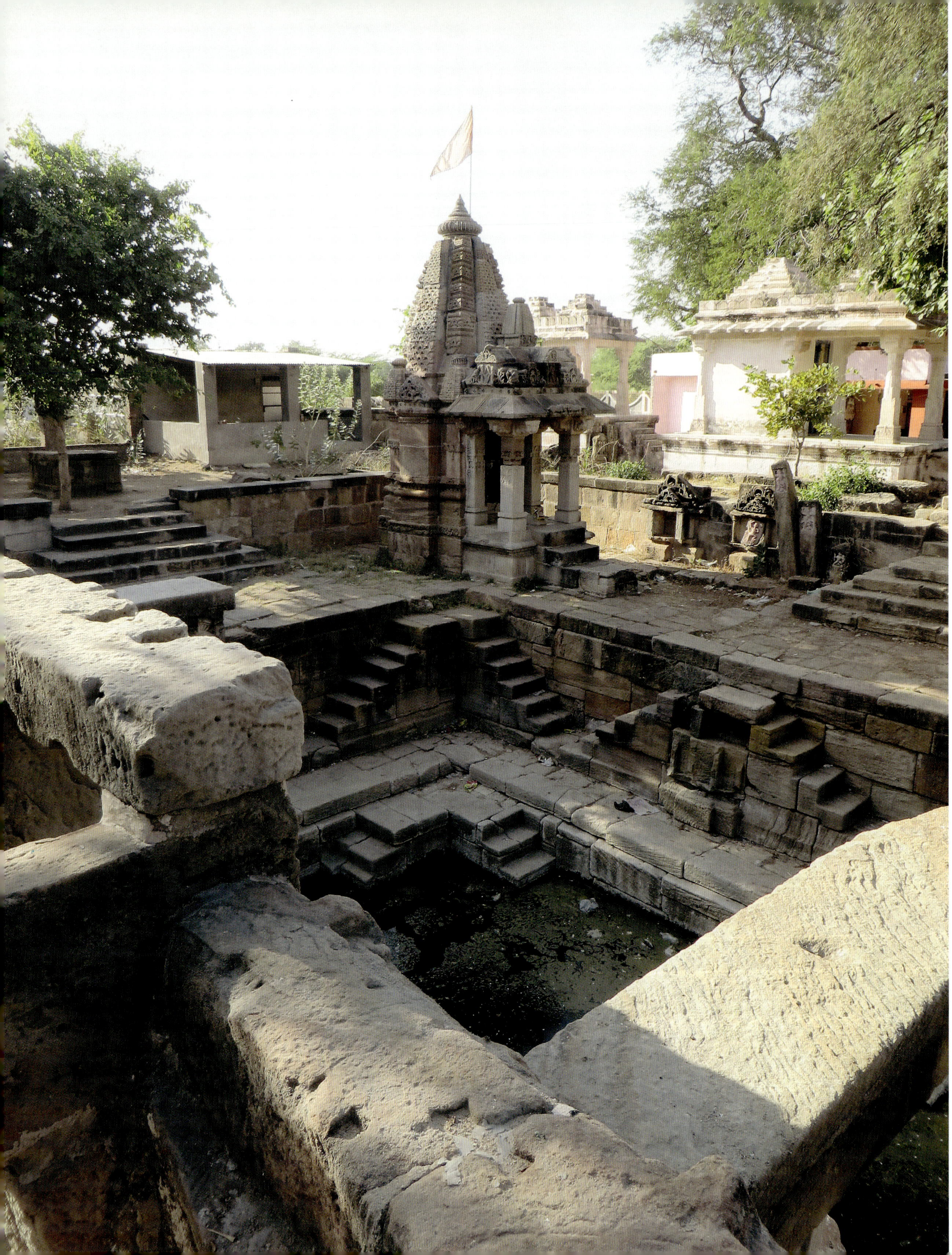

GANGVO KUND
(GANGA KUND)
DEDADARA, GUJARAT
10th CENTURY
22°46'3.19" N
71°45'50.38" E

In Hinduism, the Ganges is a sacred river, and many other bodies of water in India, no matter how distant from 'Mother Ganga', are considered to be connected to, or symbolic of, it. The names of many stepwells throughout the country reflect this powerful link, and Gangvo, another early kund, is an example.

Gangvo Kund is at the centre of a peaceful compound and is ringed with shrines that are still in use. The tank itself is anchored by four remarkable freestanding shrines, one at each corner, each topped with a towering, ornate *shikhara*, or roof, which is seen in some form on every Hindu temple. Additional, smaller shrines surround the well, mini-structures of pediments and columns that are set into the steps – as is the case at many kunds. But Gangvo has a unique feature: a wall with large supports to facilitate the lifting of water. The variegated sandstone blocks used here, and in the rest of the structure, are unlike the uniformly hued ones typical of most stepwells. It is an attractive, unusual treatment, and the same may be said of some of the stone steps. Look carefully and see that many were hewn so that the tread and riser are one piece, not the usual separate slabs. The masons were showing off.

There are a large number of ancient 'hero stones' arranged around the property, leaning against shrines or sunk into the ground. These carved and inscribed plaques have a long history in India, each commemorating an honourable death in battle. They are often found at sacred sites such as this, in the same way that headstones are arranged in the graveyard around a church.

The kund is an important part of the local community; the shrines and the Hanuman temple at the compound entrance are visited regularly and are well cared for. Swimming takes place in the well when the water is high, and a monsoon festival (which I have not had the opportunity to witness) brings everyone out to bathe.

Steps and blocks form a masonry puzzle at Gangvo, with 'hero stones' arranged nearby to commemorate ancestors fallen in battle (above). A large shrine stands at each corner of the kund (opposite).

LOLARK KUND

VARANASI, UTTAR PRADESH
c. 1000?
25°17'27.53" N
83°0'20.84" E

High above Varanasi's famous ghats (stepped embankments), the dramatic Lolark Kund appears as if out of nowhere, embedded in a small plaza surrounded by shrines. It is one of the most distinctive water structures I have seen, combining the classic deep-funnel kund form with wide flights of steep steps. The tall, narrow arch separating the pool from the well is extraordinary, and powerfully emphasizes what is described as one of the oldest sacred sites in one of the oldest continuously inhabited cities on Earth. The kund is located near the confluence of the Ganges and Asi rivers, and it is referenced as being 'very old'. This must certainly be the case, yet much of the structure and the steps are modern, and the arch could be medieval – so any date is basically arbitrary.

Lolark Kund is dedicated to the Hindu sun god, Surya, and its water is believed to have special powers of fertility: it is said that women who take a dip in it will be blessed with a child, specifically a son. A few devotees frequent the well throughout the year, but on one designated day during the monsoon festival in August or September, thousands of couples throng the kund. Women struggle down the dizzying steps, trying to reach the sacred water. After bathing, they leave their wet clothing behind, along with a piece of fruit or a vegetable that they pledge never to eat again. An abundance of jewellery is also thrown into the water, and is later retrieved by priests in order to fund what must be a colossal clean-up effort.

Crowds are so dense during the festival that stampedes have been known to occur, and it is almost impossible to glimpse the pool itself. The arch, like an all-seeing eye, makes a particularly striking backdrop whether Lolark is empty or filled to capacity. Thankfully, the three precipitous flights of steps are equipped with modern railings to clutch.

A pool of sacred water lies behind Lolark's unique archway, a tall, narrow slit in an otherwise stark wall. After bathing, devotees leave their sodden clothes behind.

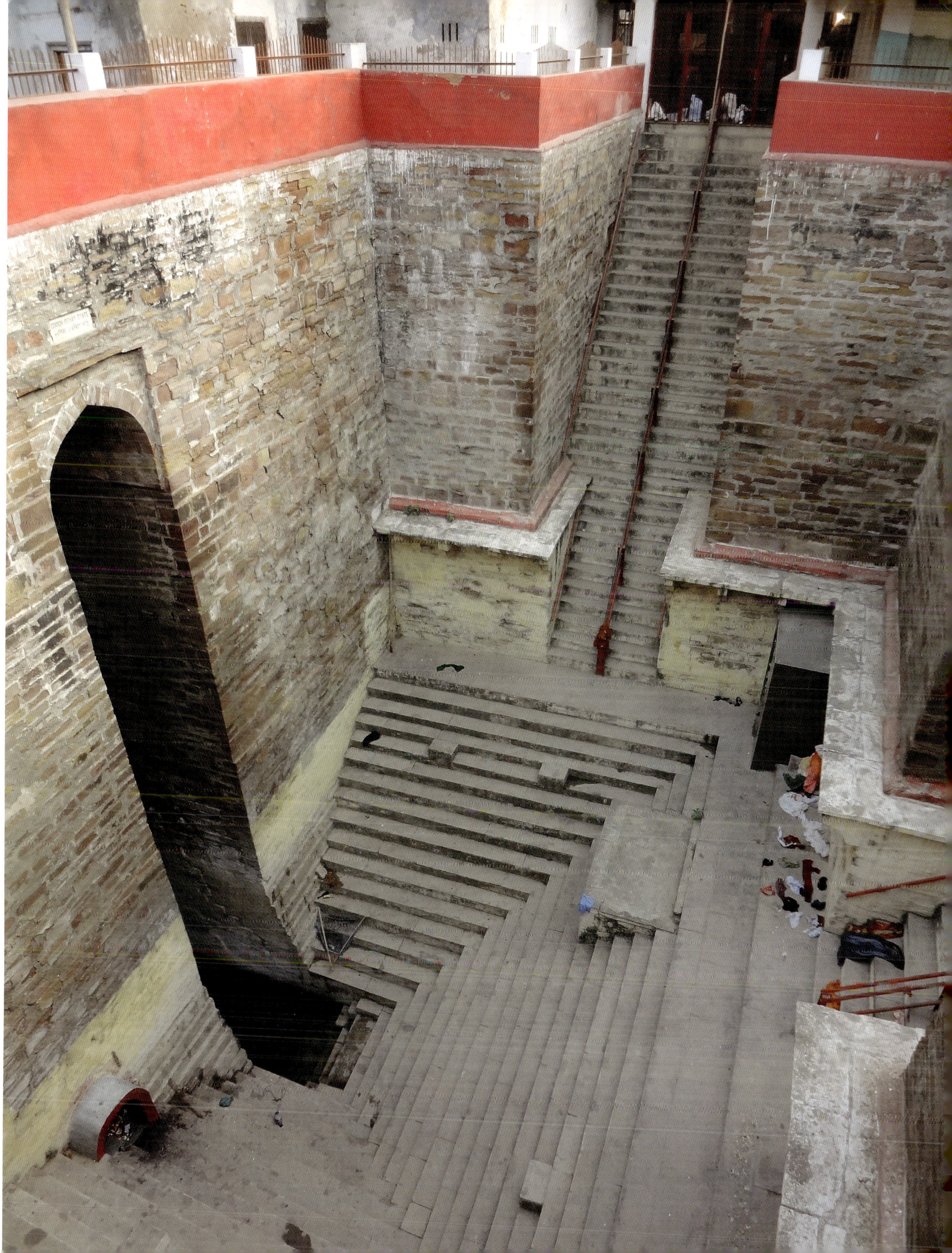

MATA BHAVANI NI VAV

ASARWA, GUJARAT
MID-11th CENTURY
23°2'39.47" N
72°36'24.71" E

One of the questions I am asked most frequently is, 'Are stepwells still used?' Yes, they are, whether for water, shelter, storage or worship. Shrines are important in many baolis and vavs, even if they are limited to a small niche in an otherwise neglected well, and regardless of whether water is present. It is most exciting to experience stepwells that are still active temples, filled with bustle, colour and aromas that surely approximate what they were like hundreds of years ago.

Mata Bhavani ni Vav provides evidence of how one stepwell lived, died and was reborn, thanks to a community that essentially commandeered and transformed it to meet its needs. It was a spiritual coup, in keeping with the fierce, eight-armed Hindu goddess after whom the vav is named. Bhavani always rides a lion or tiger, and holds a variety of weapons and the head of a demon.

Built in the mid-eleventh century during the rule of the Solanki dynasty, before the foundation of Ahmedabad, Mata Bhavani (which is located within blocks of the much later Dada Harir Vav; pp. 106–107) was far from the busy capital, Patan. At the same time, the most elaborate and costly of all stepwells, Rani ki Vav (pp. 52–57), was constructed in Patan, but there the similarity ends. Mata Bhavani is a simple, utilitarian, three-storey well, its original ornamentation kept to a minimum. 'Original' is the key word here, because Bhavani – which could be dubbed the 'Eliza Doolittle of stepwells' – might have begun life relatively plain, but it is now transformed through the addition of joyously glitzy paint, sculpture and tinsel. This is a protected heritage site, so it is, strictly speaking, illegal to alter the original structure or to encroach on a designated area with new construction. However, there is little or no regular enforcement of such rules, and in this case, that is a good thing.

The community that has grown around Mata Bhavani did not merely encroach on the stepwell; it restored it to its original purpose, as an active temple thriving at the centre of local life. People sleep in the vav to escape the heat, children play around it, animals wander about, and the site is filled with a colourful array of shrines. The well cylinder, which is now a shrine to the goddess, is accessible only to priests once they cross a little bridge. The rest of the vav is open to all, through a tall gateway surmounted

Ganesh (opposite, top) is one of many deities venerated at the highly embellished vav. Contemporary flags and sculpture adorn a pavilion that overlooked water almost a thousand years ago.

by welcoming painted deities. The steps into the well are flanked by a pair of vibrant concrete 'guardians' standing atop modern tiled pedestals emblazoned with images of the goddess.

Every part of Mata Bhavani is embellished, draped and garlanded. Myriad deities reside in niches for those worshipping the elephant-headed god Ganesh, the fierce goddess Bhairavi and others. At the very bottom of the steps, potted plants surround a tiny pool with just a puddle of water. The cool subterranean space is neither deep nor large, but it is easy to see why Mata Bhavani was reclaimed and resurrected. When I last visited, the local ASI officials were considering removing the contemporary additions, but in this instance such intervention would diminish the impact of the vav. It is far better that it serve the community than be allowed to crumble, ignored and unloved, or worse, become filled with trash.

49

RANI BAOLI

NADOL, RAJASTHAN
c. 1051–75
25°22'25.29" N
73°27'1.14" E

The little town of Nadol is in the Pali district, which was for centuries an important trade centre with an abundance of noteworthy temples. Consequently, there was a constant parade of traders and pilgrims moving through the area, necessitating the building of stepwells and the public beneficence of affluent locals. It would take days to see all the baolis in this historic region, but sadly most are disappointing in their current state. Even a unique one, such as Rani Baoli, is nearly beyond saving, expiring slowly like a sick animal. Many historians and other experts have noted the baoli's significance, and some years ago it even belonged to a group of nine stepwells considered for nomination as protected UNESCO World Heritage sites. That effort had to be abandoned, and Rani's future looks no brighter.

Located down a dirt lane just off the main road through Nadol, the well is hard to spot at first glance because of the trees growing in and around it. The vegetation threatens to take over entirely within the next decade, but the features that remain visible underscore the baoli's singularity. As one descends the steps past filth-obscured niches, an inventive approach to extra cross-bracing materializes. In order to support the structure, the masons fitted horizontal sandstone braces between the columns. It is a clever design, and one that has worked for a very long time; miraculously, nothing has collapsed at Rani – so far.

The other remarkable feature at Rani is the mysterious circular structure at the back of the baoli; were it not for its dilapidated state, it would allow access to the well cylinder. It is thought that the well was operated by a Persian wheel system, in which oxen turned a pulley to haul up buckets of water. Today the only way to enter this odd structure involves climbing some steps to pass through a small doorway.

Plants and litter are gradually consuming Rani Baoli. The unusual circular stone chamber (right, top) may have housed a pulley system. Ingenious masonry struts shore up the first pavilion (opposite).

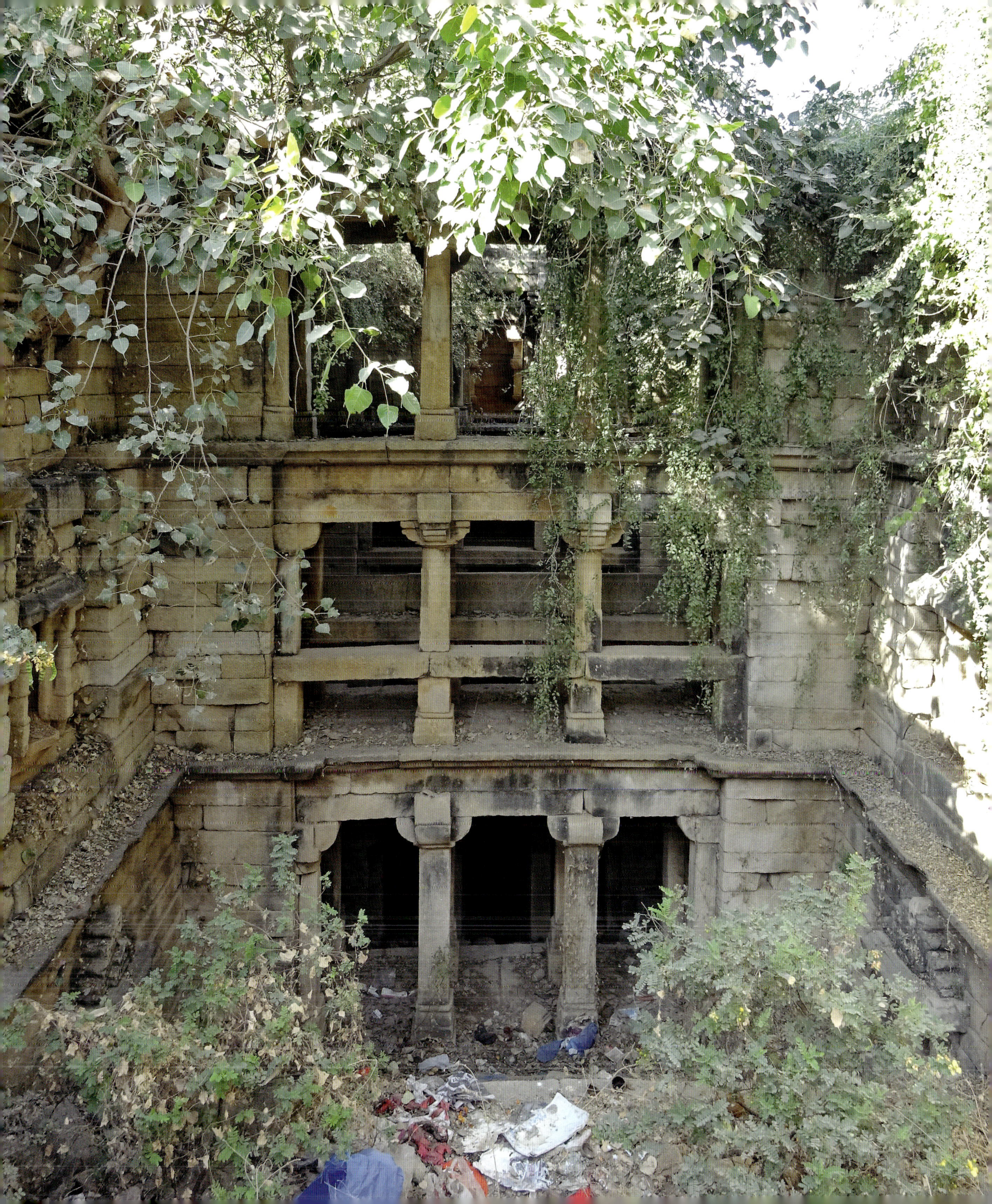

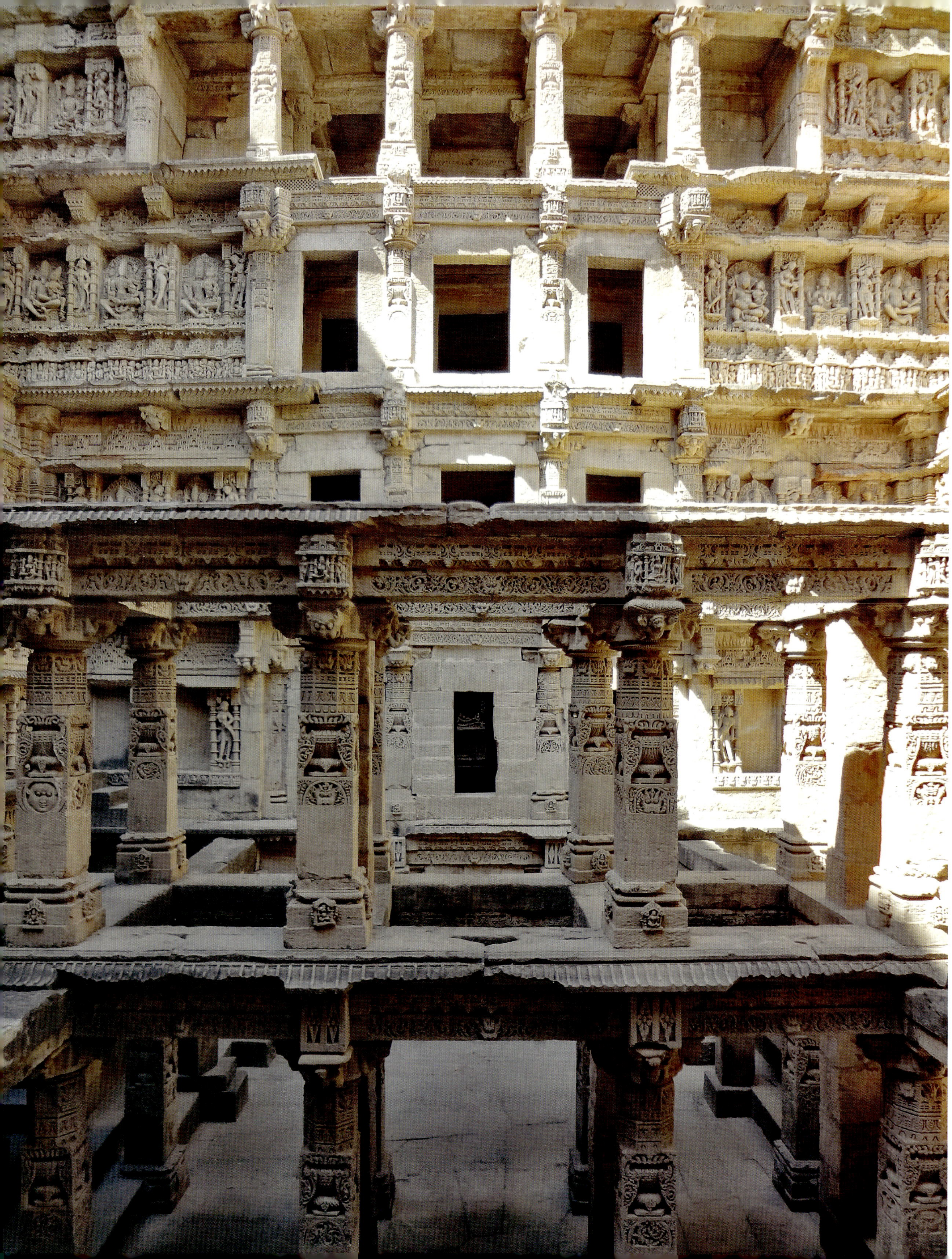

RANI KI VAV

PATAN, GUJARAT
c. 1063
23°51'31.99" N
72°6'6.36" E

Rani ki Vav is truly the queen of all stepwells. It is certainly the most lavish in terms of ornamentation and expense, and the grandest in terms of size. After many centuries of obscurity, it is finally getting its due – as is made evident by the fact that there is even a Rani ki Vav Facebook page. Commissioned by Queen (*rani*) Udayamati around 1063 to honour her powerful late husband, Bhimdev, this outstanding monument was granted UNESCO World Heritage Site status in 2014. It is now one of thirty-five UNESCO sites in India, and since it is an easy hour's drive from the busy city of Ahmedabad, perhaps new fans will be lured to see it.

At 64 metres (210 ft) long and 27 metres (89 ft) deep, Rani ki Vav would impress by scale alone. But it is the sculptural decoration that takes one's breath away. Hundreds of sculptures and reliefs of deities, their consorts and animals, as well as a variety of patterns, are rendered in astonishing detail; adorning almost every surface, they are considered some of the finest sculpture of their era. Incredibly, each block of stone was hauled from a quarry 140 kilometres (87 miles) away. It is no wonder that ornate columns, stone blocks and some of the deities were cannibalized over the centuries.

Rani expert Kirit Mankodi estimates that the vav took between fifteen and twenty years to build; however, disaster struck soon after completion. Rani's source of water was the nearby Saraswati River, but the river changed course, and the well filled with mud and silt. At some point, sections of the structure collapsed, and it began to disappear. By the nineteenth century, only part of the cylinder and some column stumps were visible above ground. It was not until the ASI undertook serious conservation work in the 1980s that the full scale of the stepwell was uncovered. To get a glimpse of some of Rani's pilfered elements, visit the much smaller Bahadur Singh Barot ki Vav (pp. 204–207) a few kilometres away. Columns and sculptures were hauled there in the early 1800s – a somewhat easier journey than that between the quarry and Patan in Udayamati's time.

Seen from above (right, top), Rani ki Vav resembles a deep canyon, but at ground level it is invisible until one is just a few feet from the edge. Inside, superb craftsmanship is evident in every detail.

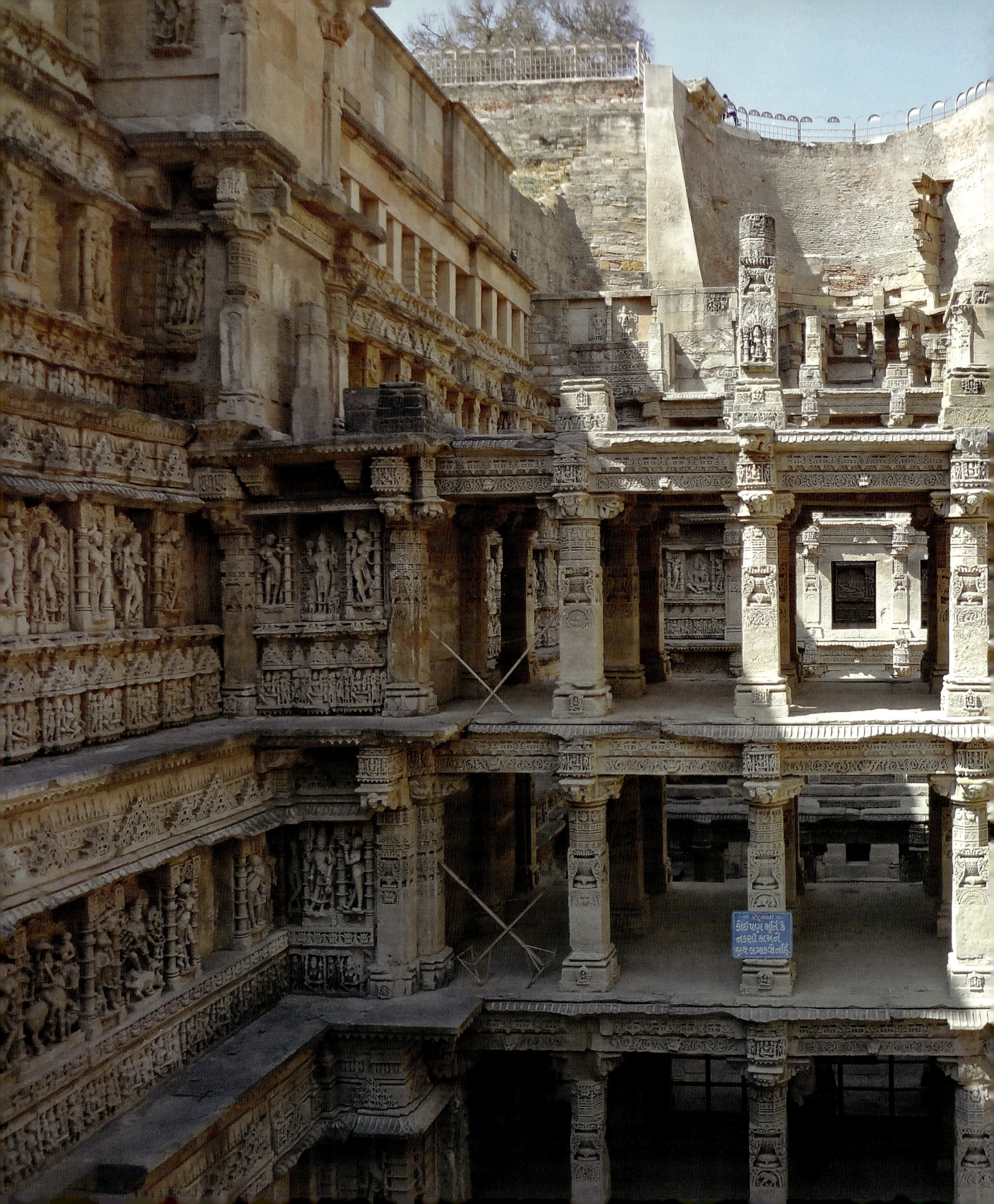

More than 600 sculptures form a dense veneer that covers each wall of Rani ki Vav. Enormous pavilions shored up the walls, but these eventually collapsed after the nearby river altered course, and the site filled with mud and silt.

KUNDVAV

KAPADVANJ, GUJARAT
c. 1120
23°1'23.26" N
73°4'16.31" E

The small city of Kapadvanj lies about 70 kilometres (43 miles) east of Ahmedabad. Centuries ago it was wealthy owing to its location along an inland trade route, and some significant architecture is still to be found in the old city centre. The region was ruled by the Solanki dynasty, whose members were consumed with building some of the most noteworthy and elaborate structures in India. Siddharaja Jayasimha (r. 1094–1143) expanded the Solanki empire and was a great champion of art and culture. Among the structures he commissioned in Kapadvanj are a number of stepwells and also an ornate *toran* (arch) that is worth a visit in itself.

The name Kundvav says it all: this stepwell takes the funnel-like form of a kund. It is located right in the city centre, at the base of a looming tower. Many old buildings surround the 900-year-old structure – in fact, are built right up to its edges – and the well itself is in a neglected state and strewn with rubbish. Kundvav is said to have more niches than any other stepwell; there are over 130 in total, embedded in each level and in each set of steps. Even though the deities inside the niches have long since disappeared, there is a marvellous staccato visual rhythm wherever the eye rests – except that it rests on litter, too. Two of the three original little pavilions overlooking the water still stand guard, their roofs and eaves barely holding up; sculpted deities and *kichaka* (dwarf figures) cling to the columns.

It is sad to see the extraordinary arch trapped in this utterly forlorn setting. Considered one of the finest such examples in Gujarat, this would have been the very grand entrance to what was once an important destination. Unfortunately, the arch – with its elaborate reliefs of battling elephants, intricate patterns and a host of deities with eroded features – is so hemmed in that it is almost impossible to take a decent photograph.

Older locals recall swimming in the five-storey pool decades ago, and recount the legend of the stepwell's inception: Jayasimha's mother had a skin ailment that was cured by the Kapadvanj spring. Clearly a good son, Jayasimha built Kundvav soon after her recovery.

Once a place of ritual, Kundvav is slowly dying. The top floor of a neighbouring house is the only place where one can obtain a clear view of the complete structure and the monumental arch.

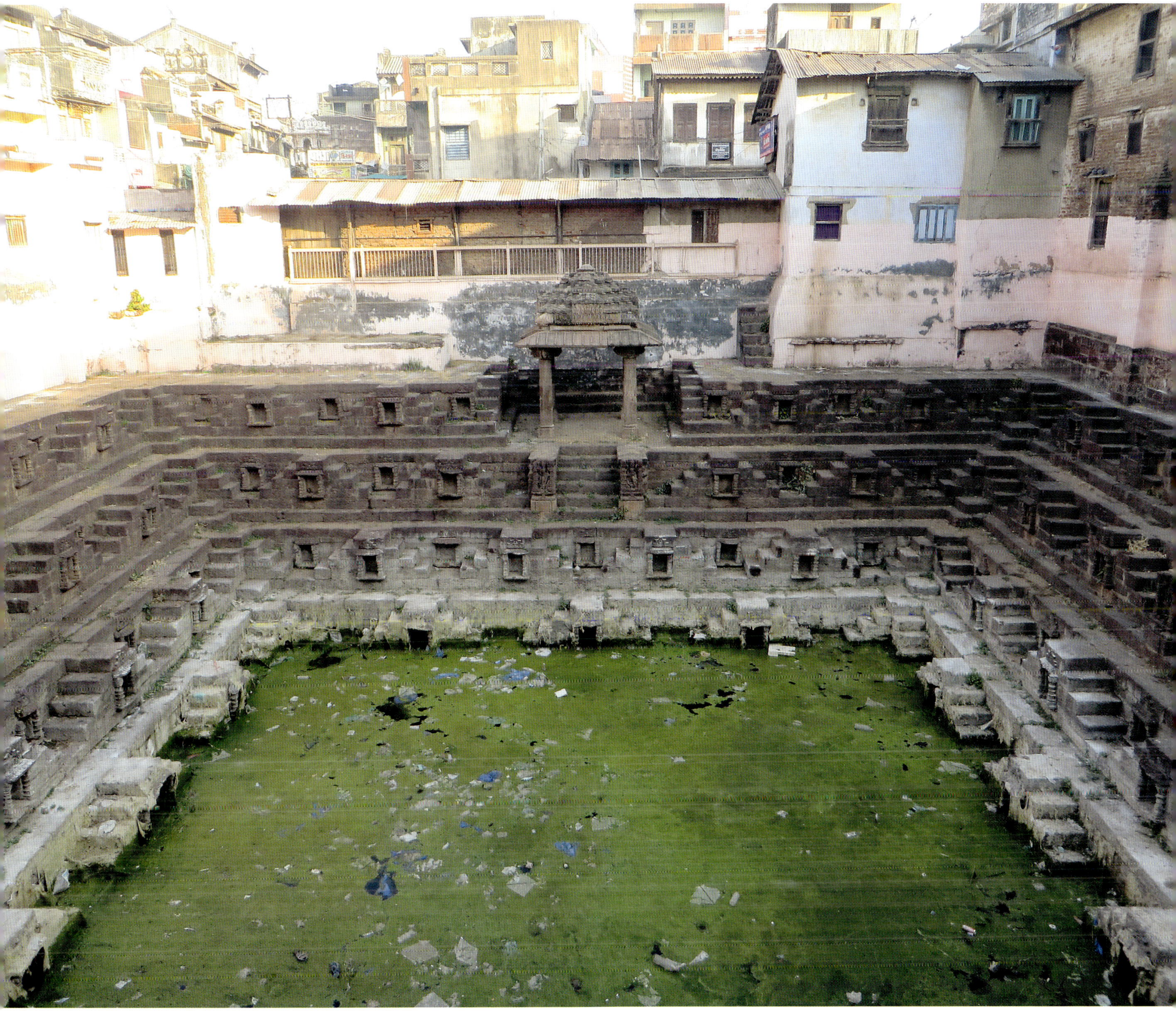

BATRIS KOTHA VAV

KAPADVANJ, GUJARAT
c. 1120
23°1'23.65" N
73°4'17.21" E

Batris Kotha is another project built during Jayasimha's reign, but this stepwell was as modest as Kundvav was grand, the latter's niches, deities, pavilions and monumental arch being still powerful enough to suggest their original impact. Batris Kotha has no aristocratic connections, and now, squashed uncomfortably between tall buildings, it stifles the imagination. It has even less visibility than most stepwells, and there is no vestige of its spatial relationships, no clues about its position in the landscape or its profile as visitors approached.

One thing is certain: the well is deep. Its name means 'Thirty-Two Storeys', and that probably seemed the case by the time anyone reached the bottom. Today, with the tank full of murky water and the well cylinder inaccessible, the depth is not discernible. However, as one stands on the top step, the incline is so steep that there seems to be no staircase left, just a sheer drop off a cliff. The first pavilion tower, or *kuta*, appears far below, two levels down.

At Batris Kotha, as is typical of a utilitarian stepwell, decorative elements are subdued, and if there are alcoves for deities or shrines, they are now obscured. On the second, taller, pavilion tower, a carved stone balcony displays a simple but dynamic pattern of lozenges and rectangles. This would have been the most ornamental feature of Batris Kotha, and was a popular decoration at many stepwells. Here, the pattern is rather overshadowed by the green vines that are draped across the red sandstone. Although the vines enhance the scene, they will ultimately damage the structure.

Many of the huge masonry blocks that formed the walls at Batris now lie in piles near the steps. They were removed to make way for newer buildings layered on top of the old. In comparison to these mighty stones, however, the modern brickwork looks positively flimsy.

Batris Kotha is somewhat forlorn but beautiful. Barely visible through the greenery (right, top), the stepwell plunges to an unknown depth. Masonry blocks were removed to accommodate new construction (right).

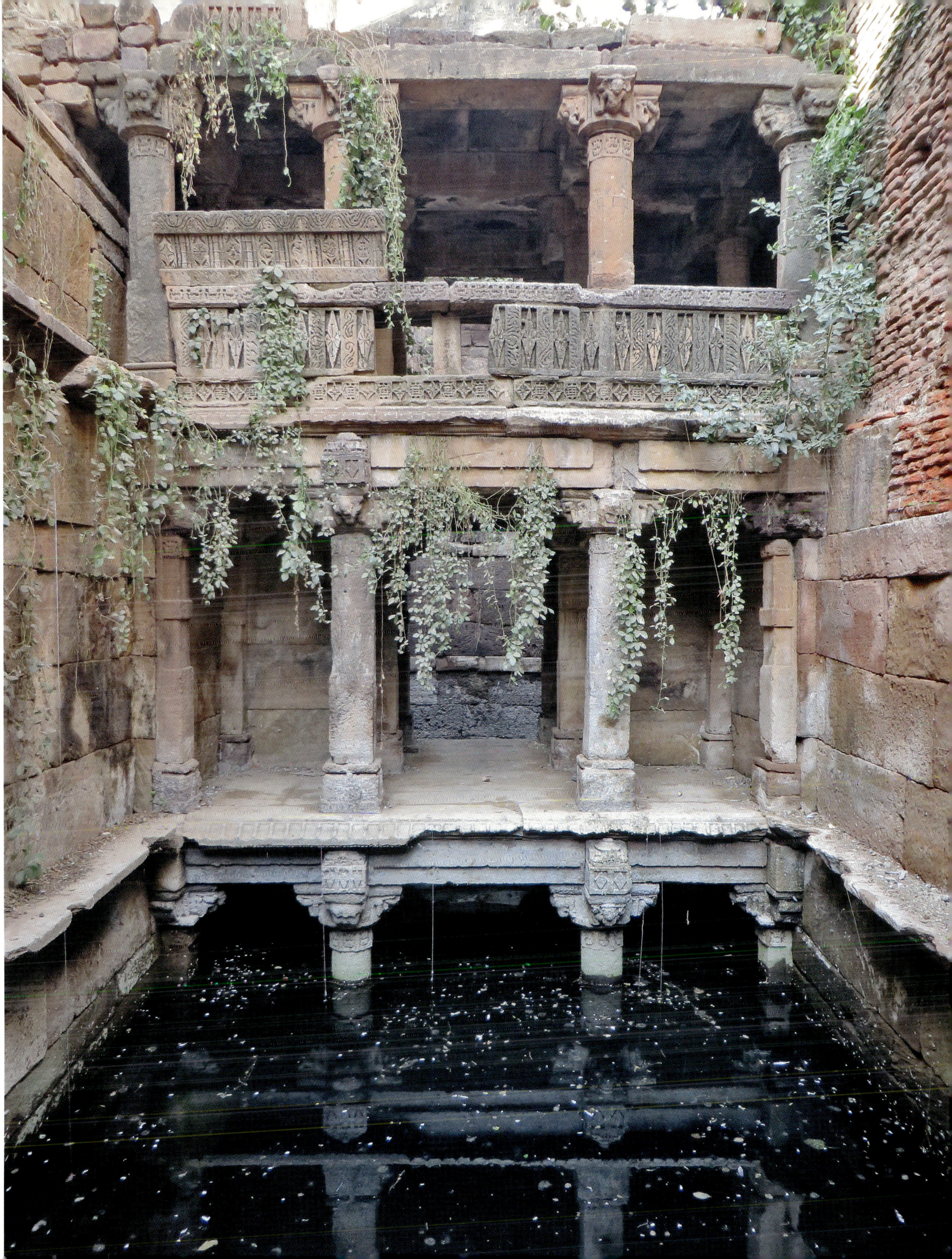

DHANDHALPUR VAV

DHANDHALPUR, GUJARAT
c. 1120
22°23'29.3" N
71°21'37.77" E

The population of Dhandhalpur hovers around 3000 inhabitants. The town is thought to have been founded by Siddharaja Jayasimha to commemorate his remote birthplace, some 200 kilometres (125 miles) from Kapadvanj. The vav is believed to have been built by the same Solanki ruler as a gift to the townsfolk, who required a source of irrigation and somewhere to water their animals; their needs were somewhat different from those of the wealthier city dwellers who used Kundvav and Batris Kotha.

The scale is impressive. Three chunky pavilion towers project above ground level, making the vav easily visible to anyone in need of water. If Jayasimha were indeed the patron, he held back the artistry that he lavished on his beloved Kundvav. But there is one unique, if subtle, feature: each tower is topped by a small corbelled dome, flanked by pyramids, as seen in later vavs such as Madha and Rataba (pp. 70-73, 96-99). This unusual design certainly pushed the architectural envelope a little. *Kichaka* (dwarf figures) and *kirtimukha* (lion faces) stare down from the capitals on the columns that support the roof of each tower. The clear water teems with tiny fish and, nearby, the original stone water trough continues to attract cattle.

Dhandhalpur Vav is in need of help. Although it has protected status, it is risky to explore; one shake and it could fall down. The columns are deeply eroded, and dangerous cracks can be seen under the pavilions; one chunk of stone is on the verge of dropping. After 900 years, it is a miracle that the vav has not toppled. With a little luck, maybe it can press on for another hundred years or so.

The domes and pyramids atop the pavilion towers at Dhandhalpur reflect diverse construction styles. Erosion weakens the structure surrounding a frieze of deities (above). In spite of its perilous state, the well contains surprisingly clear water.

GELMATA NI VAV

BHADLA, GUJARAT
c. 13th CENTURY
22°11'10.94" N
71°6'7.59" E

Visitors to Gelmata ni Vav pass the shrine to Babero and his offerings of cigarettes (below, centre). After drinking the sacred water, they often leave behind piles of stones that signify prayers (opposite).

Protected by the Gujarati government, Gelmata ni Vav, in the small town of Bhadla in Rajkot district, is a popular destination for pilgrims and families eager to pay their respects to the goddess Gelmata and to partake of the waters blessed by her. The local priest explained the legend of this L-shaped vav to me; similar stories are repeated at many other stepwells. An evil spirit, Babero, lived on a nearby hill and kept killing the locals. This upset Gelmata, who, as a form of the fierce goddess Durga, arrived and in turn killed the malevolent spirit. But Babero's ghost returned and, having transformed into a good-hearted entity, apologized profusely for his bad ways. As penance, Gelmata suggested that he build a stepwell for the populace, which he did overnight. Just before visitors descend into the well there is a little shrine to honour Babero, and because he enjoys smoking, devotees leave lit cigarettes for him.

As one goes down the first flight of steps, past Babero, piles of pebbles teeter on a narrow ledge, each left by a visitor hoping to have a prayer granted. Such piles are frequently seen at holy sites, and at Gelmata they enrich an environment that is teeming with life and devotion.

The masonry in the narrow, three-storey vav employs a wide variety of shaped sandstone blocks, but the joints between the stones – in fact, much of the walls – are now eroded. A very dark, covered space, created by a turn of the corner under the first tower, makes a series of niches – and indeed everything else – difficult to see. It is a transformative experience to emerge once more into the bright sunlight; the transition from dark to light marks a powerful physical and psychological boundary as one nears the sacred water.

The corridor ends abruptly in another dark pavilion at the water's edge. There is a quasi-barrier in place, but it is largely ignored as everyone crowds forwards to scoop up the blessed water. Adults and children take a drink; the babies get a dribble, too, and then, the pilgrimage complete, the procession reverses up the steps, past Babero, who is still smoking.

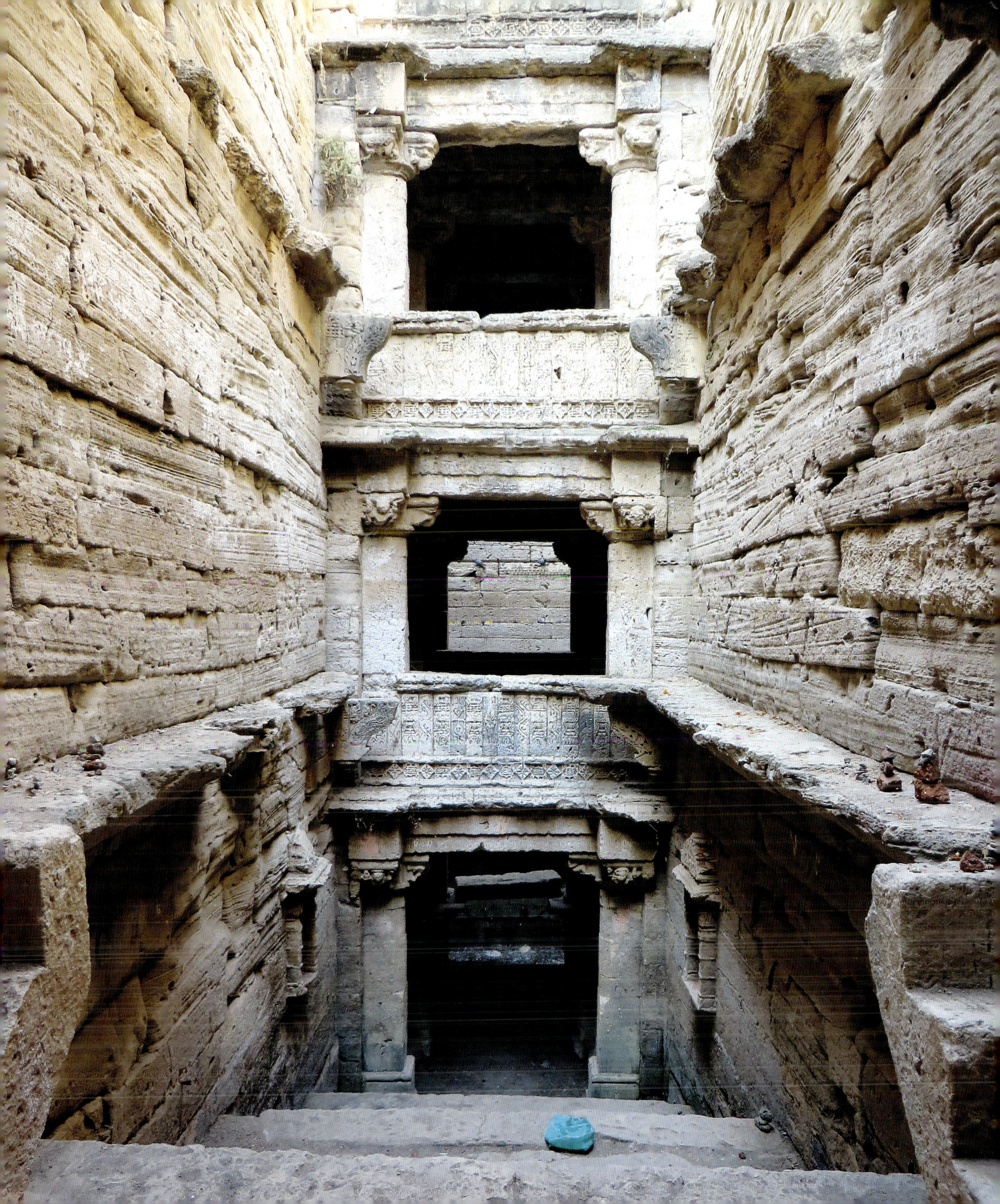

GANDHAK KI BAOLI

DELHI
1211–36
28°31'14.94" N
77°10'53.97" E

In common with all ancient major cities in India, Delhi was once home to many stepwells – more than 100 by current estimates, built during various reigns over the centuries. Of the few that survive, Gandhak is the oldest. Ignominiously named after the smell of sulphur, which no longer emanates from its water, it – like many stepwells – was said to have medicinal powers. Gandhak was constructed around the time of the creation of the Delhi Sultanate, a far-reaching, pre-Mughal Islamic kingdom. Sultan Iltutmish (r. 1211–36) made Delhi his capital. It is believed that the well was built for Bakhtiar Kaki, an influential Sufi mystic and scholar, whose teachings inspired the ruler. Hearing that there was no place for the Sufi to bathe, Iltutmish commissioned the well as a gift.

The narrow, five-tiered well sits in the village of Mehrauli, now part of greater Delhi. The drastically depleted water table had caused the baoli almost to dry up until the ASI led a recent programme of desilting. Now that the water level has been restored, local people are often to be found here, washing, swimming during the hot months and occasionally camping out. The architecture is simple, with just a discreet four-columned portico partitioning off the well cylinder.

In spite of the efforts to resurrect one of Delhi's oldest monuments, it is still in danger from the community growing rapidly around it. Illegal construction continues to encroach on the site, and traffic passes directly by the walls; the situation is difficult to control at best. When you are next in Delhi, see Gandhak while you can.

Gandhak is believed to be the oldest baoli in Delhi. Its water level has fluctuated over the years with the changing water table, but the well is still used for washing and bathing.

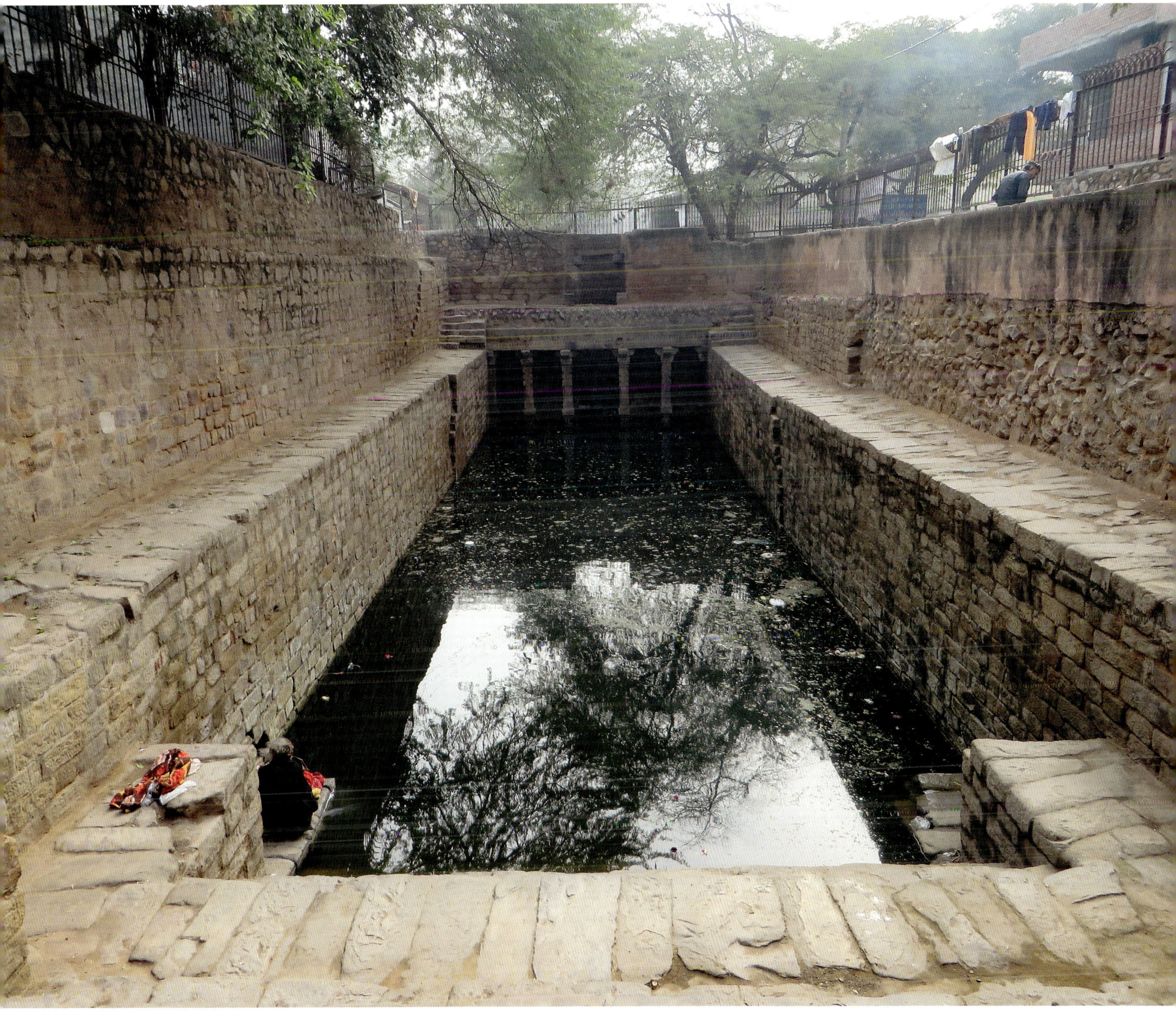

RA KHENGAR VAV

VANTHALI, GUJARAT
c. 1230
21°29'31.26" N
70°23'4.03" E

A sign for the Department of Gardens at Junagadh Agricultural University makes no mention of the unusual vav that waters the surrounding lush greenery. And the little government sign nearby does not offer any factual details; however, in their research the scholars Julia Hegewald and Jutta Jain-Neubauer are in agreement about the general date of construction given above. What is certain is that Ra Khengar (there are various spellings of the name) was a king in this region during the thirteenth century, and the vav's somewhat flamboyant details correspond to those found at other structures dating from that period. Sadly, the well is also a layer cake, with an 800-year-old base and unpalatable modern frosting. At some point the vav was appropriated as a convenient foundation for new construction: a tidy office with a double portico and tiled roof bridging the site and overlooking the ancient cylinder. The first view of Ra Khengar, straight down the steps, is of the concrete arch supporting the architectural addition above. Such are the vagaries of government protection of heritage sites, but at least the arch and new building are centred.

Ra Khengar may not be large, but it has one particularly exuberant feature: a spacious gallery around the cylinder, similar to that at Indaravali Baoli (pp. 136–39) but more impressive by virtue of its elegance. It displays fine workmanship and provides close-up views of the massive stone supports used to haul up buckets of water, where some of the most accomplished carving can be seen. Unfortunately, this passage is accessible only from a walkway on the top floor of the well, and to reach it, one must pass through modern doorways cut directly into the cement bridge.

The beautifully crafted, highly animated sculpture at Ra Khengar is worth close examination. Carved geese parade around columns, where fierce *kirtimukha* (lion faces) and contorted *kichaka* (dwarf figures) peer down from the capitals; a galloping horse and rider are fitted skilfully into an odd angle of a bracket; lively deities and beautiful flora decorate many architectural features. But what would have been superb views both towards the steps and down them, towards the cylinder, are spoiled by the new bridge, plopped unceremoniously on top of the former pavilion tower.

A modern office building and arch mar the centuries-old construction at Ra Khengar. The upper walkway provides views of the ornate supports (right, centre).

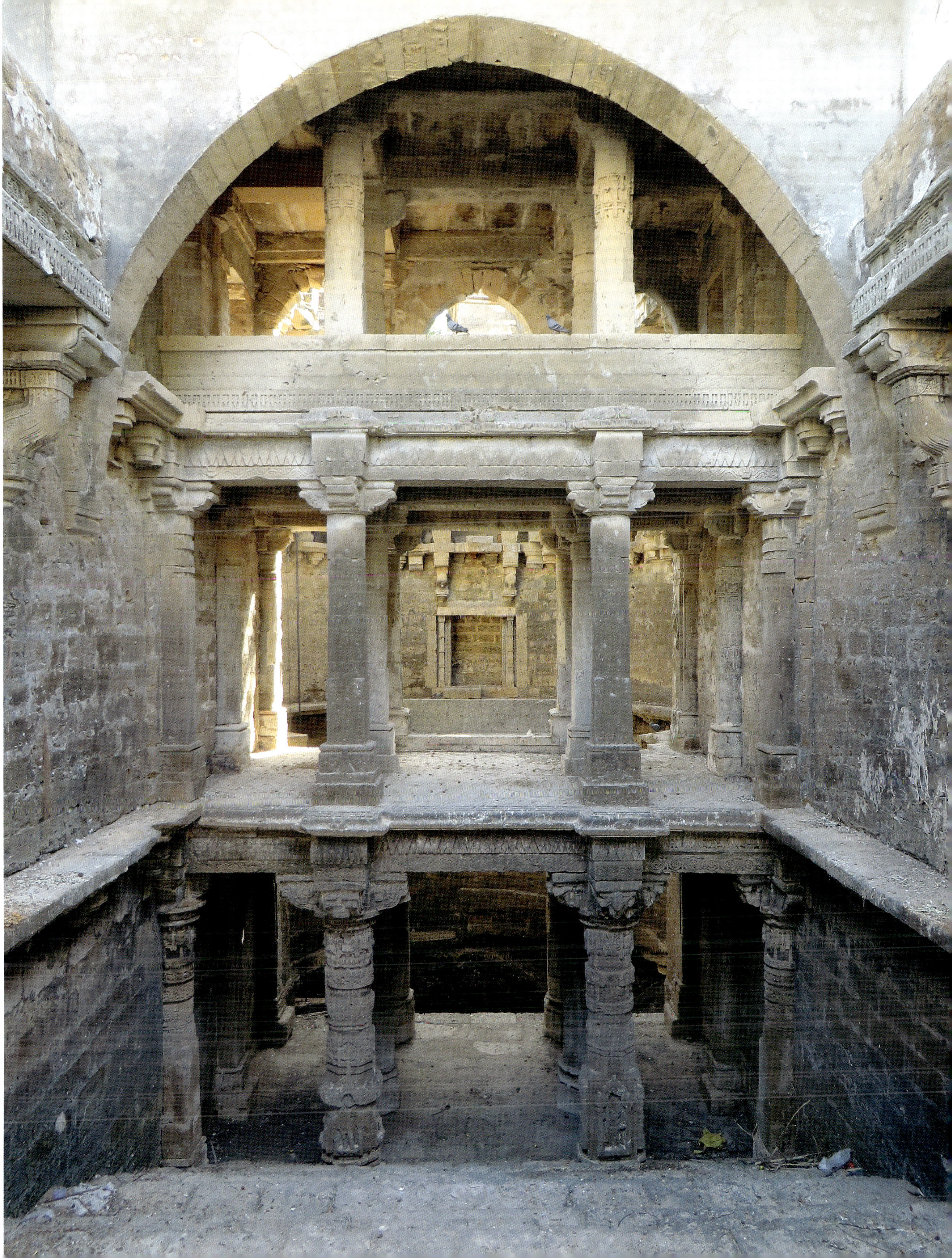

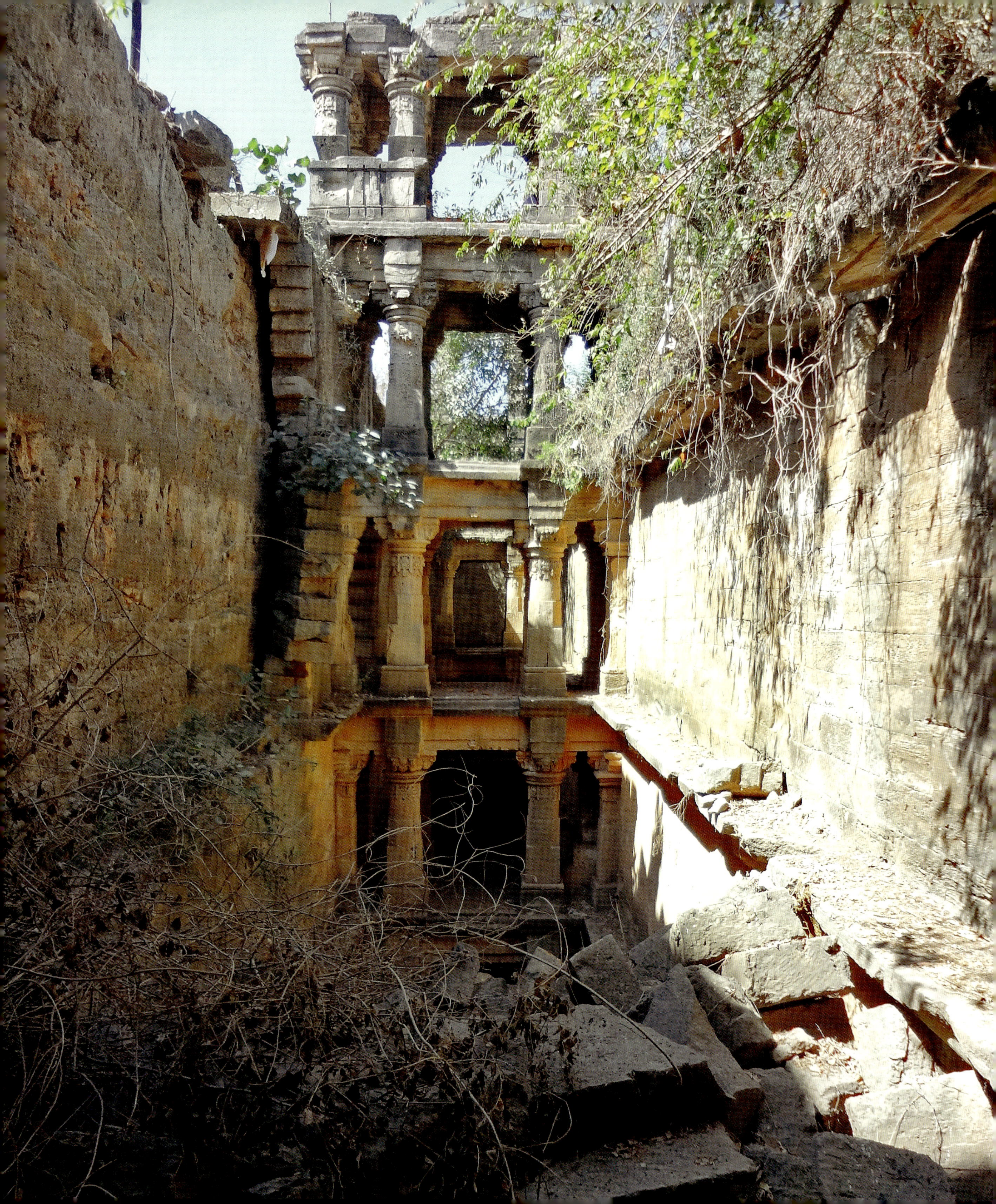

VIKIA VAV

GHUMLI, GUJARAT
c. 1250 (c. 12th CENTURY)
21°52'46.39" N
69°42'15.50" E

If any stepwell is emblematic of those that offered indispensable shade and refreshment to trade caravans and pilgrims in medieval India, the remote Vikia Vav is it. Located near the small town of Ghumli, which was an important capital from around 1220, the vav is 45 kilometres (28 miles) from the ancient port of Porbandar, and would have been a welcome oasis for weary travellers. There are a number of wonderful temples close by that are still visited by pilgrims, including the ornate, Solanki-period Navlakha Temple. However, Vikia itself cannot be described as overly decorative.

As one drives down a rocky path that is ruinous to tyres, the three monumental towers of the vav suddenly appear out of the dirt. The well's water source can be found in the Barda Hills, where a wildlife sanctuary thrives. Vikia – named after a local ruler – is an impressive five storeys deep and, at nearly 60 metres (197 ft), it is one of the longest vavs in Gujarat; but it is also almost comically squat. The large entrance pavilion, where benches overlook the first flight of steps, has a corbelled dome that has long since fallen into disrepair. Although the stocky columns seem to crouch and strain under the weighty roof, they have managed to hold it steady for more than 750 years. Each of the pavilion towers is surmounted by a covered platform with the same short, sturdy columns. A shady little shrine is maintained in the only tower retaining both a roof and floor.

Where capitals and friezes are intact, carved decoration is still visible, though badly eroded. *Kichaka* (dwarf figures) adorn capitals in the entrance and pavilion towers. That a vav as long and as deep as Vikia has only three towers is explained by the fact that it is narrow and is excavated from rocky terrain, and therefore requires less support than many other Gujarati stepwells.

Vikia Vav is in a far more precarious state today than is evident in earlier photographs. It is difficult to tell whether it has been weakened by the earthquake that struck Gujarat in 2001, by blasts from limestone mines in the vicinity or simply by the ravages of time. The well has collapsed entirely in places; the stone walls are peeling away from the sides, and there are dangerous holes in abundance.

Earthquake damage has probably contributed to the precarious condition of Vikia Vav. The sturdy-columned pavilions have managed to survive.

MADHA VAV

WADHWAN, GUJARAT
1294
22°42'33.69" N
71°40'28.17" E

Stories of human sacrifice abound in stepwell lore, along with tales of tunnels many kilometres long and baolis constructed overnight, as in the case of Gelmata (pp. 62-63). In the historic walled town of Wadhwan, the romantic but grim folktale of Madha Vav is so entrenched that it became a song describing the formerly accursed stepwell, which remained dry after its consecration. The townsfolk consulted a fortune teller, who suggested that a double sacrifice would break the spell. A pair of young newly-weds, the patron's own son and daughter-in-law, volunteered and, wearing their wedding clothes, entered the vav. The water rose with their every step, and at the seventh step they were submerged and drowned.

According to a worn inscription on the gateway to the vav, the stepwell was constructed in 1294 by Madhava, a government official during the reign of Sarangdev Vaghela (1275-97), and he paid for some exceptional stonework. Two perforated screens flank the entrance to the first pavilion, each divided into sixteen squares; each square has a different intricate – though badly disintegrating – pattern. In no other stepwell have I seen anything comparable to such delicate stone patchwork, and the deep, perpendicular niches are just as beautifully crafted. This is an astonishingly grand way to enter the main body of the stepwell, with the friezes that surround this entrance being similarly decorated, although the lively forms are difficult to decode. The niches in the pool itself are likewise heavily embellished, and house pairs of carved deities. But thanks to the selfless newly-weds of long ago, Madha is full of water, so it is not possible to proceed very far. The view is unobstructed, however, and the eye is drawn through all six pavilions towards the distance – sadly, not before stopping at the mass of detritus that has built up in the water and beneath the exquisite niches.

The pyramidal corbelled roofs atop the pavilions are another notable feature at Madha (and seen also at other vavs in the region). They are wonderfully sculptural, though nearly impossible to make out thanks to dense vegetation and the buildings packed either side of the vav. The generous (if incredulous) neighbours kindly allowed me to traipse through their homes for clearer views.

The pyramidal roofs of the pavilions at Madha Vav are also found at other stepwells in the region. The entrance to the first pavilion is flanked by intricately carved panels and shrines (right).

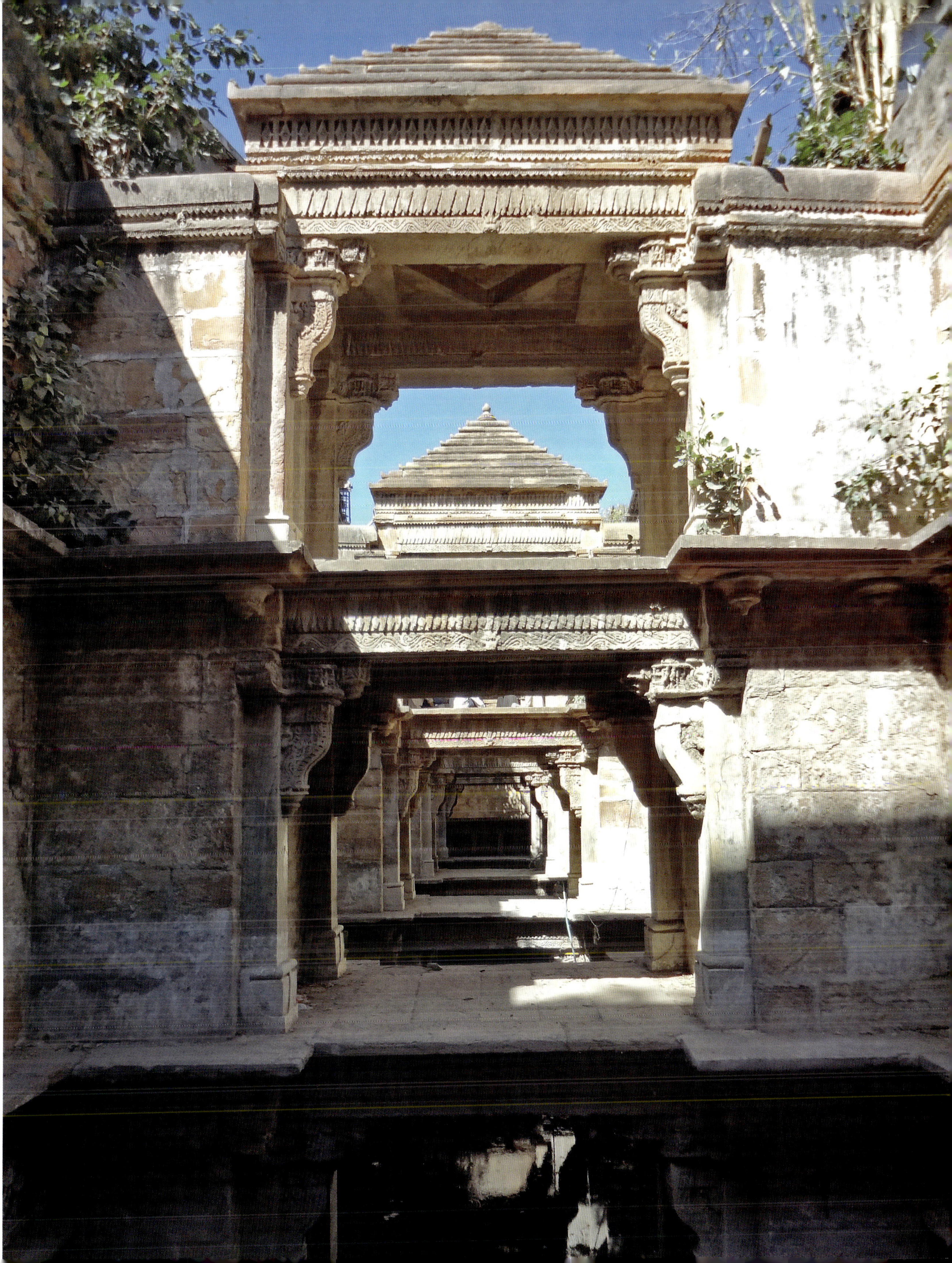

The parade of roofs set among foliage indicates how densely the neighbourhood has grown around the vav over time.

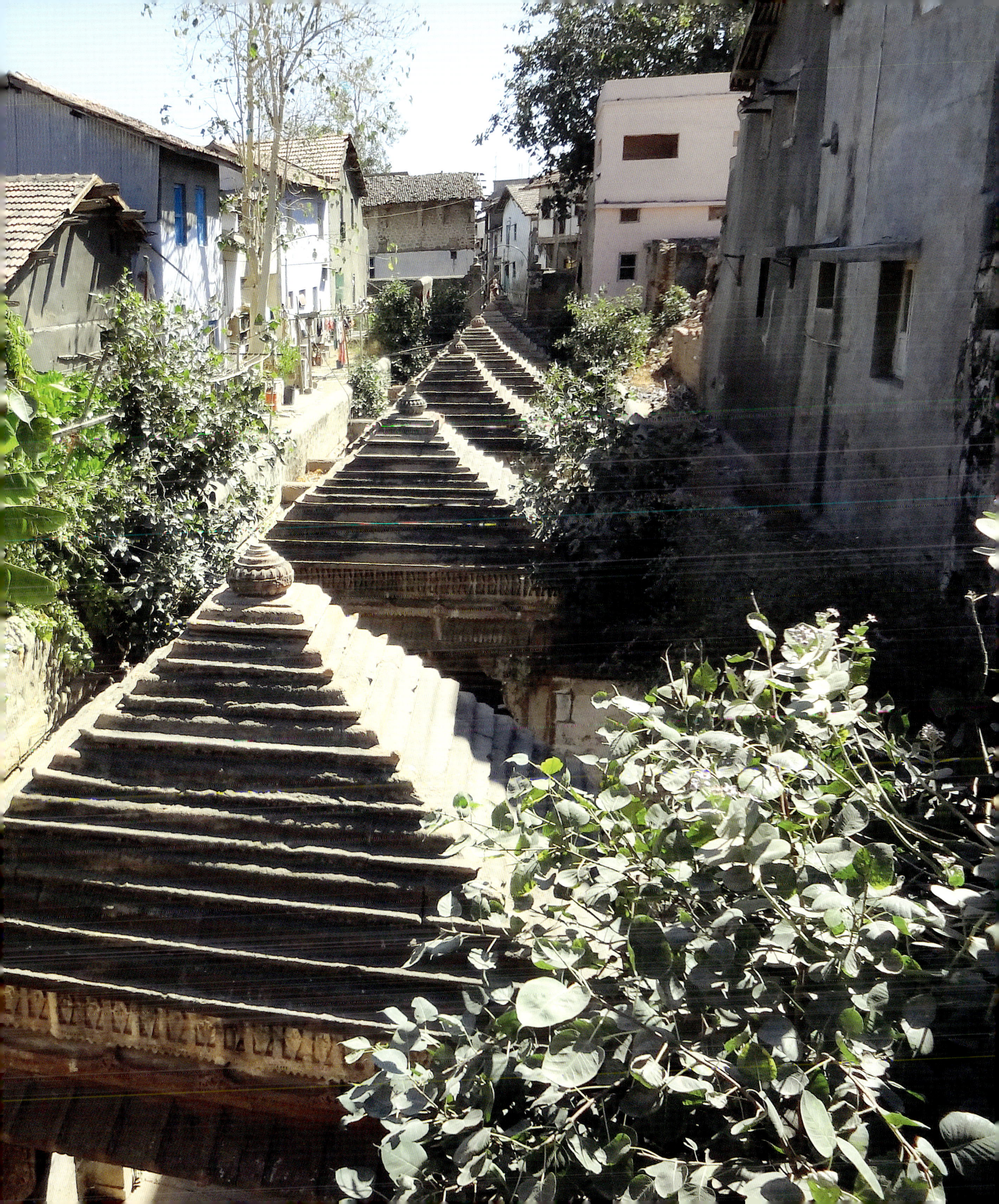

RED FORT BAOLI

DELHI
c. 14th CENTURY
28°39'32.17" N
77°14'27.56" E

Around 100 stepwells are estimated to have been built in Delhi. While only a handful remain, the surviving wells are fascinating and easily accessible, and have been priority restoration projects for the ASI. But hardly anyone knows about them. This handsome example, at the popular Red Fort in the city centre, is adjacent to a nondescript colonial-era barracks building, and has little to announce its presence except a metal fence. It is fortunate that the fence is there (even though the gate can be locked unexpectedly), since the stone perimeter is flush with the ground, and it is easy for non-vigilant visitors to topple in.

The existing fort dates to the seventeenth century (there were earlier forts on the site), and the baoli is thought to pre-date the current fort by some 300 years. While there is no record to substantiate this, the documented history of the well records that, prior to Partition in 1947, three Indian National Army officers awaiting trial were imprisoned here. Iron bars and bricked-in arches are still visible, but the toilet was – thankfully – removed.

Two mirror-image stepped entrances, set at a right angle to each other, give this two-storey baoli particular flair, but it is the use of stone that is most unusual. Perhaps there were many such masonry baolis in Delhi at one time; however, those that survive are typically constructed from rough rubble. Look closely, and a subtle alternating pattern is revealed. The use of open and blind arches also contributes to the considered elegance of the structure, and it is disappointing that the sophisticated patron is unknown – but that is, of course, normal in the case of stepwells.

The steps terminate at a small, circular pool (set within a square surround) that is fed by an adjacent octagonal well shaft. An arched gallery runs round two edges of the pool. Although not uncommon, such a feature makes any stepwell more striking, and this one affords some interesting views.

Post-Raj, the Indian Army took possession of the well at the Red Fort, and it became a weedy dump until 2002, when stewardship changed hands again and the ASI took control. The plants were cleared, centuries' worth of silt was hauled away, and water appeared again in the baoli, to be used for irrigation. At the time, a plan was announced to convert the structure into an exhibition space dedicated to India's struggle for independence, but that has not yet transpired.

Chambers converted into prison cells line the stepped corridors to the pool (above). When the water is high, it overflows from the well shaft into the pool (opposite).

75

FEROZ SHAH KOTLA BAOLI

DELHI
MID-14th CENTURY
28°38'9.44" N
77°14'40.75" E

Like Rome, Delhi is made up of many different layers, formed centuries apart; in fact, it is claimed that it is the site of seven previous cities. The fourth was Ferozabad, built next to the Yamuna River (which has since shifted much further east) as the new capital for Sultan Feroz Shah Tughluk (r. 1351–88). At the time, the sultan's *kotla* (citadel) had a beautiful walled garden, and today it is still a peaceful, much-needed green oasis in the centre of Delhi. With its ancient ruined monuments, it is a delightful place to visit, but it is particularly popular on Thursday evenings, when many people, local and otherwise, arrive to beseech *djinns* (related to genies) to grant their wishes. Candles and little notes abound.

The *djinns* arrived long after Feroz Shah had gone. He built this baoli as a private well for himself and his court; it is an early version of what would be seen centuries later as more complex 'retreat' wells, also found in gardens and palace grounds. Plunging up to six storeys underground, they, too, were circular and thus inward-looking, exclusive rather than inclusive. They were meant for private pleasure, away from public or just prying eyes.

This baoli, of rubble construction and two storeys deep, is currently undergoing restoration. However, the rhythmic parade of Islamic pointed arches is still prominent on the ground-level promenade. Below, a complex arrangement of passages, walkways, pilasters and chambers gives the visitor a sense of what it must have been like to spend the day at the palace pool. The water, still being pumped, now refreshes the surrounding lawns.

Visitors to the citadel leave behind incense and letters seeking help from the resident *djinns* (right, top). The rough rubble masonry of the baoli is common in Delhi stepwells.

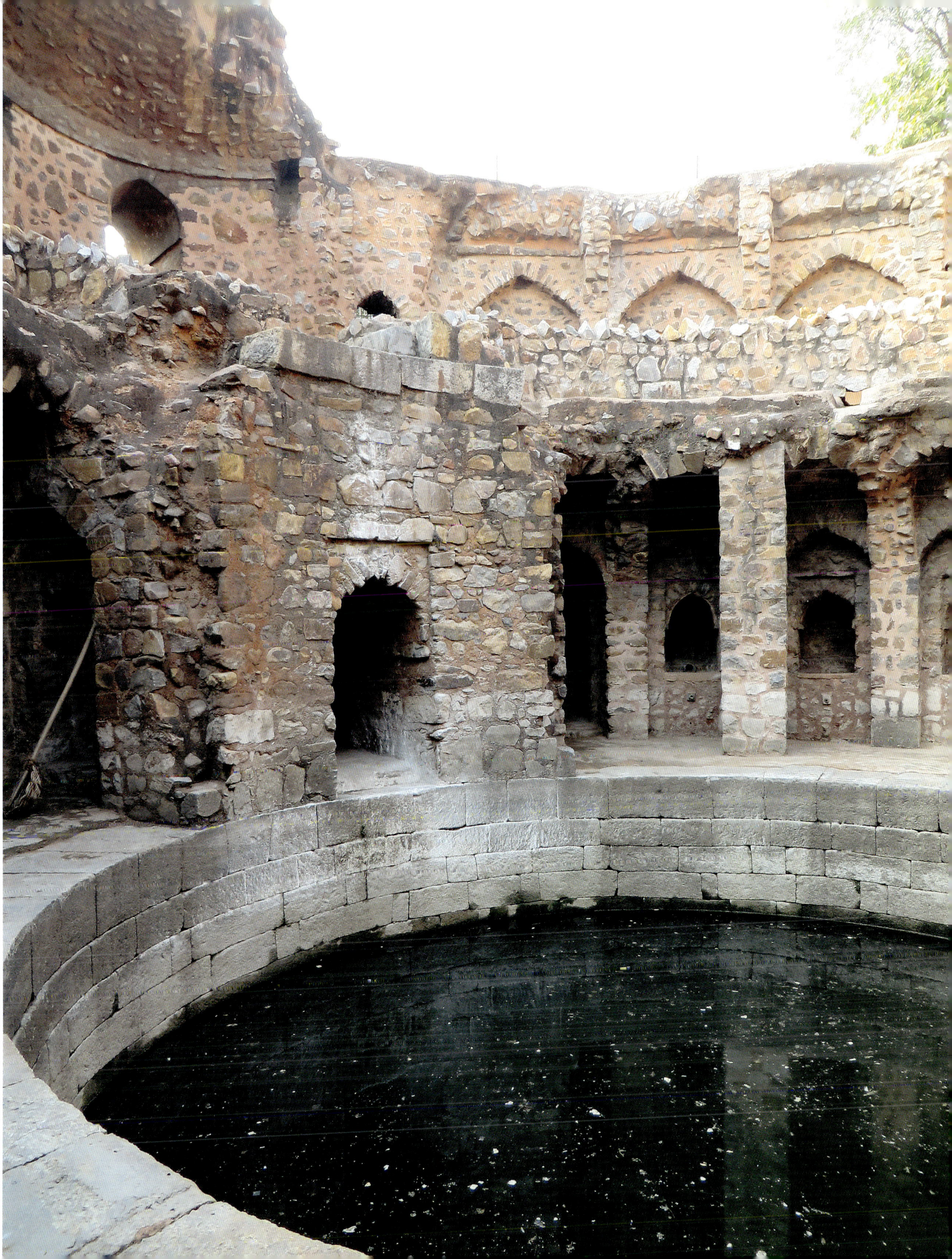

ADI KADI VAV

JUNAGADH, GUJARAT
c. 15th CENTURY (4th/10th/14th CENTURY)
21°31'35.46" N
70°28'15.66" E

Adi Kadi has one of the most wide-ranging spreads of possible dates cited in stepwell literature, but it is easiest to stick with the date (or century) of construction listed by the local government, which protects the site. The well's dramatic location, at the rocky Uparkot Fort, adds to its mystery, as does the nearby, equally enigmatic Navghan Kuvo (pp. 26-29), which also has debatable dates.

Viewed from above, Adi Kadi looks like a long, narrow incision in the rock, with a deep gouge at one end; it is an unusual, attenuated stepwell form. Hewn out of sandstone, the vav has more than 100 steps that descend towards the water at a gentle incline, rather than the more typical, frighteningly steep approach. Along the way, the passage narrows into a constricted canyon, with the resulting erosion of the walls creating intense abstract patterns that the architects could never have imagined.

This rather surreal corridor ends at the deep well shaft, the entrance to which is marked by an enormous block of stone and a natural rock bridge. It is a strikingly odd sight. The echoes of flapping pigeons intensify the somewhat unnerving atmosphere by the water's edge; this could vie for first place in a competition for 'most haunted stepwell'. According to one of the two myths associated with Adi Kadi (very similar myths are connected to many other wells), a double human sacrifice – in this case, poor Adi and Kadi, both young virgins – was required to ensure the flow of water. The second, less grisly, story claims that the two girls were water-bearing slaves for a local king. Either way, their names live on.

An elongated corridor of age-worn steps descends to the water, past eroded and striated walls. A huge stone block and a natural rock bridge mark the entrance to the well shaft (overleaf).

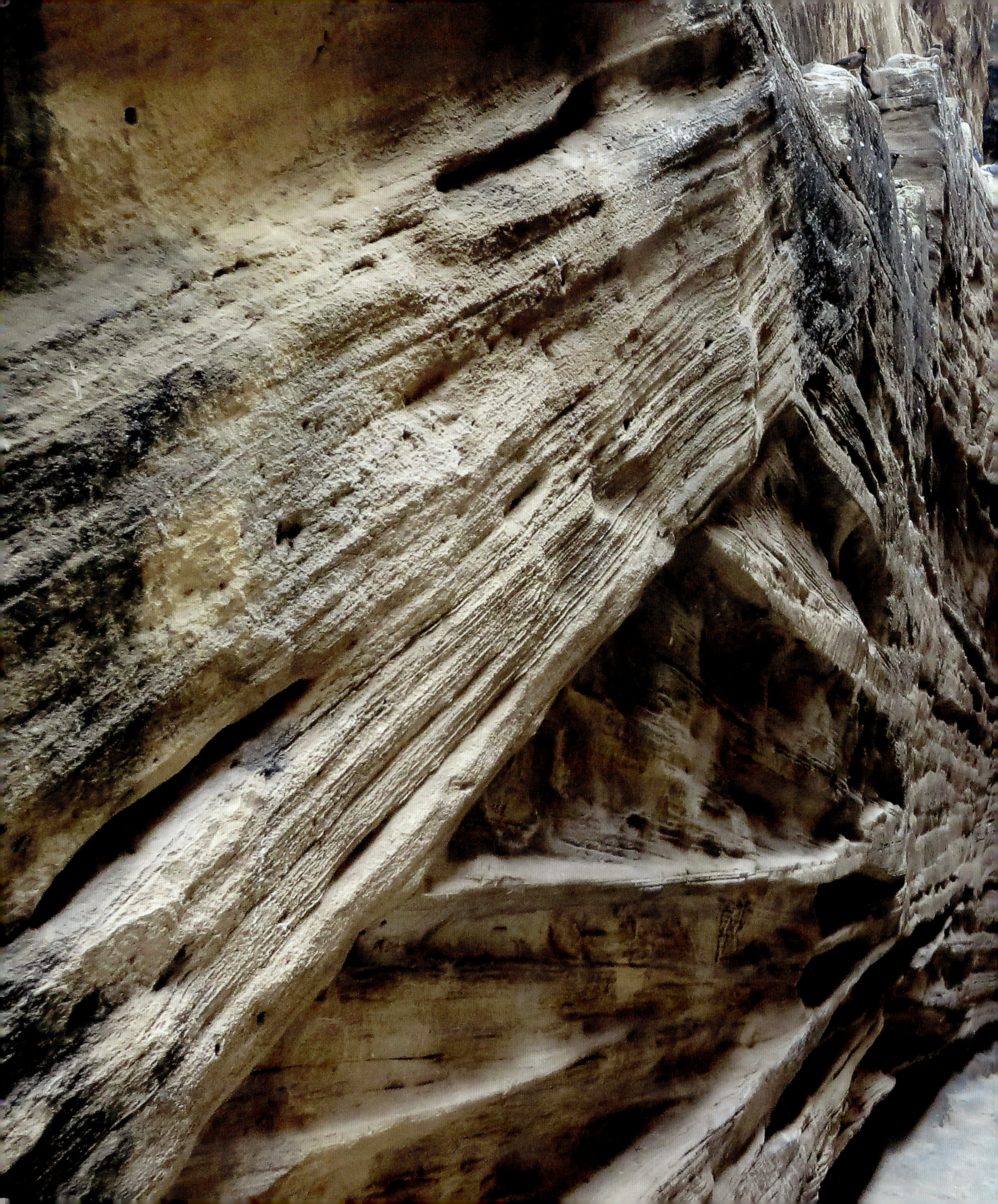

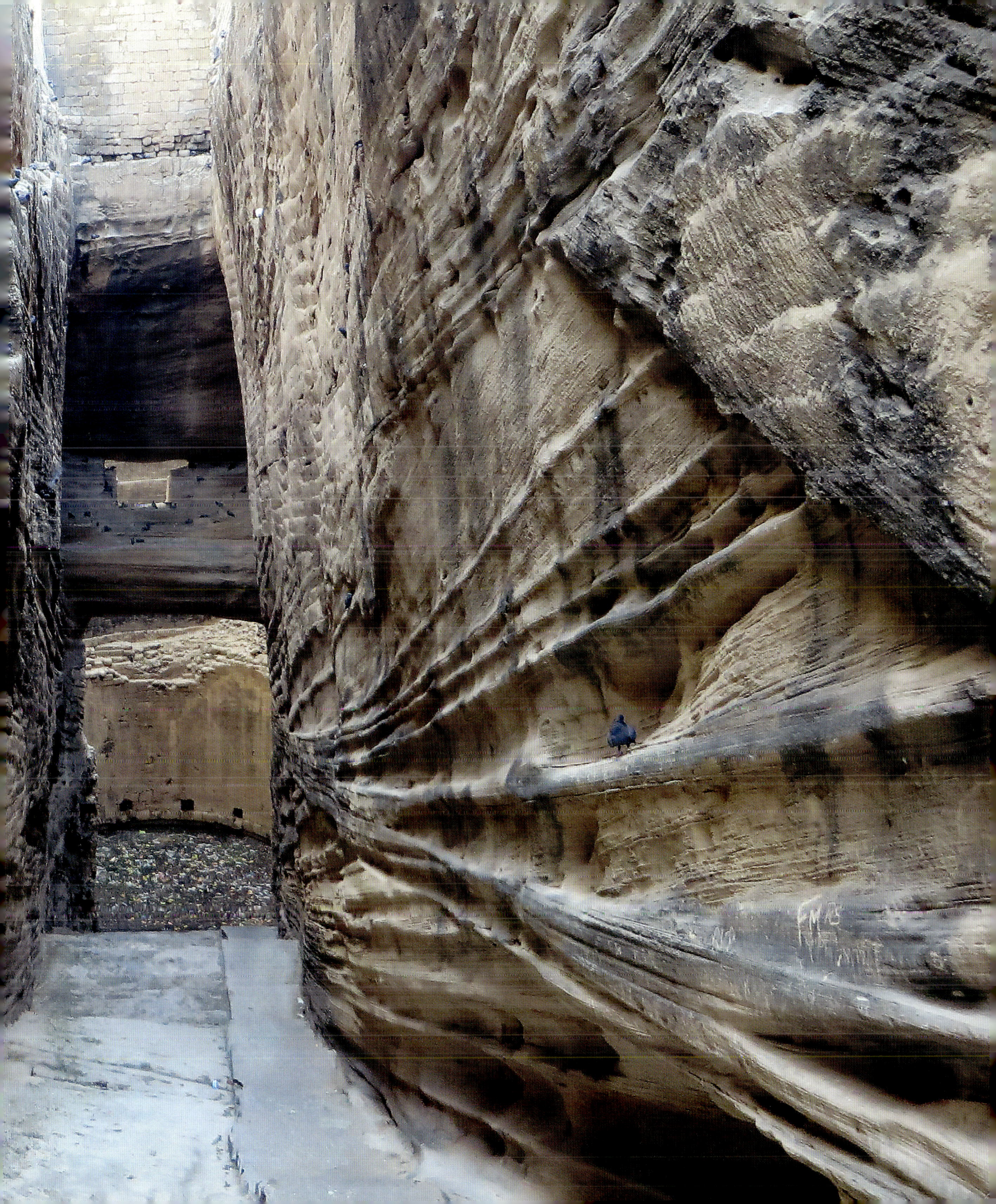

SARAI BAWADI

AMER, RAJASTHAN
15th CENTURY
26°57'55.83" N
75°52'7.12" E

This is what happens when good intentions go awry. A *sarai* - or caravanserai - was a humble roadside inn for travellers. There were several such inns and adjoining baolis along the popular route between Amer (which is today some 8 kilometres/5 miles from central Jaipur) and Agra. Behind the peaceful pool and graceful loggia at this pretty *sarai* is the well cylinder. The small village that borders the well avails itself of the water by running pipes into the cylinder.

The conservation architect Manas Sharma, who ascertained that the well was built in the fifteenth century, explains that the landslide that obliterated half of the structure was a fairly recent occurrence. A public-private initiative in 2008 identified this baoli as being among several around Amer and Jaipur that were in dire need of help (the nearby Kale Hanuman Baoli, pp. 184-85, was another). Sarai was in a terrible condition, the most urgent problem being a retaining wall that required stabilization. Unfortunately, the workmanship and materials (cement in this case) were seemingly unequal to the task, and the new wall collapsed into the well.

When I visited this well, there were chunks of concrete lying everywhere. Vegetation had already sprouted, and the once beautiful structure could be accessed only through piles of rubbish. The restoration of any stepwell is a costly venture, and the effort here was laudable. But the baoli is apparently now in a worse state than before the work began. The landslide could not easily have been predicted, but it is nonetheless disturbing to see such damage, particularly when one notes the relatively pristine condition of the facing wall and the loggia. It is difficult to know how to proceed; perhaps in the future generous new patrons will clear away the rubble and try again.

At Sarai, there is a startling contrast between the baoli's restored areas and the relatively recent landslide. A row of niches in the wall remains intact.

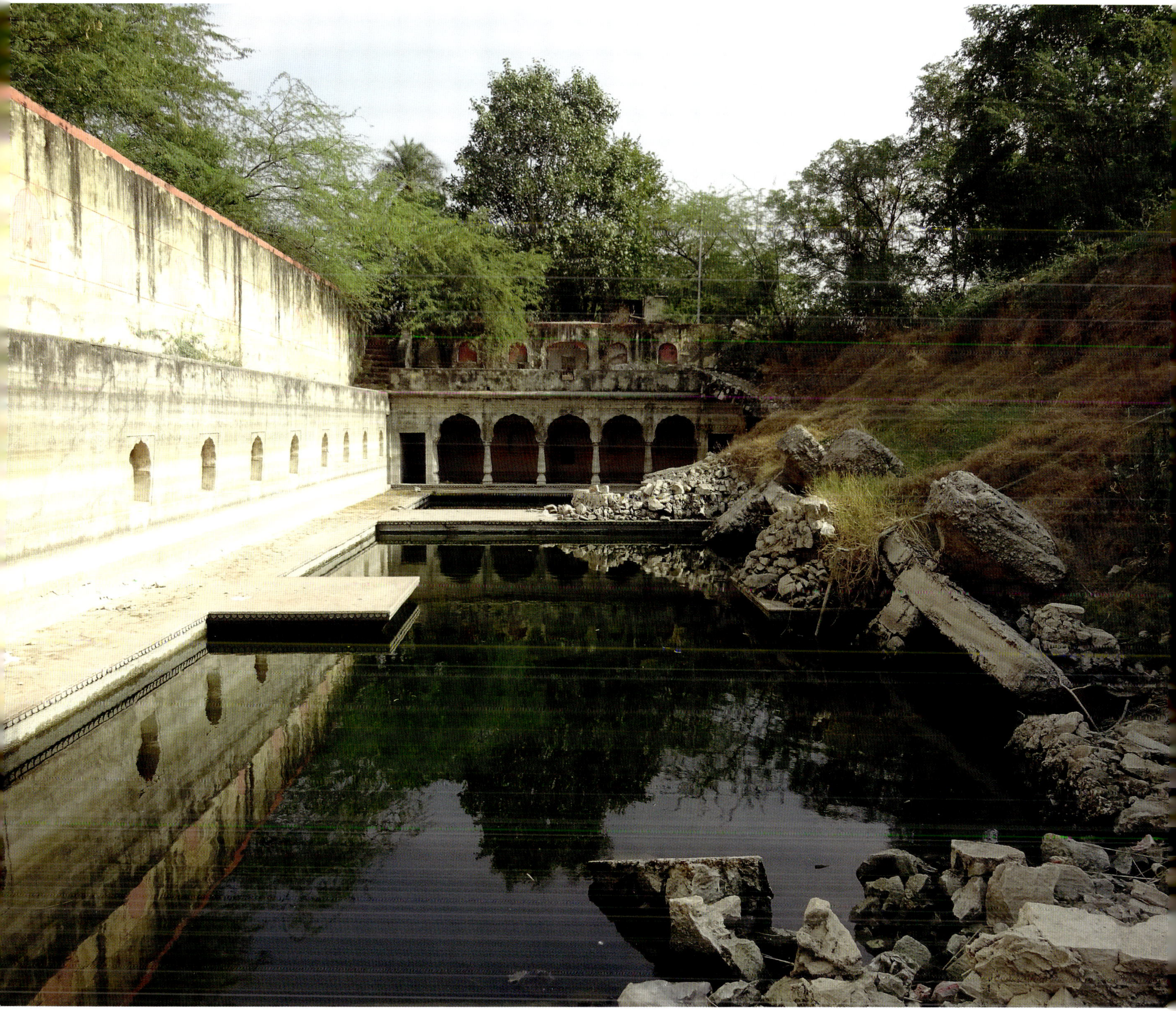

AGRASEN KI BAOLI

DELHI
c. 1400
28°37'33.75" N
77°13'29.76" E

Located on a quiet residential street, a few blocks from one of Delhi's most chaotic shopping areas and in the shadow of modern high-rises, Agrasen ki Baoli perfectly illustrates the way in which many stepwells hide in plain sight. It is surrounded by an unremarkable stone wall and attracted little attention until the popular Bollywood movie *PK* (2014), starring Aamir Khan, was filmed there. These days there are plenty of visitors to this once-secluded oasis in the heart of the city, and the baoli boasts its own website.

In fact, Agrasen was an oasis until the early twentieth century, when New Delhi absorbed the old village where the baoli was sited. For centuries it had been a utilitarian well, offering respite and shelter to travellers coming in and out of Delhi. They could hole up in the alcoves and corridors available on two of the four levels, their animals secure close by and plenty of water available. Simple as Agrasen may be by stepwell standards, to confront the unexpected four-storey drop is nonetheless a dramatic experience for the uninitiated. If tourists in Delhi visit just one stepwell, it is almost always Agrasen, owing to its proximity to hotels, a government handicrafts emporium and the shops around Connaught Place.

According to a local legend, the original patron of the baoli was the semi-mythical Emperor Agrasen, who supposedly lived more than 5000 years ago. While no solid evidence of his existence has been found, there was enough faith in the legend that the baoli was rebuilt around the turn of the fifteenth century by a member of the Agarwal community, who claim to trace their lineage to the emperor.

Another local legend has it that the baoli is one of the most, if not the most, haunted places in Delhi. Many stepwells are associated with stories of ghosts, and there is no denying that when they are devoid of people, and one is left with only the dark water below and the echoes of pigeons cooing and flapping, they can be spooky, even sinister places. Agrasen is far less eerie now that it is full of tourists, film buffs and students, who lounge for hours on its steps.

A famous image taken in 1971 by the renowned Indian photographer Raghu Rai depicts a young boy flinging himself off the edge of the baoli to swim in the water below. The water reaches nearly to the top, but the well's decayed condition is clear. Today, after the restoration efforts of the ASI, it looks positively pristine, even though the process of desilting and recharging the water is not complete. When that work is finished, Agrasen will function as an important cistern in a city desperate for water.

To combat relentless thrust, the well narrows noticeably towards the bottom (opposite, left). Agrasen ki Baoli is now a popular tourist destination, although some believe that it is haunted.

NAVLAKHI VAV

VADODARA, GUJARAT
c. 1405
22°17'44.4" N
73°11'29.01" E

Navlakhi Vav is one of the most unusual, visually confounding of all stepwells. It is located in the grounds of the flamboyant nineteenth-century Laxmi Vilas Palace, and tourists wander through the gardens, oblivious to the fifteenth-century treasure sited inconspicuously among the trees a few yards away.

A dedication plaque at the well states the date of construction and identifies Zafar Khan, nawab (governor) of Gujarat, as its patron. No one knows why the vav was situated in this spot or why, as in the case of any L-shaped well, it took that particular form. But the earth in this location was apparently softer than most soil in Gujarat, and therefore required more support than usual. As a result, the pavilion platforms that would normally hold back the walls are supplemented by a grid of narrow stone beams. The framework continues all the way down the five-storey well, and must have demanded complex engineering at every intersection.

The approach and entrance are unimposing, marked by a delicate little cupola and a low parapet; a short flight of steps leads to a large, multi-columned platform. Since this is an Islamic structure, there is no figurative decoration, but some simple geometric and floral carvings enliven the otherwise restrained columns and ceiling. The cross-bracing is by far the most ornamental aspect.

This entrance would originally have led directly to the pool. However, at some point a wall of brick and cement was erected between the columns, with a single doorway punched through. It is an uncomfortable transition, but it has to be said that passing through the opening certainly adds to the spectacle of the view beyond. The addition is as mysterious as it is troubling, with vestiges of the embedded columns visible here and there.

Looking down into the well from the parapet, one obtains a more rational view of what is going on with the cross-bracing, and sees that the stone grid connects four pavilions. But here is another mystery: how to reach the pavilions? Since they appear to be accessible only from the narrow cross-braces, only the sure-footed or intrepid should try.

The low parapet and shallow steps at Navlakhi Vav disguise structural complexity within. The profusion of cross-beams confounds the eye (opposite), but is certainly a feat of engineering.

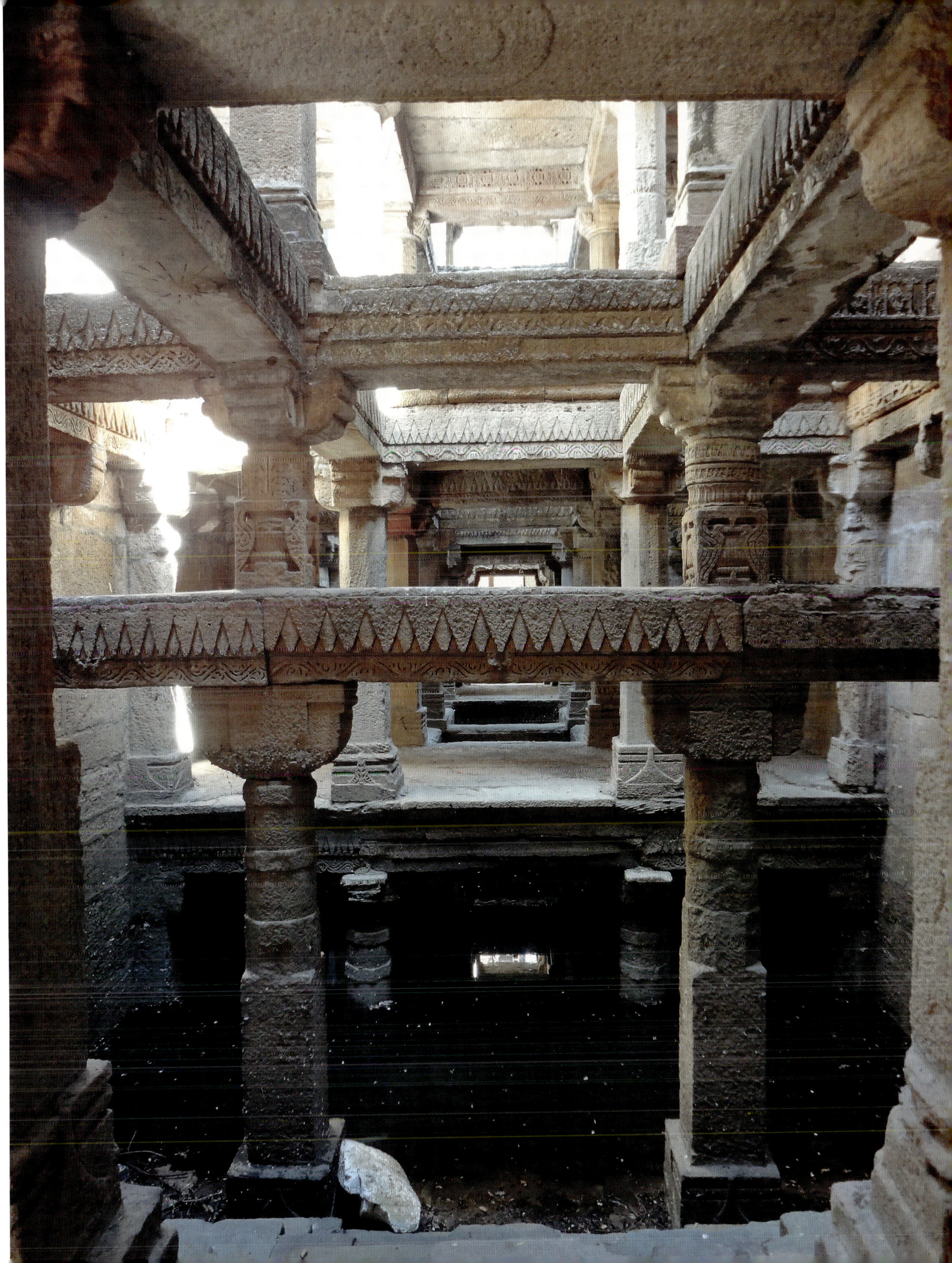

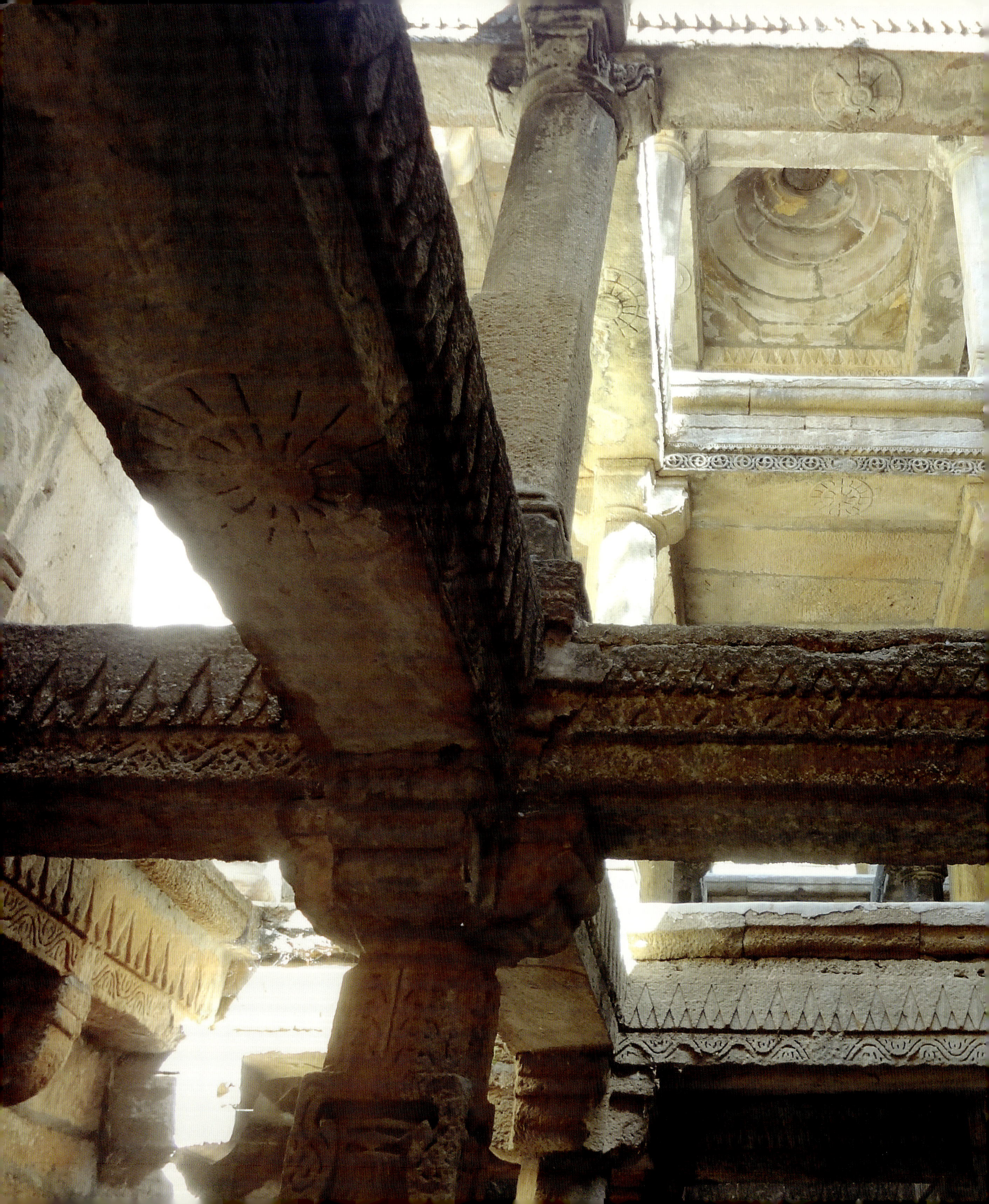

The short, mismatched columns differ markedly from their unadorned neighbours. They were undoubtedly appropriated from a different structure.

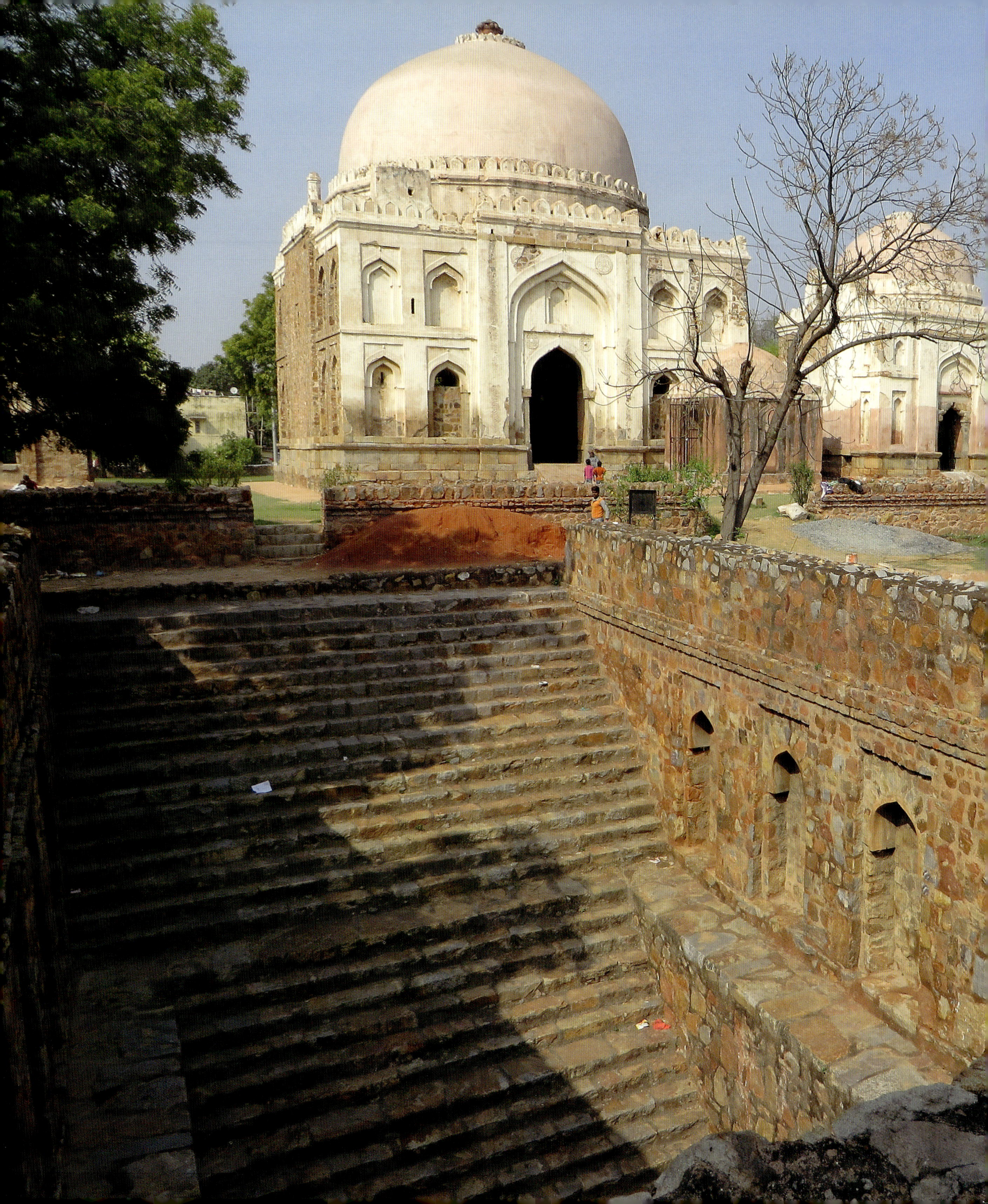

WAZIRPUR BAOLI

DELHI
1451–1526
28°33'45.06" N
77°10'29.85" E

Rama Krishna Puram – otherwise known as R.K. Puram – is a huge residential development in Delhi, begun in the late 1950s. It is almost a city within a city, and a small patch of park in Sector Five is an oasis, a place where families and couples can loll on the grass against a backdrop of dazzling sixteenth-century tombs and a small mosque. Actually, this is not unusual in Delhi; tombs are found on golf courses or in shopping areas, and have even been turned into office buildings. What makes the Wazirpur Monument Complex special is the surprise stepwell right in the middle. Compared to other wells in the city, this two-storey baoli is more a shock than a thing of extraordinary beauty, but the setting makes Wazirpur the most inviting. It also garners the most attention, thanks to the park's popularity. Children, in particular, enjoy playing in, on and around the baoli.

As in the case of many stepwells, little is known about Wazirpur. It is thought to share the same date of construction as the mausoleums, between 1451 and 1526, when the tomb-loving Lodi dynasty ruled the Delhi Sultanate. The group of monuments was built at some distance from any civic centre of the day; it was urbanization and the extension of New Delhi that transformed their pastoral origins.

Two small domed towers rise above the baoli's rear wall, and could be mistaken for tiny sepulchres themselves were they not attached to a well. Without them, there would be no way of discerning the presence of a stepwell behind the low rubble wall. The rest of the structure is modest in comparison to its cousins Red Fort, Agrasen and Rajon (pp. 74–75, 84–85, 122–23). From the top of the steps, there is an unobstructed view down to the circular pool at the bottommost level. In the dry season, this little pool would have to suffice.

Dignified Lodi mausoleums provide a picturesque backdrop to the unpretentious two-storey stepwell.

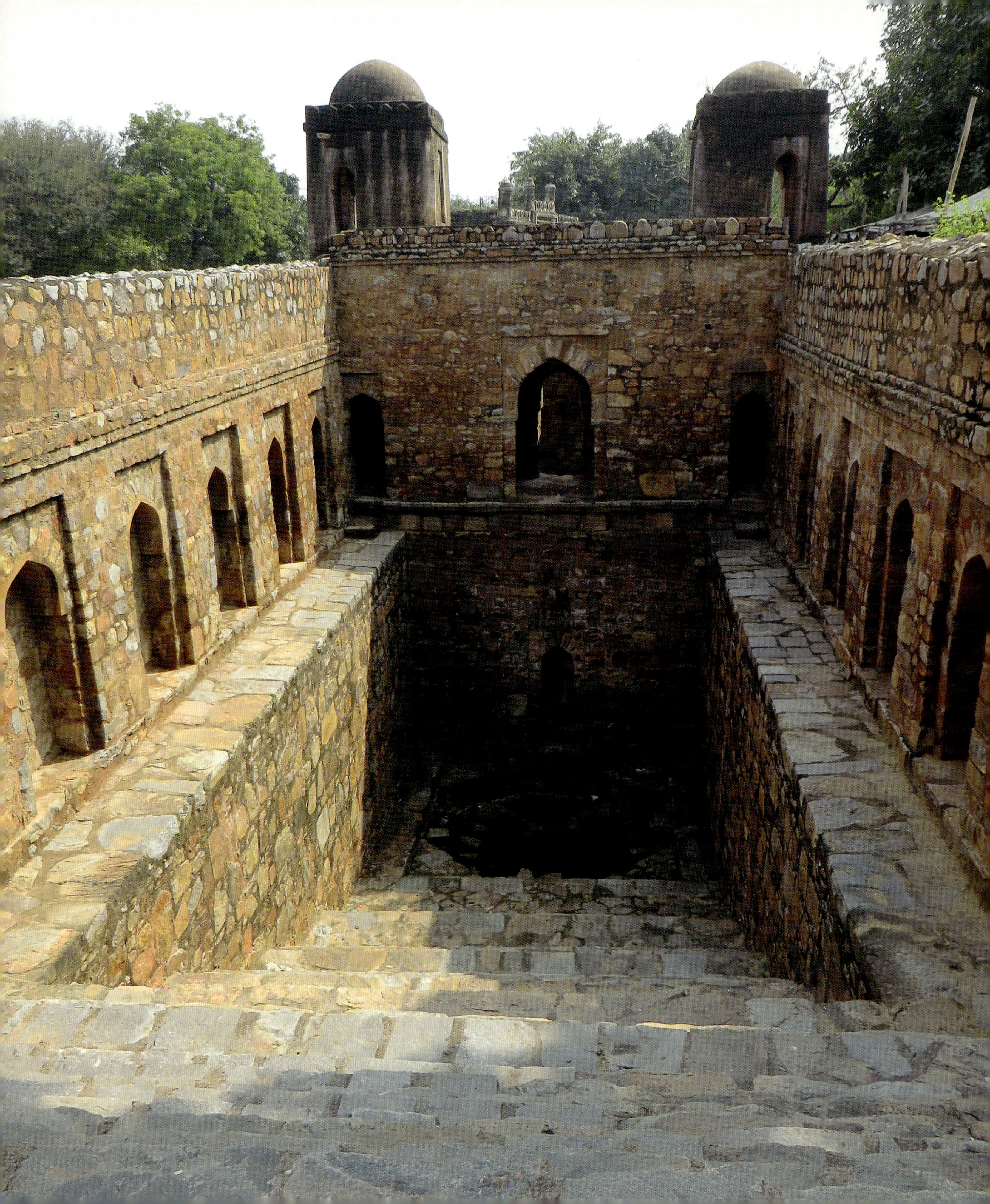

Blind arches enliven the walls, which terminate at a pair of vaulted towers (opposite). The well's cylinder is now blocked off from the pool (above).

SAMPA VAV

DEHGAM, GUJARAT
c. 1480
23°11'37.73" N
72°52'45.32" E

Sampa Vav is tucked away in a small town an hour's drive from Ahmedabad, and what little information can be gleaned about it apparently has not helped to establish the date of its construction. There are three possible dates from which to choose, proposed by three respected scholars, and the one cited here was reached by means of triangulation.

The stepwell – quite long and five storeys deep – is distinguished in a number of ways. It has three entrances: a main one and two, much narrower, side entrances. This cruciform arrangement is unusual, but not unique; it is also seen at the larger, flashier and better known Rudabai Vav (pp. 103-105), just over 30 kilometres (19 miles) away. As in the case of Navlakhi Vav (pp. 86-89), Sampa required some extra engineering. There are stone struts between the pavilions and, although the construction is not as complex as that of Navlakhi, the views inside Sampa are still interrupted, the foreground and background playing push-pull as the eye tries to adjust.

There is little in the way of ornamentation, perhaps because Sampa's patron preferred to spend money on scale. The brackets supporting each cross-beam are delicately carved, and at the centre edge of each pavilion platform, a tiny pair of animals, such as elephants or birds, face each other. The main corridor of the vav houses an important shrine, lavishly adorned with garlands and flags, and a sacred stone. Less recognizable than many other deities, the goddess depicted here, Bahuchara Mata, is identifiable by her rooster *vahana* (the animal transport unique to each deity). She is generally regarded as the patron deity of India's 4000-year-old, ill-treated hijra community, now legally recognized as a 'third gender' (referred to in the West as transgender, intersex or eunuchs) but still highly discriminated against. At Sampa, the role of the goddess concerns fertility. According to the local people, whenever there is a marriage, 'everyone' turns out for a ritual devoted to Bahuchara Mata. Considering that the town has more than 40,000 inhabitants, that is quite a crowd.

For more than 500 years, Sampa Vav has endured as a centre of prayer and ritual. Stone struts, less exuberant than those at Navlakhi, help to keep the earth at bay.

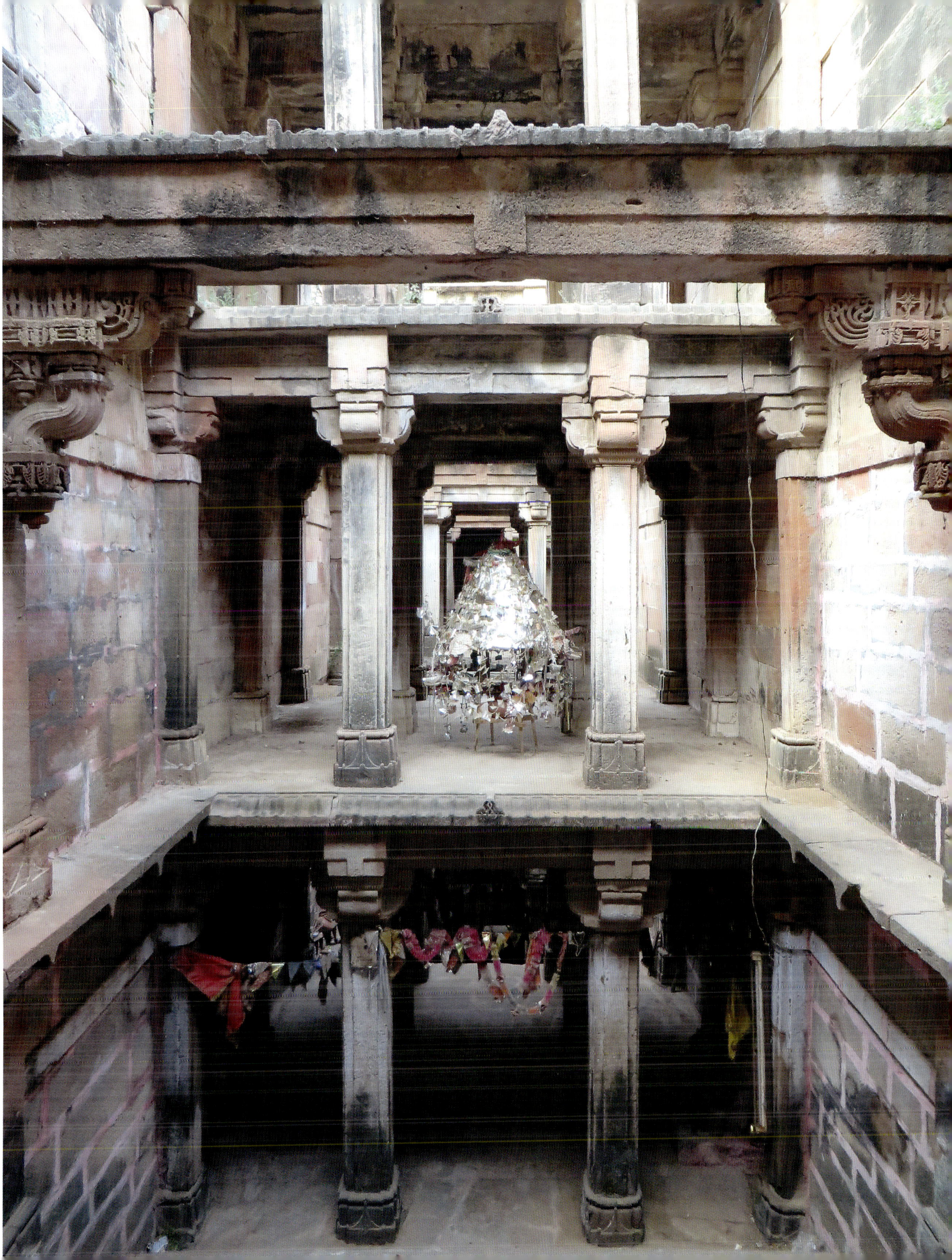

RATABA VAV
(RATALA VAV, RATBA VAV)
RAMPURA, GUJARAT
c. 1482
22°35'51.18" N
71°32'34.99" E

From a distance, the six distinctive pyramidal *shikharas* (roofs) of Rataba Vav resemble toadstools peeking above the red earth. As they come into clearer view, the extreme length and narrow width of this dramatic vav unfolds, until it becomes so elongated that it is nearly impossible to take in the entire structure at one glance. Once you are inside, the structure is utterly hypnotic, a series of unobstructed frames that seem to stretch into infinity.

Rataba was built two centuries later than Madha Vav in Wadhwan (pp. 70-73), 85 kilometres (53 miles) away, but the similarity is striking. Other stepwells in the region reflect this style, too: pavilions that span a narrow space and are topped by square, corbelled *shikharas*. In larger stepwells – for example, the Dhandhalpur and Sampa vavs (pp. 60-61, 94-95) – multiple columns and even struts were necessary to shore up the expanse, while engaged pilasters alone were used at both Rataba and Madha. Perhaps the geology dictated such design decisions, or maybe it was cost, or both, but at Rataba there is nothing to distract from the sweeping view except a worn stone frieze with what appear to be erotic scenes. The water level makes it impossible to descend further than the third storey.

Pilgrims, families and other visitors to Rataba leave offerings in different forms and to different deities. Most prominent is a vibrant Shiva shrine beneath the first *kuta* (pavilion tower), bedecked with banners, beads, tinsel, peacock feathers and garlands of coconuts. A reclining Vishnu – who more often appears within well cylinders – rests on the floor, carved into a chunk of stone, the origin of which is unclear. A narrow ledge close by has become an extension of the shrine, with several icons of Ganesh, the Remover of Obstacles, adorned with jewellery and flowers. Small wooden carvings of body parts, which are commonly seen at other important stepwells, are displayed on the ledge in the hope of securing good health, curing illness, conceiving children or providing ample breast milk.

There are plenty of contemporary intrusions at Rataba, as at Mata Bhavani in Asarwa (pp. 48-49). But the tilework, cement and electricity have not commandeered the entire edifice, the high water precluding access beyond the third pavilion tower. A lone and precarious support props up an equally precarious roof and, outside, a closer look at the marvellous pyramidal crowns is alarming. One is partly destroyed, others have deep, worrisome cracks, and all are showing signs of erosion. However, large and small stacks of stones (signifying prayers) are carefully balanced on top of these roofs, accompanied by leaning hero stones (see p. 45), attesting to Rataba Vav's particular sanctity.

The pyramidal roofs at Rataba Vav support stacks of stones that represent prayers. The Shiva shrine is adorned with ritual objects (opposite, bottom). The telescoping views can be disorientating (overleaf).

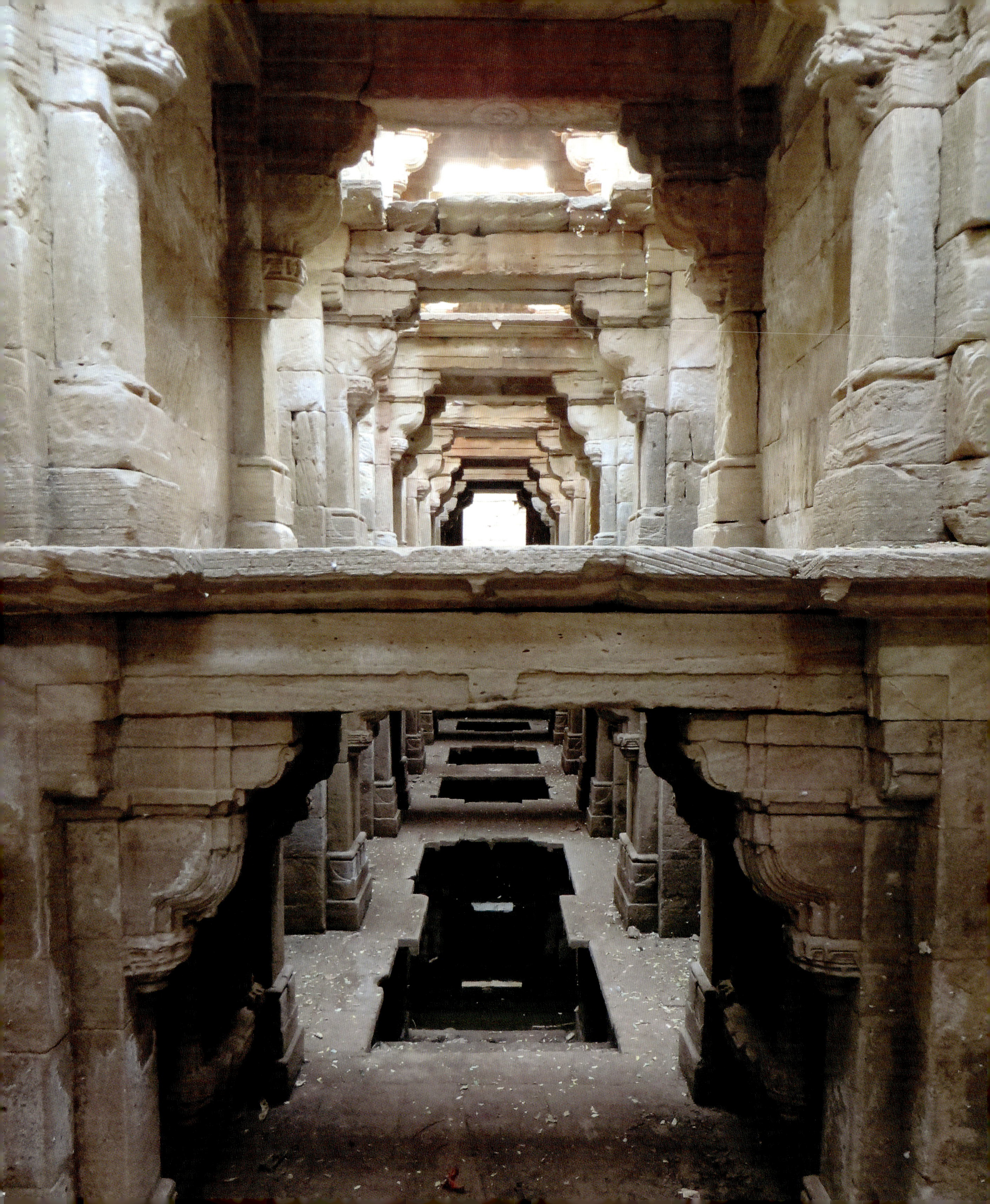

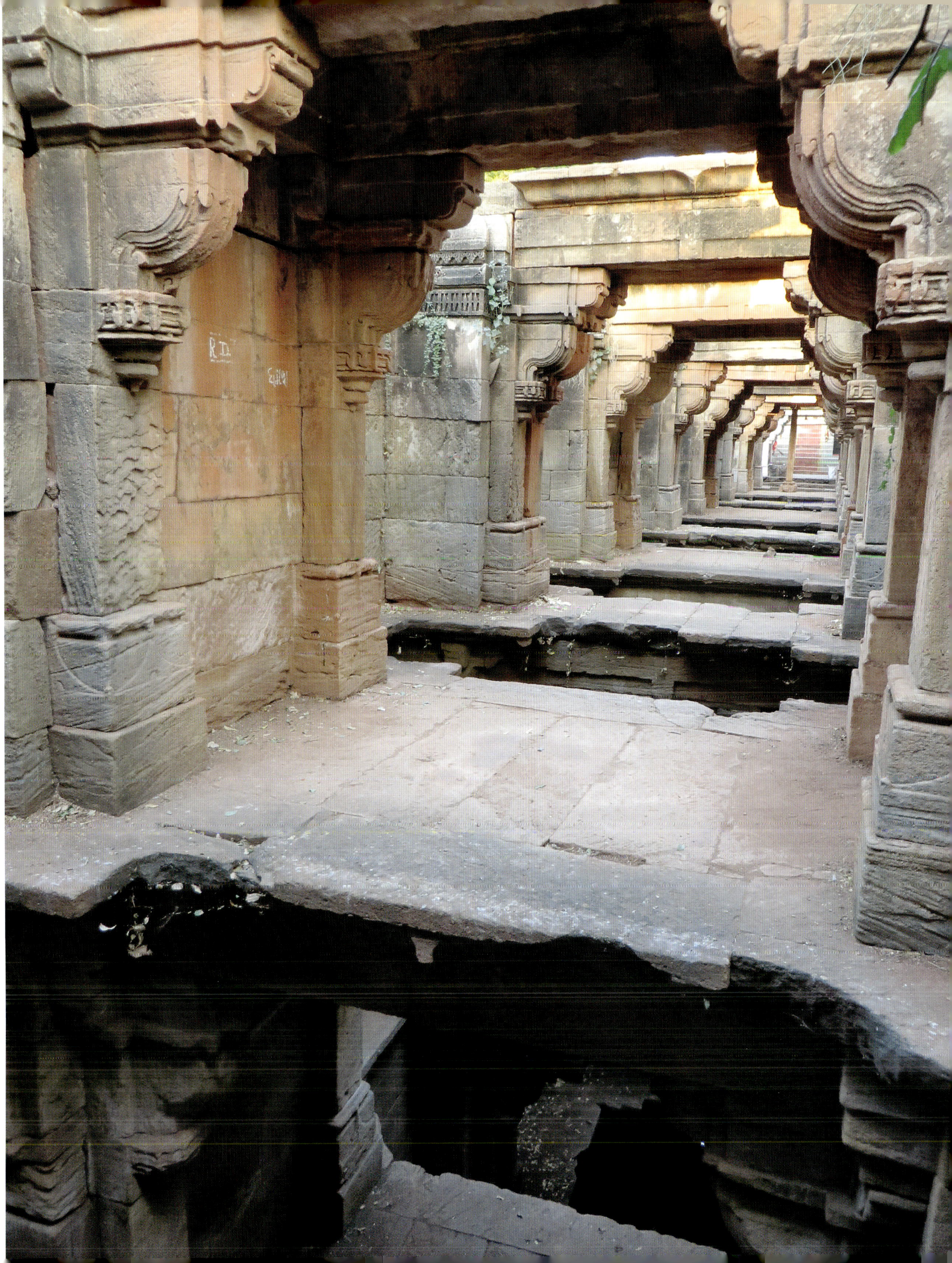

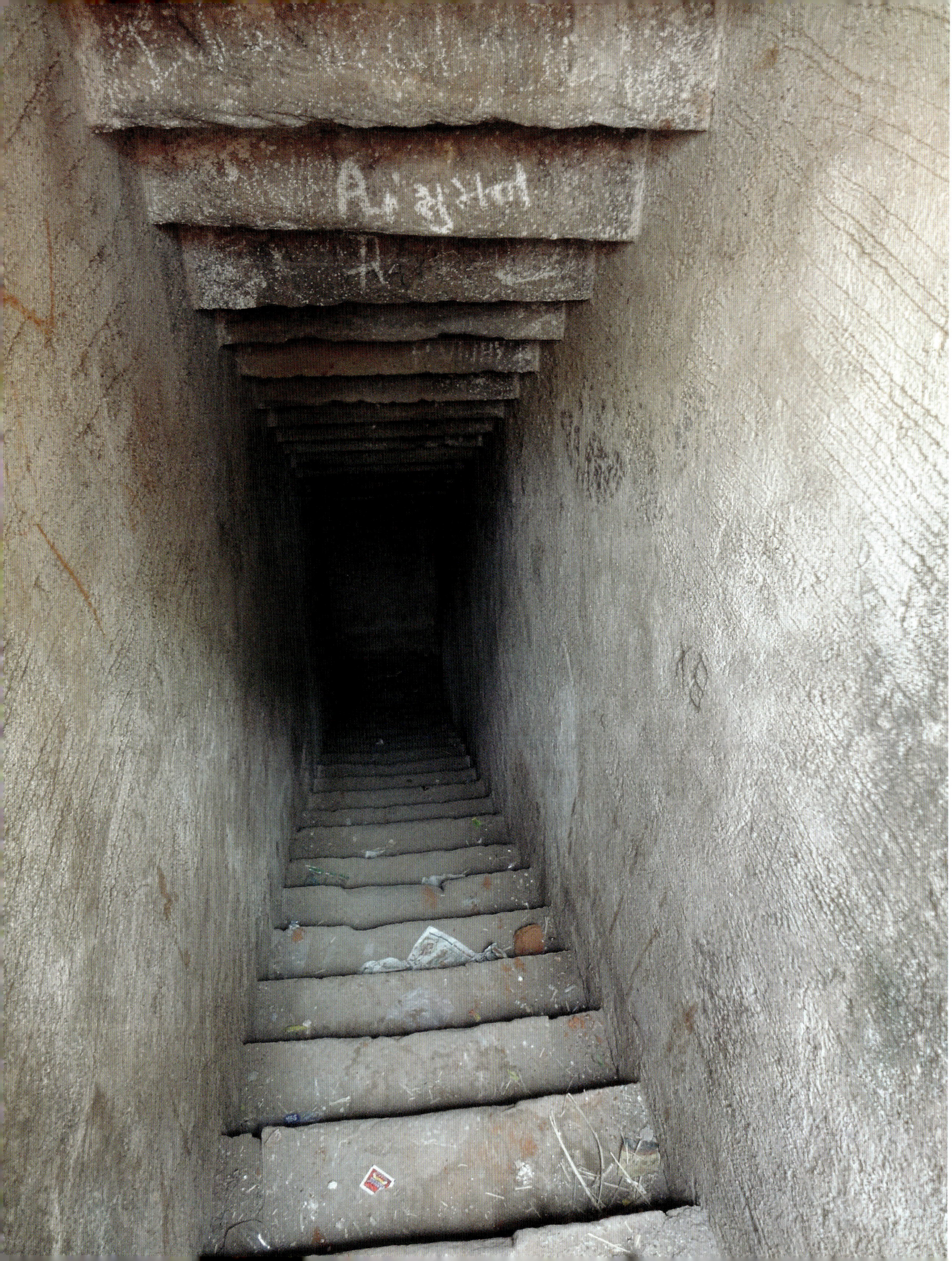

BHAMARIA VAV

MEHMEDABAD, GUJARAT
c. 1495–1511
22°48'42.81" N
72°44'57.26" E

A peaceful, overgrown garden outside the town of Mehmedabad, an hour's drive southeast of Ahmedabad, is believed to have been a pleasure retreat during the reign of Sultan Mahmud Begada (1458–1511; it was probably built not by Begada himself, but by some other wealthy individual). Within this garden, Bhamaria Vav was clearly a private well, as indicated by its inward-looking construction around a central cylinder. Inside, hidden from view, a complex series of stairs, rooms and corridors stretches underground some six storeys, although the exact depth is unknown.

Like Akbar's Baoli at Agra's Red Fort (pp. 142–43), which was built in the late sixteenth century, the exterior of Bhamaria offers few clues as to the treasure underground. With its low, unobtrusive profile, it could easily be mistaken for a bunker. At some point, small domes were apparently visible above ground, but they have disappeared, and all that now remains up top is the apparatus for drawing water from the octagonal well shaft.

Only on entering the structure and descending via a narrow, somewhat creepy staircase can one absorb the full impact of this remarkable edifice. Two huge, parallel stone arches span the entire space, supporting the equipment above. Surprisingly ornate windows are built between the arches, overlooking the well cylinder. The open roof lets in the only natural light; the rooms – four per floor – that hug the structure's outer walls are completely windowless. When the retreat was in use, these dark spaces were illuminated by oil lamps positioned in small arched niches in the walls. Nowadays, the screeching sounds of a vocal bat colony make entry to the side rooms uncomfortable indeed.

The narrow steps that descend into Bhamaria Vav open on to its large cylinder (right). Windows pierce the shaft, lighting the spaces behind the cylinder wall and allowing access to the water.

CONCEPTUAL COUSINS: INDO-ISLAMIC WELLS AROUND AHMEDABAD, GUJARAT

All within 30 kilometres (19 miles) of one another and of the former capital of Gujarat, Ahmedabad, three stepwells in different cities share enough DNA to allow them to be grouped together as what the scholar Morna Livingston has aptly dubbed 'fusion wells'. This term refers to a specific, highly creative style that melded features from both Indian and Islamic design, and the results were among the most impressive wells in India. The trio were constructed within a few years of one another, around the turn of the sixteenth century and during the reign of Sultan Mahmud Begada (otherwise known as Begadha, Beghara or Begda), who conquered a large swathe of Gujarat from his base in Ahmedabad.

These three wells – each five storeys deep – reflect an extravagant union between skilful Hindu construction and taste for ornamentation, and the architectural innovations introduced by Muslim rule. Hindu builders, unacquainted with the Islamic 'true' arch and dome (which relied on a keystone) and other structural devices, had engineered only trabeated (post-and-lintel) structures with simple corbelled cupolas. Their stepwells housed sculptures of many deities. The Islamic world had its own long history of creating beautiful water structures, and as Muslim rulers began to dominate India, the destruction of stepwells was forbidden, even as temples were being pulverized. Since every citizen required water, the stepwells built during this period were conceived specifically to appeal to both Hindus and Muslims. Figuration, prohibited in Islamic art and architecture, was still present – even depictions of the Hindu pantheon – but was dramatically scaled down, until it was eventually phased out. Domes, octagons, spiral stairs and other architectural features used throughout the Islamic world were now incorporated into stepwells, and, in the omnipresent niches formerly occupied by deities, artisans turned their exceptional, centuries-old skills to depicting flowers, trees and other carvings that found favour with both faiths. The travellers and pilgrims who stopped at these wells on the roads around Ahmedabad must have been transported by their beauty, in much the same way as a Renaissance cathedral would have amazed its congregation.

RUDABAI VAV
ADALAJ
c. 1499
23°10'0.04" N
72°34'48.42" E

Among this family of stepwells, Rudabai Vav in Adalaj is the most famous and most frequented by tourists. It is also the most complex and flamboyant, shrouded in a romantic legend (although there are several versions of this story): its patroness, Ruda, was a comely Hindu queen whose husband had already begun work on the elaborate stepwell when he was killed in battle by Sultan Begada. The sultan was subsequently smitten by Ruda's beauty, and the widow promised to marry him on one condition: that she could complete the stepwell in honour of her fallen first husband. Begada agreed to the terms, but upon its completion, Ruda inaugurated the well by throwing herself in.

The truth about Ruda is unknown, but she funded a spectacular cruciform vav (an earlier, less ostentatious example is Sampa Vav; pp. 94–95), with three entrances converging in an octagonal rotunda open to the sky. Either side of the main staircase is an exquisitely carved balcony with a frieze depicting battling elephants, archers and warriors on horseback. The columns that mark the descent of the steps are similarly dense with sculpture.

An octagonal shaft pierces all five storeys, culminating in a square pool. Stone benches with slanted backs were built into each level, allowing users of the well to socialize and look down at the water.

Rudabai Vav – which hides behind a nondescript wall at ground level but descends five storeys into the earth – epitomizes the profound experience of being in a stepwell. The octagonal shaft is an Islamic contribution, but the extravagant carving and figuration are Hindu.

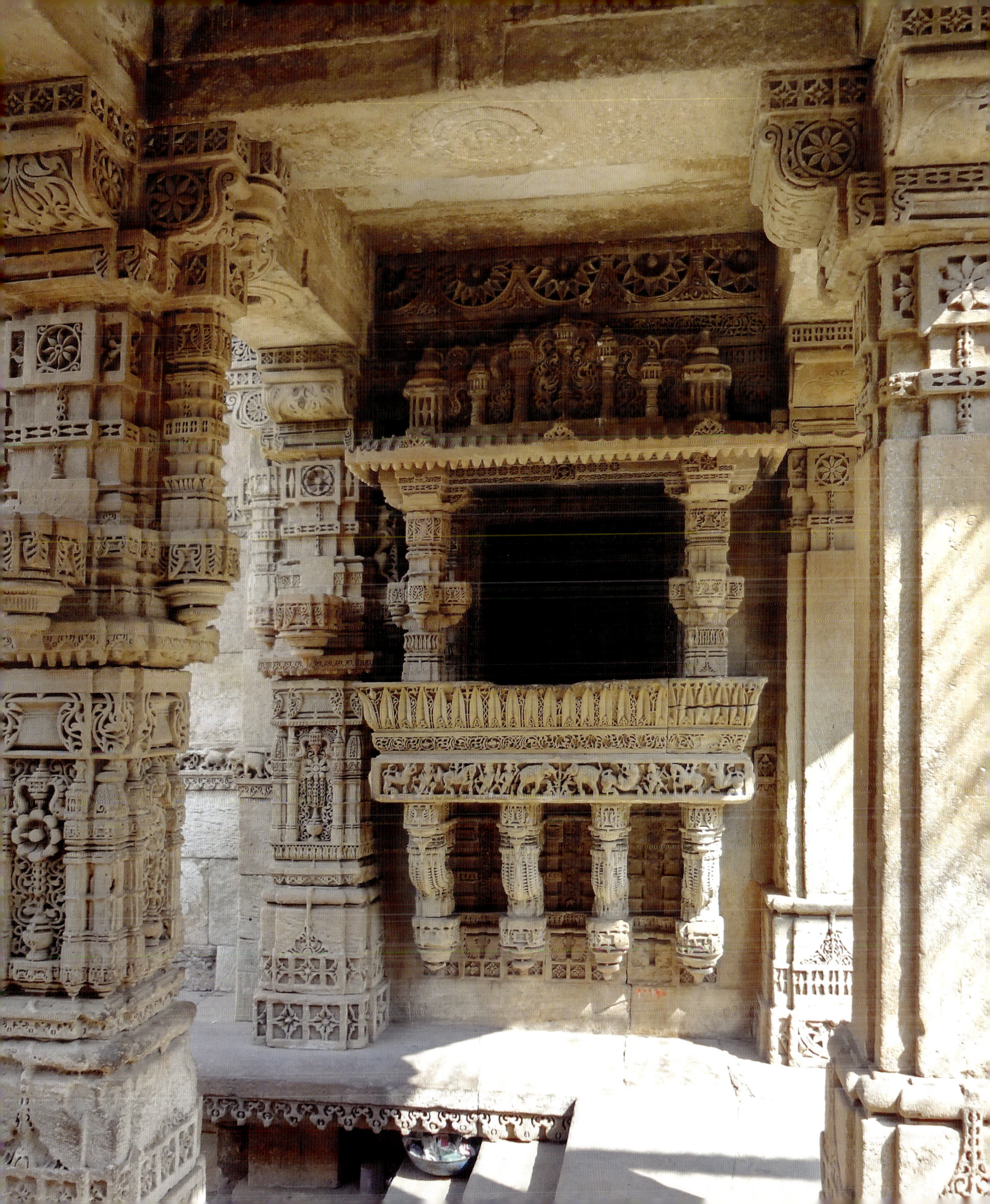

DADA HARIR VAV
ASARWA
c. 1499
23°2'26.55" N
72°36'21.31" E

On a dedication panel, Dada (or Bhai) Harir is described as 'the general superintendent at the door to the king's harem'. Whatever her specific duties were, she paid for a resplendent monument. It is not as large as Rudabai Vav, but the plan and craftsmanship demonstrate that the tastes of Dada Harir and Ruda overlapped. The fact that Ruda was Hindu and Dada Muslim probably accounts for the more immediately apparent Islamic additions and the absence of figurative sculpture. The large, domed entry pavilion, smaller domed *chhatris* (umbrella-like canopies) and a carved tree of life in a niche in the well's cylinder all point towards a lessening of overt Hindu ornamentation.

Madame Harir is buried nearby in a pretty tomb, where visitors occasionally pay their respects. There is also a mosque dating from the same period. The well-preserved and well-attended compound houses exceptional architecture, even if a rusted metal fence abuts it to one side. Photos from thirty years ago show that the compound was then positioned in a relative sea of emptiness.

The similarity with Rudabai Vav is pronounced, as can be seen in the octagonal shaft and the view through the corridor. But a domed entry pavilion (above) and *chhatris* set Dada Harir apart.

106

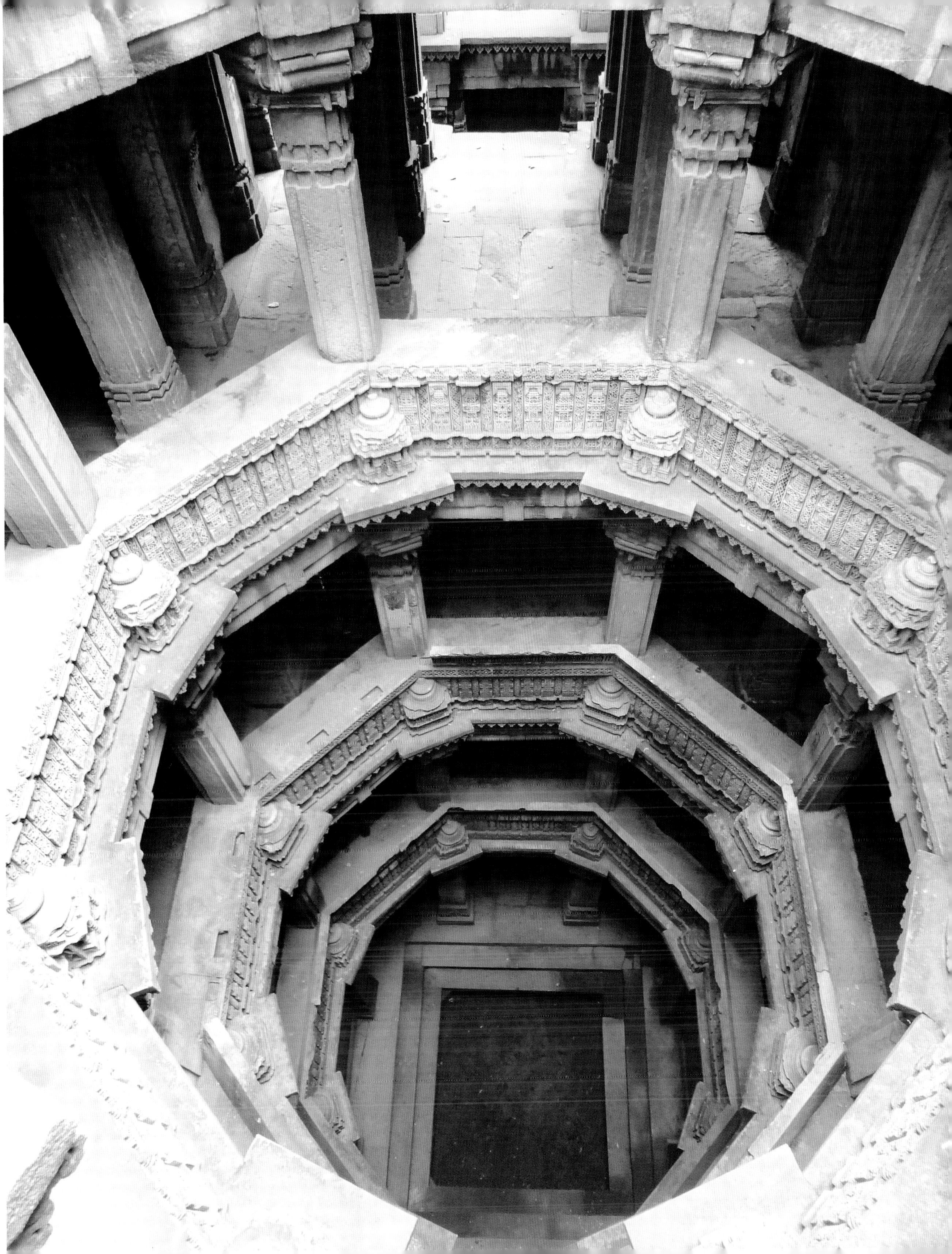

AMBAPUR VAV

AMBAPUR (ALSO KNOWN AS BUDTHAL)
c. 1500
23°9'6.27" N
72°36'39.08" E

In a dusty little village only 5 kilometres (3 miles) from Adalaj and adjoining a modest Shiva temple, Ambapur Vav suffers in near obscurity, as if it were Rudabai's impoverished relative. Although it is a beautiful and significant stepwell, it does not boast the same level of flashy craftsmanship as Rudabai; it is much smaller, with a conventional single entrance, and also lacks a tragic myth. Consequently, Ambapur is overlooked by nearly everyone who visits Adalaj.

Nonetheless, the narrow well is graceful in its comparative restraint, its tall walls punctuated from top to bottom by carved niches – a distinctive feature. Many of these niches are now stripped of the stone flowers and stylized trees they once housed; those still embedded have an unmistakable similarity to the ones on view at Rudabai and other wells built during the reign of Mahmud Begada.

It is somewhat ironic that a sign by the gated entrance declares that the stepwell is protected under the Gujarat Ancient Monuments Act, with a hefty fine of 5000 rupees (at the time of writing, that is about £60 or $75) 'for anyone defacing or removing part of the structure'. Graffiti, several dangerous holes and a partial collapse of the structure make Ambapur's future appear uncertain. An ill-tempered monkey helps to guard the property.

Especially noteworthy at Ambapur are its elegant proportions and the unusual configuration of its steps.

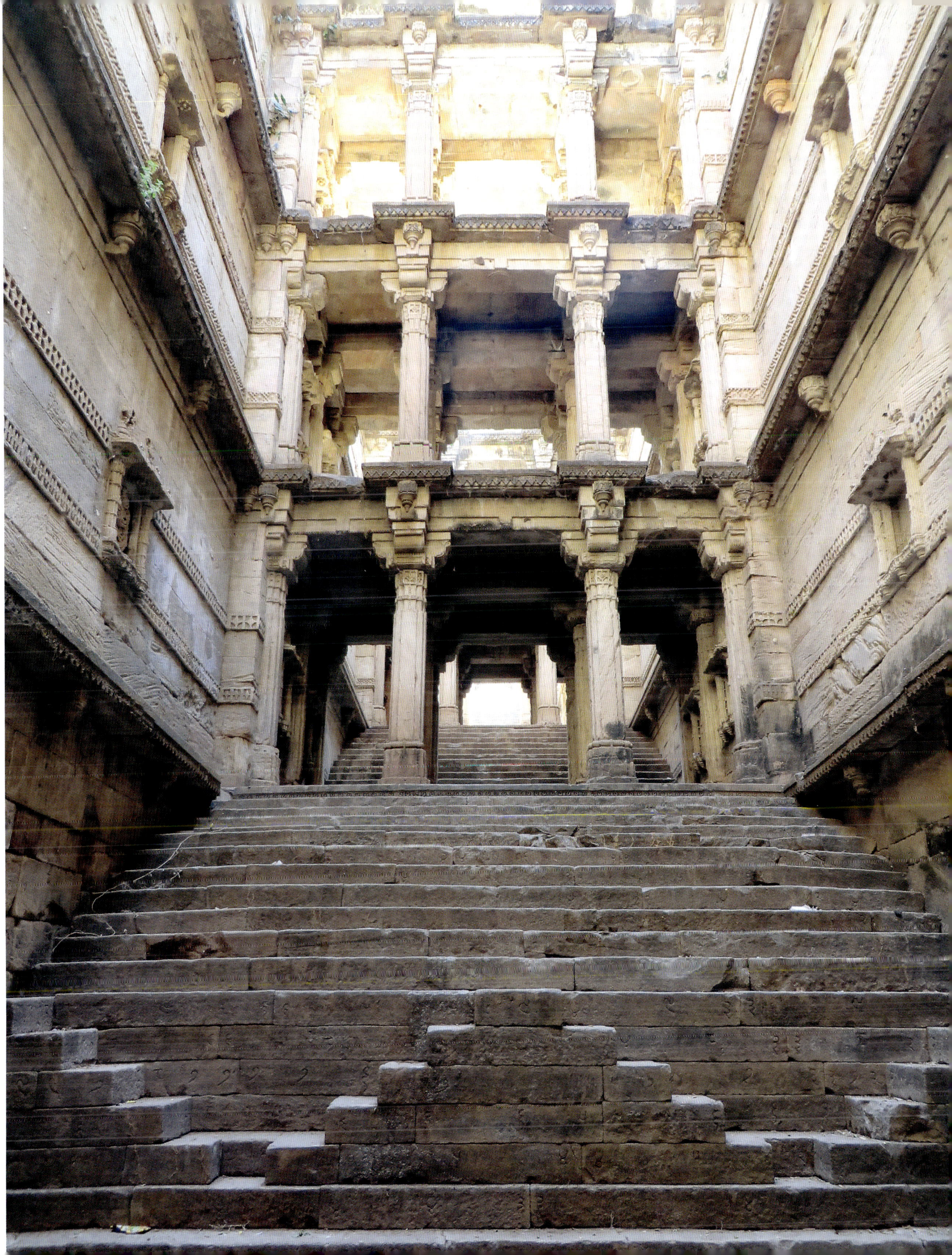

UJALA BAOLI

MANDU, MADHYA PRADESH
LATE 15th/EARLY 16th CENTURY
22°21'29.87" N
75°23'45.36" E

To say the immense fortress of Mandu in Madhya Pradesh has an epic history does not begin to describe the almost Shakespearean drama that has taken place within its 30-plus kilometres (more than 19 miles) of defensive walls. Mandu was caught in a violent tug of war between dynasties and kingdoms throughout the fifteenth and sixteenth centuries, and witnessed ancillary emotional struggles: sons poisoning fathers, friends poisoning friends, and beloved consorts taking their lives in preference to being taken captive by enemies. But through all this conflict and strife, there was no skimping on the architecture, and some of the most unusual and sophisticated buildings of medieval India can be found at Mandu. There are also numerous water features, many of which were stylistically more advanced than those constructed at other fortresses of the time. Among the tanks, reservoirs, fountains and channels that fed many of the remarkable structures were a few stepwells, the most stunning of which is Ujala Baoli.

Ujala (which means 'light') was built away from the centre of activity at Mandu, in a spot where few tourists stray today. It is an eccentric-looking baoli, strangely asymmetrical, with its broad main stairway set to one side and perpendicular to another stairway into the well: a series of narrow steps that zigzag down a three-storey wall from both left and right, accompanied by arched niches all the way down. This is an arrangement that is predominantly associated with kunds, and seems redundant so close to a wide staircase.

A pair of imposing structures face each other on opposite sides of the baoli, one with supports for hauling up buckets of water, the other with interior chambers and a surprisingly bulbous-domed pavilion on top. The profusion of open and blind arches and dark interior spaces in both these towers is confusing, and lends the play of light and shadow over the façades a surreal, ominous quality, reminiscent of a Giorgio de Chirico painting. As for the serene green water, its depth may extend another storey, judging by what may be another flight of steps, with the tips of the submerged arches tantalizingly visible just above the surface.

As mysterious as it is beautiful, the plan at Ujala Baoli is inexplicably odd. Broad entry steps transition abruptly to narrower ones (right), and additional steps meander down another wall (opposite). Small chambers occupy the tri-level structure (p. 113).

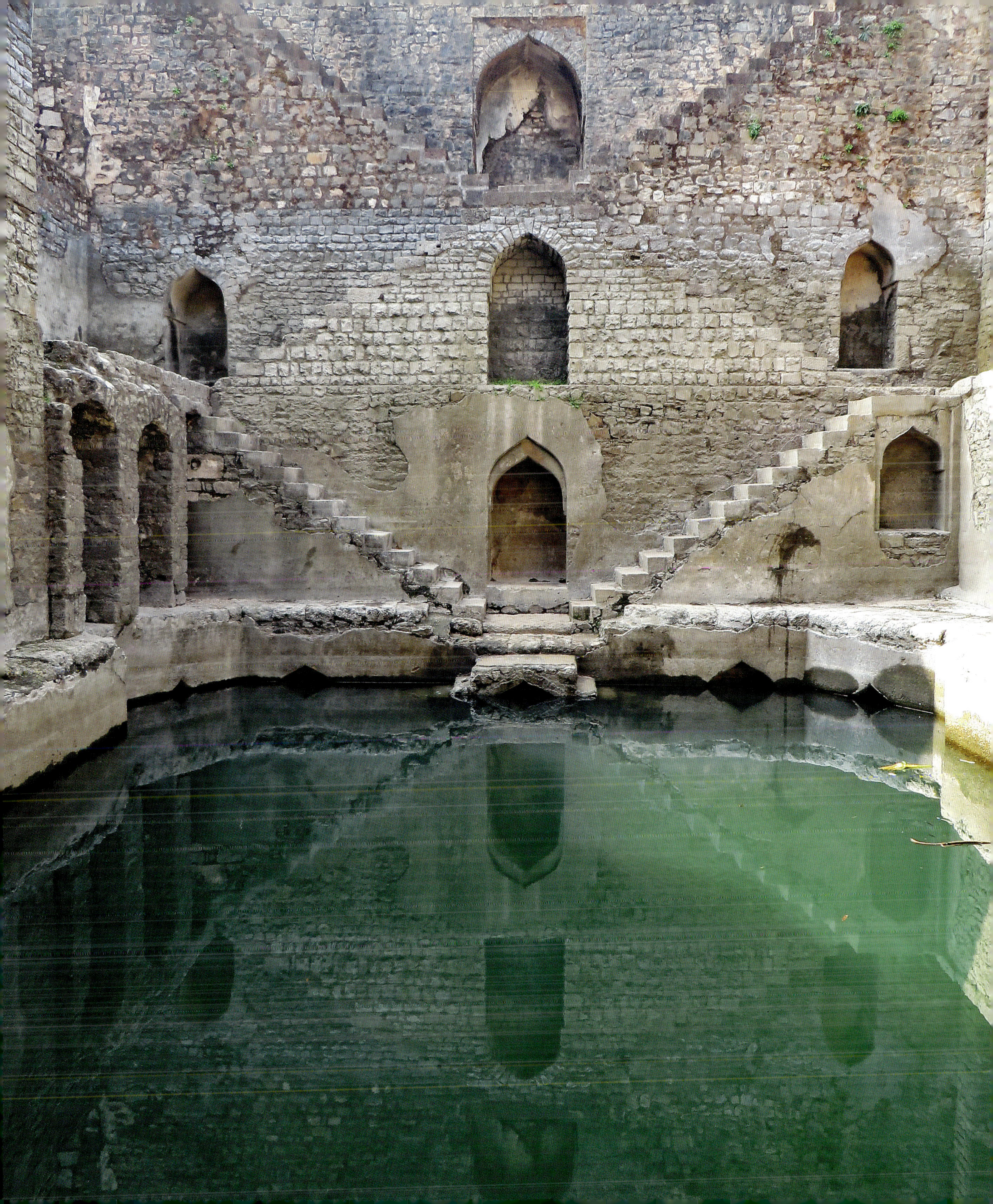

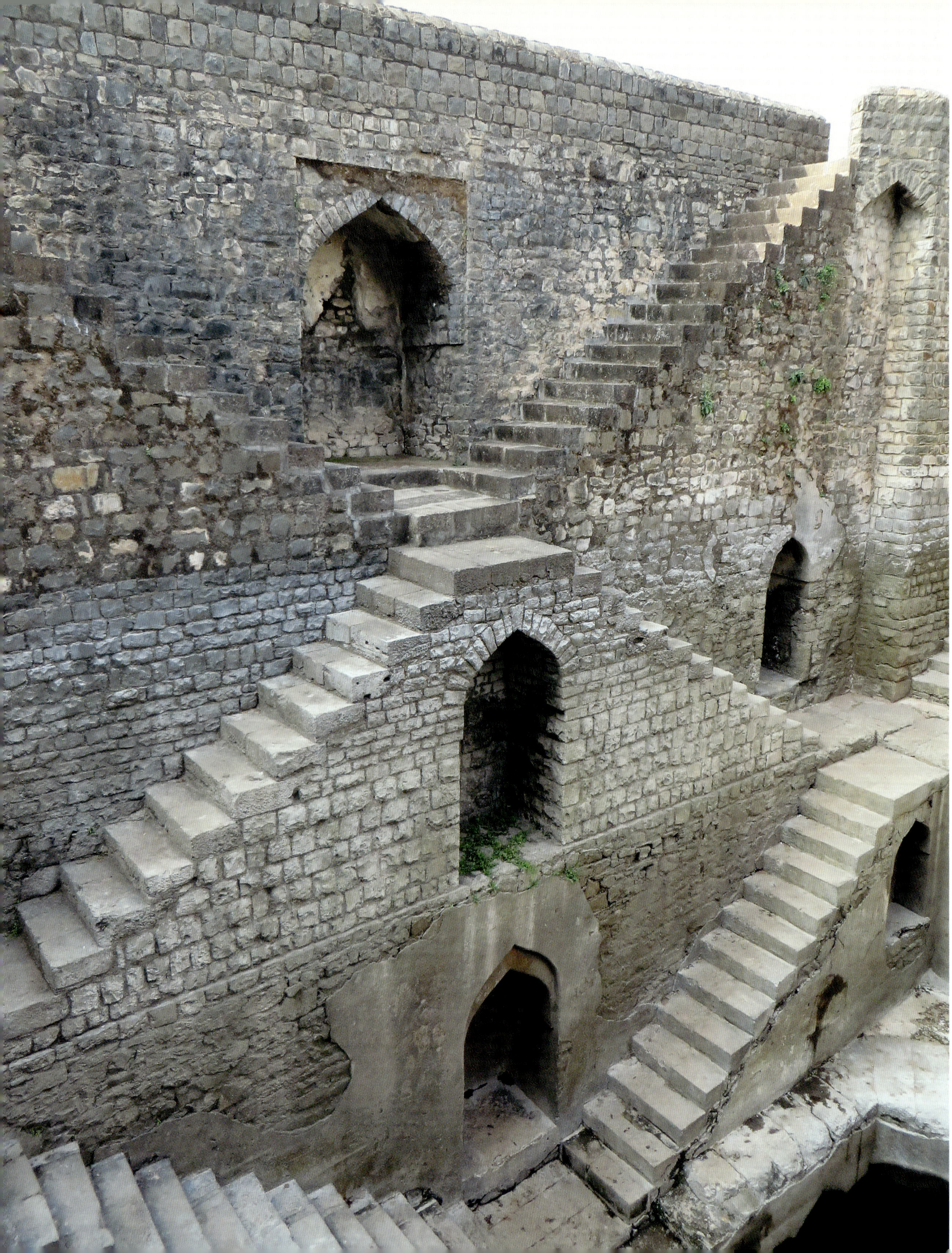

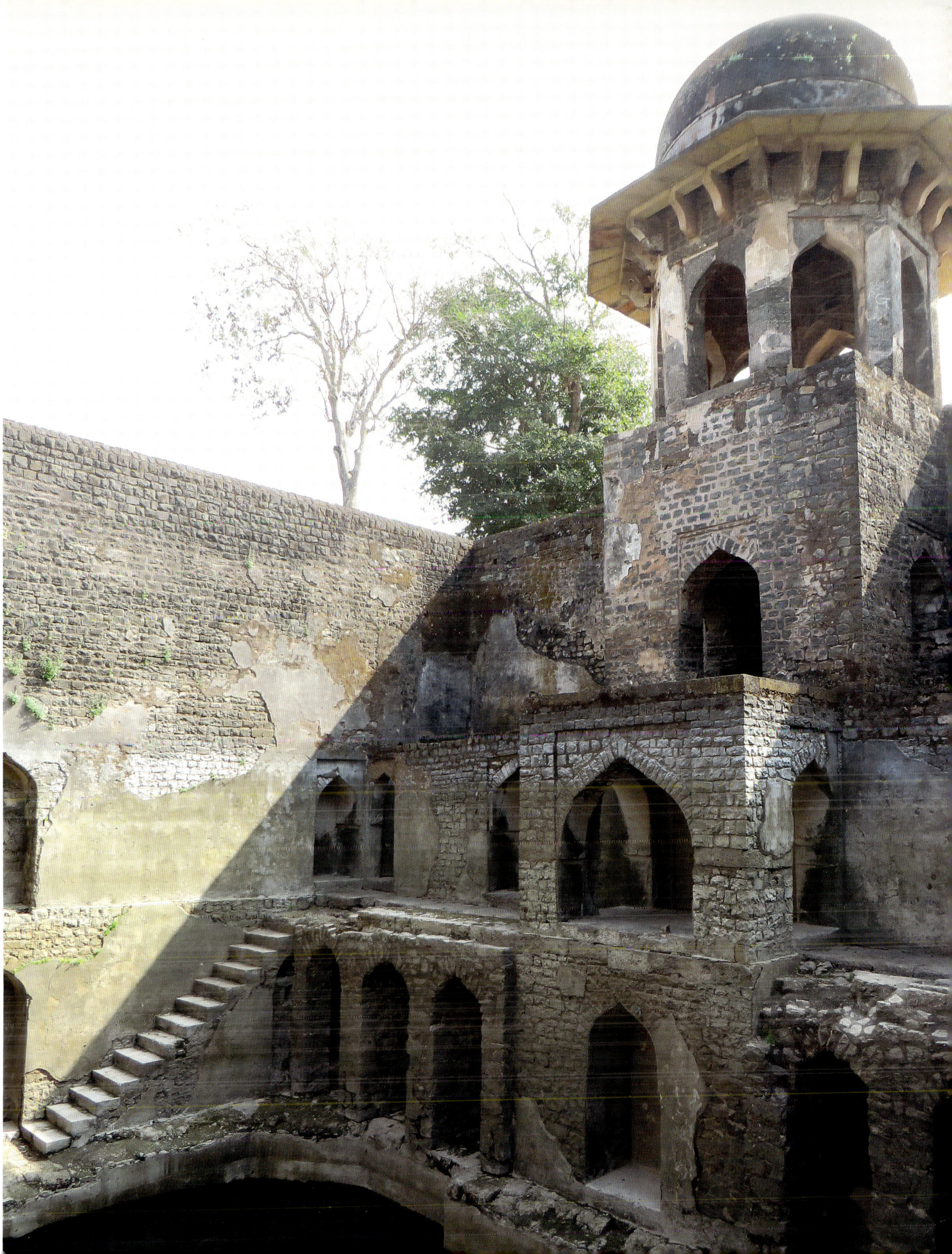

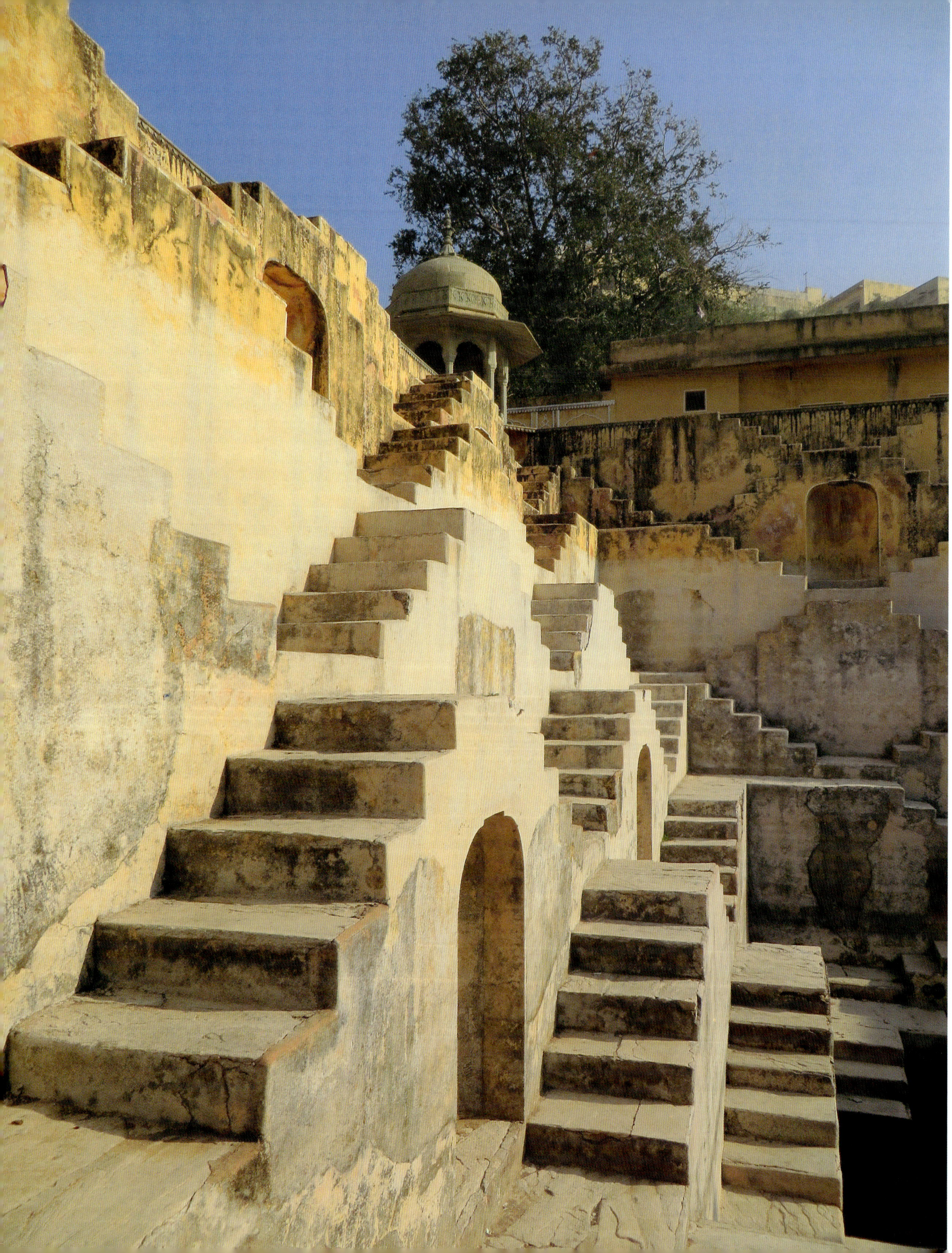

PANNA MEENA KA KUND
(PANNA MIA KUND, PANNA MIAN KUND)

AMER, RAJASTHAN
c. 16th CENTURY (17th/18th CENTURY)
26°59'28.02" N
75°51'4.43" E

Nestled in the Aravalli Hills, Panna Meena ka Kund has views of Jaigarh Fort, an eyrie perched high in the distance (below, pictured at top right).

Jaipur's top tourist destination, Amer (or Amber) Fort, sits on a craggy hill 13 kilometres (8 miles) outside the city. Thousands of tourists visit daily, choosing one of three ways to reach the citadel: walk up, drive up or ride an elephant to the top. Pachyderm transport is only one-way, however, and the journey down through the narrow streets is made painfully slow by the volume of traffic inching along. What most people do not know is that the buses and cars pass right by a little oasis as tranquil as the fort is raucous.

Panna Meena ka Kund is especially pleasing. It differs from other examples of kunds in this book such as Katan Baoli, Chand Baori and Dabhai Kund (pp. 36-39, 40-43, 160-61), each of which is remarkable structurally but daunting in scale and depth, with tiers of steps that seem to invite calamity. By comparison, Panna Meena feels unintimidating, even cosy, and its clear, green water is easy to reach. Jaunty yellow and white hues, remnants of a years-old paint job, infuse the edifice with a sunny disposition, enhanced by the lively pattern of stairs and recesses.

The origin, date and spelling of this stepwell are, as ever, open to some interpretation. While the sixteenth-century date given here is the one that is most commonly used, later dates of construction also crop up, along with theories about the well's patron. The most compelling tale points to Panna Myan (*panna* means 'emerald' in Hindi), who was allegedly a powerful eunuch in the court of either Raja Bishan Singh (r. 1688-99) or his son, Jaipur's founder Sawai Jai Singh II (r. 1699-1743). But it hardly matters if there is any truth in this account while you are basking in the sun or feeding the fish in the serene pool.

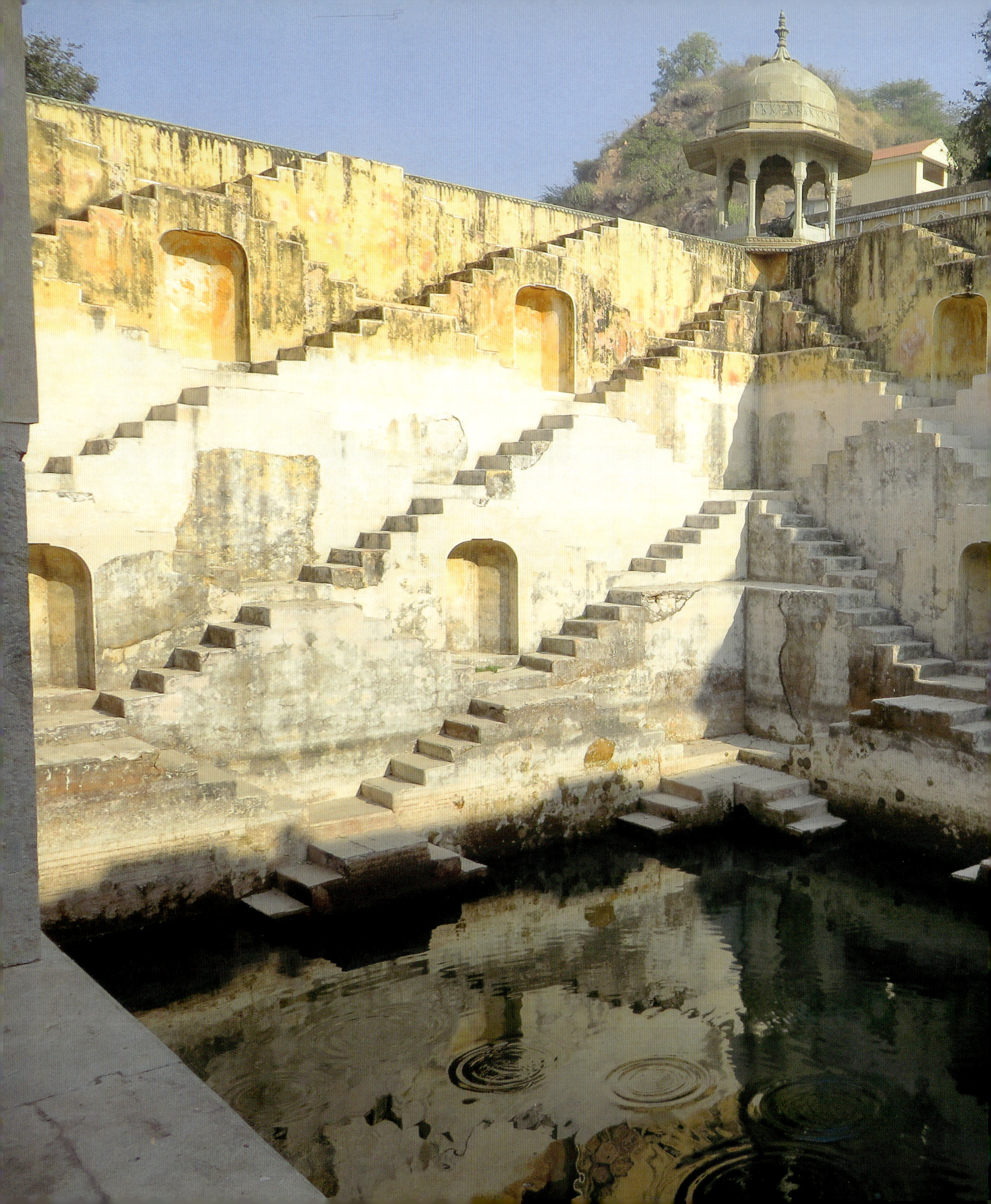

The kund's steps form shifting patterns, depending on the position of the viewer. The mottled yellow and white hues provide a luminous contrast with the green water.

HELICAL VAV

CHAMPANER, GUJARAT
EARLY 16th CENTURY
22°29'3.17" N
73°31'4.45" E

This is one of the humblest stepwells in India, yet its simple form makes it also one of the most beautiful. The otherwise nameless Helical Vav can be found outside the fortress city of Champaner, Gujarat, amid a complex of structures that reveal a tangled political history. Wrested back and forth between Hindu and Muslim rulers for centuries, in 1484 the city and the adjoining hilltop fortress of Pavagadh finally wound up in the hands of Sultan Mahmud Begada. Begada was a prolific builder of extraordinary monuments, and in Champaner he spent a quarter of a century renovating earlier structures while creating magnificent new ones of his own. In 2004 the Champaner-Pavagadh Archaeological Park received UNESCO World Heritage Site status, the only other such site in Gujarat being the eleventh-century Rani ki Vav (pp. 52-55), four hours' drive away.

Champaner was once nicknamed the 'City of a Thousand Wells' on account of its extremely sophisticated water-harvesting systems, which included numerous stepwells dating from various regimes. Of those that survive, Helical Vav is my favourite, even if its photogenic, sinuous stairway is of a type not uncommon in other wells across India; such flights of steps are the most efficient way to access water in circular wells. The simple, low parapet and pleasant setting, among trees and lawns at the base of a hillside, make this an especially peaceful place. Viewed directly from above, the well resembles a keyhole. Do not be fooled by the unassuming design, however: with only the ancient brick wall for support, and with the murky water below, descent of the winding stairs is precarious work.

There is little information about this well, and it is easily overlooked off the main road into Champaner, where it would have been used by travellers entering and leaving the city. An ASI sign provides visitors with very basic details, suggesting that the vav's form recalls a 'coiled snake'.

A plain, unassuming wall obscures the simple curl of steps at Helical Vav. The minimalist form of the well creates maximum visual impact.

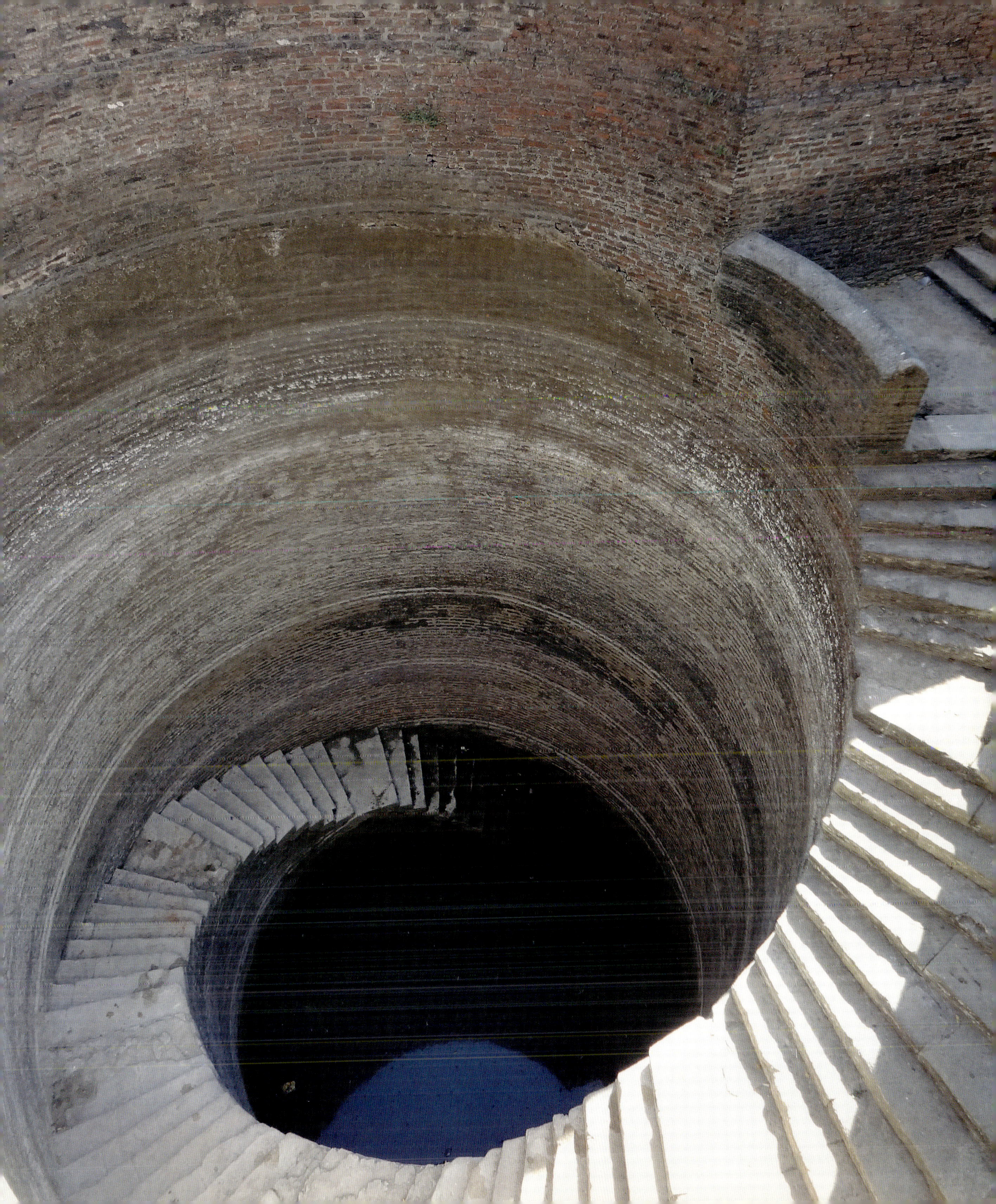

ASSI KHAMBHA BAORI

GWALIOR, MADHYA PRADESH
c. 1500
26°13'44.6" N
78°10'6.15" E

Many stepwells have descriptive names; in this instance, Assi Khambha simply means 'Eighty Pillars', a reference to the columns in the pretty gallery around the top of this unusual well. It is situated in the grounds of Gwalior Fort – one of the most impressive forts on the subcontinent, filled with exceptional monuments dating back hundreds of years – yet Assi Khambha gets barely a mention anywhere. It is known to have been built sometime around 1500 by Maharaja Man Singh, a lover of architecture whose palace is one of the fort's main attractions.

All forts relied on wells, cisterns and other water-harvesting systems that could withstand sieges often lasting years. Being one of the most beautiful such structures (and also one of the oddest), Assi Khambha was most probably reserved for royal use only. A huge court adjoins and directly overlooks the well, which itself did not offer much in the way of shade. A small doorway accesses the gallery, one floor below ground level; but, although it is covered, the gallery is not conducive to lazing around on hot summer days. The forecourt would have been the real retreat, but it appears ponderous, almost brutal, in comparison to the delicate columns of the gallery, and thus strikes a jarring note.

Assi Khambha shares certain features with other leisure wells (if that is indeed what it was). As in the case of Bhamaria Vav and Akbar's Baoli (pp. 100–101, 142–43), pairs of staircases between the walls around the well cylinder lead down to the water's edge. Unlike those two wells, however, here there are no interior chambers for relaxation and very little light on the descent, with access to each staircase provided only by a single door that opens directly on to the stone-slab steps. In addition, there is no visible system of pulleys to haul up buckets of water. Perhaps, then, Assi Khambha is technically not a baoli at all. Many questions arise: Was water brought up by hand? Was the water used only for bathing? Who actually used the well? So far, this information has been elusive, but perhaps in the future there will be answers.

Ponderous columns in the open court loom above the well. The interior stairways are subtly demarcated by stone slabs on the inside of the well cylinder (opposite).

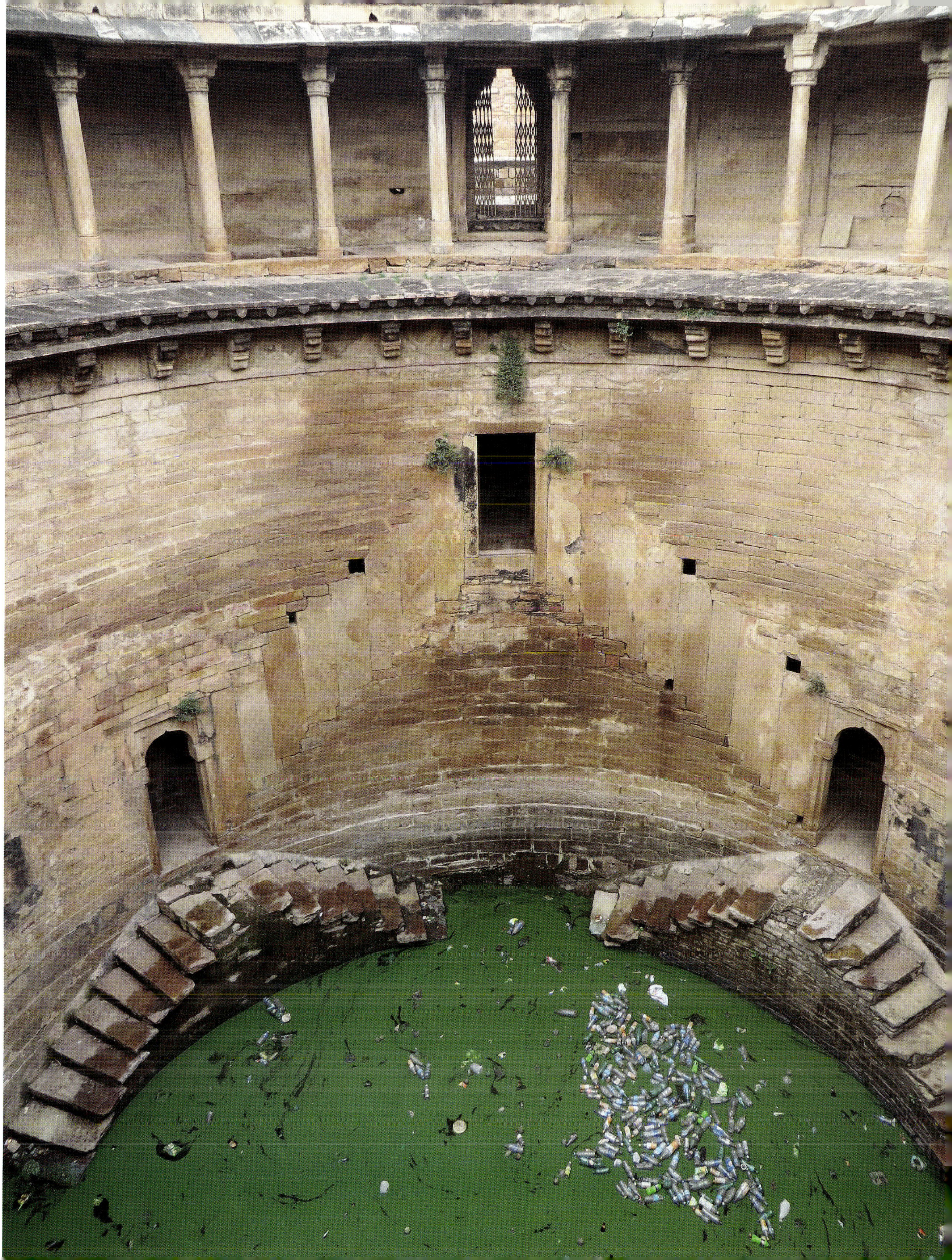

RAJON KI BAOLI

DELHI
c. 1516
28°31'13.35" N
77°11'0.27" E

Owing to its curious quirks and bucolic surroundings, Rajon ki Baoli is my favourite among the stepwells of Delhi. It was commissioned in the early sixteenth century by a politically scheming nobleman, Daulat Khan. The name is a conundrum that has spawned various interpretations, the most common being that the well was named after the stonemasons who used it. Many historians have pointed out that it seems unlikely that masons would have warranted such an extravagant baoli. A further possible explanation for the name is that it came about in the early twentieth century after a group of stoneworkers began living in the adjacent mosque. Whatever the truth, this is a splendid stepwell.

Rajon is in the often-overlooked Mehrauli Archaeological Park, which is home to many picturesque tombs. Signs for 'baoli' direct visitors down various paths, but the well - one of the largest structures in the park, albeit a subterranean one - must still be sought out in an area far from the main entrance. Aspects of Rajon's design are surely familiar: a steep, four-storey descent, a rhythmic array of niches, arcades, and plenty of space in which to shelter from the heat. But unlike other Delhi stepwells, here there is extra embellishment in the form of plaster roundels and friezes, diminutive recesses for oil lamps and - best of all - protrusions of living rock.

Rocky outcrops can be found throughout Mehrauli Park, but it is surprising to see them incorporated into the baoli. I have seen no explanation for this - was it a deliberate design decision? Did someone plan badly? Was it too late to start again elsewhere? Perhaps this is another justification for the well's name: either the masons were clever to work around the stone, or they lacked the ability to remove it. The intrusion is on the second level, along one side, crashing through the wall and resembling a lava flow occupying part of the ledge. Further along the ledge, another large stone incursion has been transformed into a set of steps (noticeably absent on the opposite side of the baoli). This is what makes Rajon a unique stepwell. And, thanks to the concerted effort made by the ASI to recharge Delhi's wells, the baoli has sufficient water to allow local labourers to wash in it.

Boulders project from the left wall, forming the base of one column (left). A small mosque at ground level adjoins the stepwell (opposite).

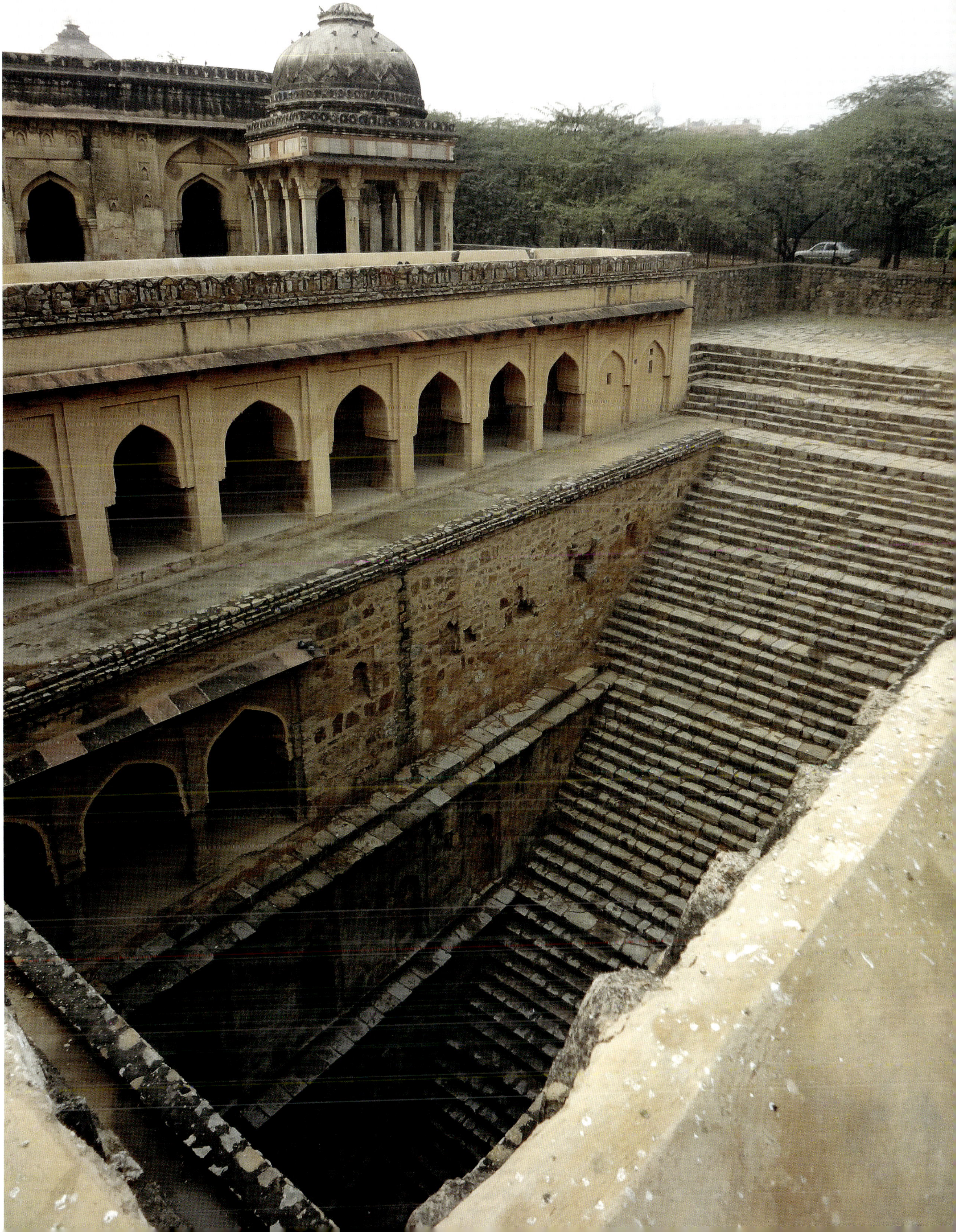

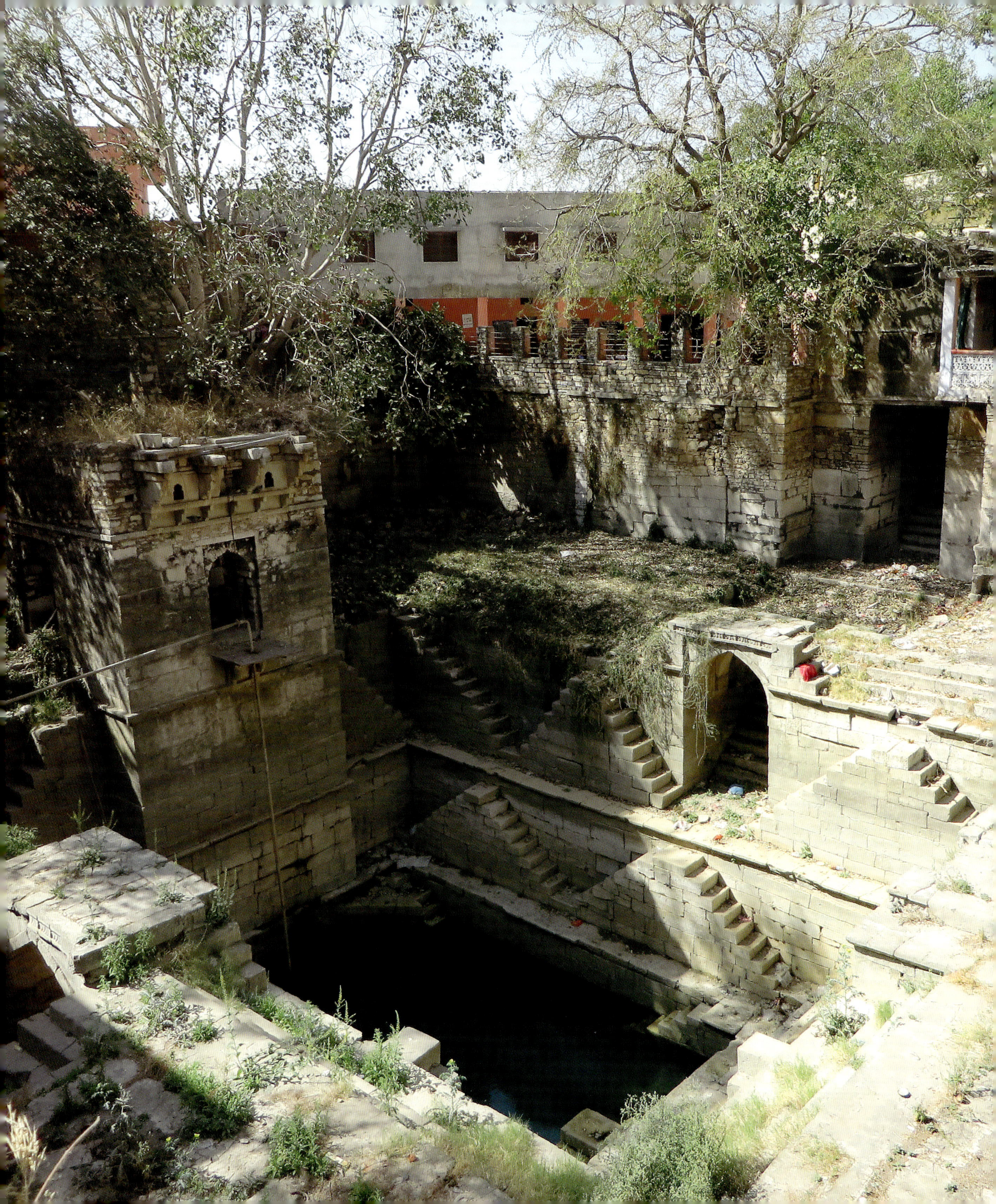

JALI VAV

CHITTORGARH, RAJASTHAN
MID-16th CENTURY
24°53'11.72" N
74°38'31.49" E

Chittorgarh Fort, a UNESCO World Heritage Site, is one of the largest citadels in India and has a hair-raising history replete with fierce sieges and mass suicides. Every day crowds of tourists pass through the seemingly unremarkable city centre, heading directly for the main entrance to the sprawling fort, which looms some 180 metres (590 ft) above the streets. And yet, just off the main road, a small passage opens on to a kund that must once have been stunning. Its patroness was Maharani Jaivanta Bai, the first wife of Maharana Udai Singh II (r. 1540-72), ruler of Mewar and founder of the city of Udaipur. Although Jaivanta was followed by twenty-one more wives, she made her mark as the doting mother of the succeeding powerful ruler, Maharana Pratap Singh. In fact, the story of the famous relationship between the two was the basis of the popular TV series *Bharat Ka Veer Putra - Maharana Pratap* (2013-15).

Although the rani's reputation endures, we know little about her gift to Chittorgarh. The district ASI office gives the local name of the stepwell as Jali Bai, but there is no other information. It is a pity, considering the unusual and complex layout of this well, right at the base of the fort. There are three separate entrances at ground level, each with a narrow flight of steps that passes beneath an Islamic arch before terminating at over-scaled pyramidal kund steps built across two levels. It is quite a steep descent to the water's edge. On the fourth side of the structure, the rectangular well cylinder, jerry-rigged with pipes and its top leaning precariously, rises above the pool's clear, blue water.

In parts - for example, the ashlar construction in the lower walls and the meticulously carved pyramidal stairs - Jali Vav looks like a finely engineered stone puzzle. But the upper, perimeter walls tell a different story: in places they are haphazardly slapped together with rubble and embedded with cannibalized remnants of earlier edifices. Fragments of deities and friezes peek out unexpectedly, adding to the mystery of this long-forgotten site.

The uncommon configuration of Jali Vav includes entry arches on three sides and tall pyramidal steps. The upper walls reveal fragments of older structures (left).

HARBOLA KI BAORI

JODHPUR, RAJASTHAN
MID-16th CENTURY
26°20'4.69" N
73°1'42.67" E

Some 25 hectares (60 acres) of orchards and manicured gardens surround the Bal Samand Lake Palace, constructed in the seventeenth century as a royal summer retreat and today a luxury heritage hotel. In the grounds, where peacocks still roam, stands a baoli that pre-dates the palace by a hundred years or so. It is in a small clearing among the trees, very close to the property's long driveway, yet arriving there is like finding an ancient ruin in the middle of a dense jungle. According to the hotel's proprietors, the significance of the name Harbola is not known. Although the baoli's date of construction coincides with the reign of Maharana Udai Singh II, there is no specific reference to the ruler.

The baoli is composed of enormous red sandstone blocks, far heftier and less refined than those used in other Jodhpur stepwells. Much thought went into the meticulous placement of the stones: large alternates with small, with no mortar between. If the sixteenth-century date were not mentioned so specifically, Harbola could be mistaken for a much older edifice. It is four storeys deep, with a tall pavilion tower at the far end. There is delicate carving on the columns, but ornamentation is otherwise minimal; because water laps up the steps, it is impossible to see what other embellishment might lurk below. One could say that the eroded masonry is sculptural in its own right, albeit in dire need of conservation.

Two small structures, originally a matching pair, mark the entrance to this unusual baoli. One retains its form as an open pavilion, its four columns decorated with the same motif as in the well itself. The other structure, now enclosed, is a little Shiva temple. Once a year, to honour the important Hindu festival of Mahashivratri, local ladies create special *rangoli*, auspicious but ephemeral designs drawn on the ground in natural white limestone and red ochre. This captivating custom has not changed for centuries.

One of the two entry pavilions at Harbola ki Baori has been repurposed as a Shiva shrine, and is still an important place of worship (left, centre). The striking – though badly eroded – stepwell is embellished for an annual celebration (opposite).

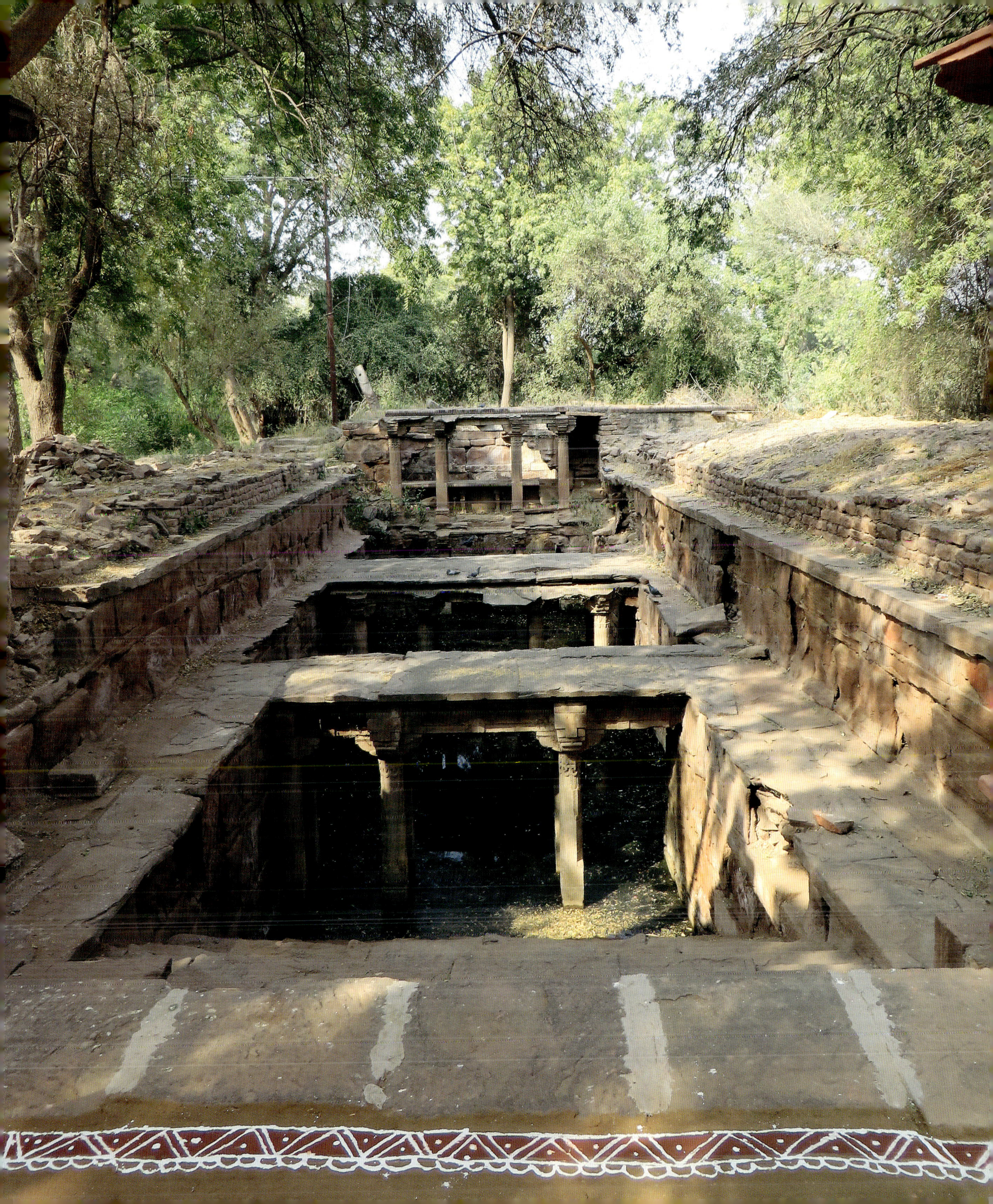

NAGAUR FORT BAOLI

NAGAUR, RAJASTHAN
MID-16th CENTURY
27°11'49.32" N
73°44'11.99" E

Built in the twelfth century, Ahhichatragarh Fort in Nagaur, Rajasthan, is usually described as one of the earliest Muslim citadels in northern India. In fact, the history of the site stretches back even further. The first, mud fort was established around 400 CE, and many successive rulers, both Hindu and Muslim, made alterations. The local state government took over the running of the site after Partition in 1947. Today it is a beautifully restored tourist destination commonly known as the easier-to-pronounce Nagaur Fort. A wildly popular Sufi music festival takes place in the grounds each year, and a five-star hotel occupies several of the fort buildings. The 'rehabilitation project' at the fort was of such high quality that it earned a place on the 2013 shortlist for the prestigious Aga Khan Award for Architecture.

Baolis within forts are always interesting on account of their strategic placement and often unusual shape or scale. The baoli at Nagaur was built directly into a rampart (apparently the eighth version), and it is not particularly easy to reach. The design is deceptively simple: a long, narrow flight of steps descends into the water. What is remarkable is the depth of the water. This rather modest-looking baoli accesses groundwater at the base of the fort walls, an impressive five storeys down. Viewing the fort from outside its walls, one sees only a massive bastion that encloses the steps and the extended cylinder of the well. In a fascinating reversal of the entire stepwell typology, this baoli is not subterranean; it starts far above ground.

The violent history of this ancient stronghold is revealed in the scavenged remnants embedded in the walls. According to the official guidebook, Rao Maldeo of Jodhpur sacked Nagaur in the 1530s, taking possession of the fort, where he obliterated the former ruler's palace. He used this royal rubble to rebuild parts of the fort wall destroyed in the attack. Judging by one beautifully sculpted fragment, the palace should have been left alone.

In an unorthodox reversal of subterranean stepwells, the baoli at Nagaur Fort was constructed high above ground level. It is a purely utilitarian well, with bees' nests the only (unintentional) adornment (opposite).

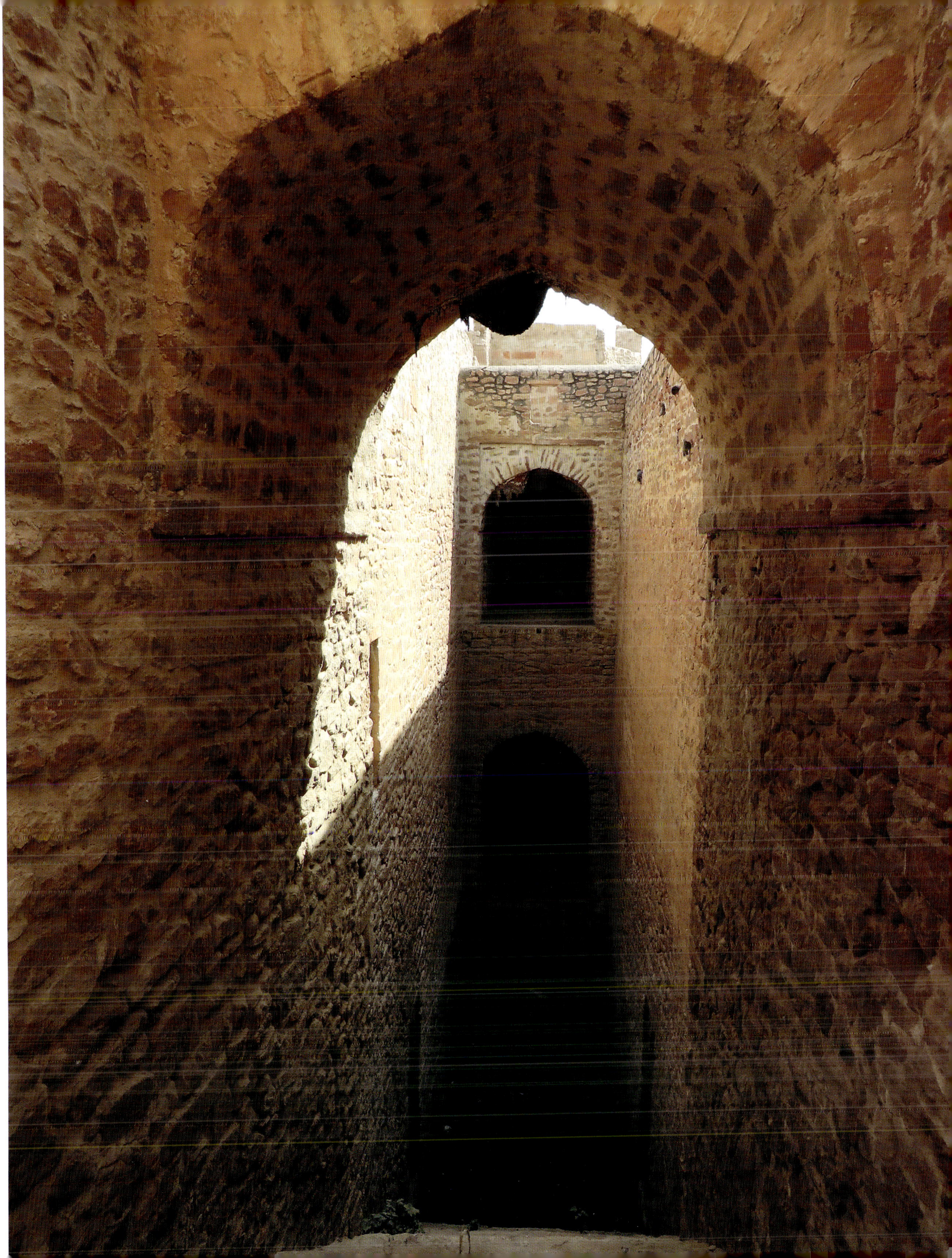

Vestiges of splendour are evident in what was once a majestic approach to the baoli (opposite). At some point, the entrance arch was partly bricked up with stone (above), obscuring the view of the arcade (above, right).

130

MIRZA ALI JAAN KA TAKHT BAOLI

NARNAUL, HARYANA
1556-1605
28°2'48.53" N
76°5'57.15" E

The Mughal city of Narnaul is midway between Delhi and Jaipur, but might as well be on the moon for all the attention it receives on tourist itineraries. Nonetheless, it is full of outstanding palaces, tombs and other monuments spanning hundreds of years and several dynasties. There are also several baolis – each entirely different – located within a short distance of one another.

According to the Haryana historian Ranbir Phaugat, Mirza Ali Jaan (or Jilan) was the physician of Emperor Akbar (r. 1556-1605), and hailed from Narnaul. However, an informative Haryana guidebook describes him as the nawab (governor) of Narnaul, who administered the city during the reign of Akbar. What is certain is that the Mirza Ali Jaan ka Takht stepwell was designed to impress. One can still gauge from what little remains of its original setting how grand it must have been; imagine it nestled in a beautiful garden, its approach marked by bubbling water courses, an octagonal pool and a fountain. At the end of this watery procession, the baoli appears, its hefty double-storeyed entrance topped by a pillared pavilion, or *takht* – somewhere to relax above the pool while catching the breeze.

The imposing scale of this entrance structure is slightly misleading; behind the massive façade is a scaled-down pool and accompanying arcade. Viewed from the front, however, the vigorous layering of columns, windows, arches and brackets makes this more than a mere gateway. There is even a decorative covered balcony, or *jharokha*. Around the back, pool-side, there is more restraint, less need to make a big impression. The simple, flat façade is pierced by dignified arches that are cleverly concealed from the front. If ladies were ensconced there, they would have been hidden from view, with curtains in place, but near the cool water; the men would have been lounging above, under a sunshade of their own.

Ali Jaan would be disappointed today by the state of his extravagant construction. No water flows to the well or any other water feature. But at least his name will be remembered – as long as the baoli survives.

SHAH QULI BAOLI

FATEHPUR SIKRI, UTTAR PRADESH
1569-84
27°5'43.05" N
77°40'1.92" E

The abandoned city of Fatehpur Sikri (meaning 'City of Victory') is a tourist must-see on the road between Agra and Jaipur. Constructed between 1571 and 1573 by Emperor Akbar, it was briefly the capital of the Mughal Empire: a city of palaces, administrative buildings, gardens and public spaces, with an enormous mosque and a gateway commemorating the conquest of Gujarat. When Fatehpur Sikri was granted UNESCO World Heritage Site status in 1986, the gateway was described as 'by far the greatest monumental structure of Akbar's entire reign and also one of the most perfect architectural achievements in India'. A sophisticated system of ponds, tanks, aqueducts, pools and an artificial lake was planned for the city, but there was ultimately an inadequate supply of water, and Akbar decamped to Lahore in 1585.

Little is written about Mohammed Quli Khan, after whom this baoli is named, but what little information can be gleaned, if true, connects to a story involving political intrigue, birthright and betrayal. It starts with Maham Anga, who was the beloved wet nurse of Akbar; in fact, she became so influential that she acted as Akbar's de facto regent. Maham Anga's son Adham Khan became one of Akbar's generals. He was eventually executed – thrown twice from a balcony – by Akbar after he murdered one of the emperor's ministers. It is believed that Quli Khan was another son of the scheming Maham Anga. Although he also became a general in Akbar's army, his life was not quite as colourful as his brother's. Today he is known chiefly on account of Adham's notoriety, and also because his tomb in Delhi was refurbished as an unconventional summer house during the British Raj.

No matter how fascinating, tales from the royal court do not explain the presence of this baoli or indeed Quli Khan's connection with it. He may now be a footnote in Mughal history, his name associated with only a stepwell and a mausoleum, but at least they are both exceptional buildings. The four-storey, L-shaped baoli is considered to be the largest and most elaborate of its kind. It is constructed from red sandstone, and at the upper level has a loggia with deep eaves projecting over plain pillars. Three levels of interior rooms run the length of the well and extend into the huge cylinder itself, creating an octagonal, multi-tiered gallery. Even more architecturally ambitious are two octagonal chambers projecting off the well, offering extra space for cool retreat – although they were inaccessible when I visited.

The baoli is located just off the main road into Fatehpur Sikri, and is currently being used to irrigate the surrounding trees, hence the tangle of pipes and other equipment, including a generator, inside. Laundry is hung up to dry and there is even a bed, but it is good to see that the well is in use.

Sited just off the main road into the Mughal city of Fatehpur Sikri, Shah Quli is thought to be the largest and most complex L-shaped stepwell. Today its water is extracted via pipes and hoses.

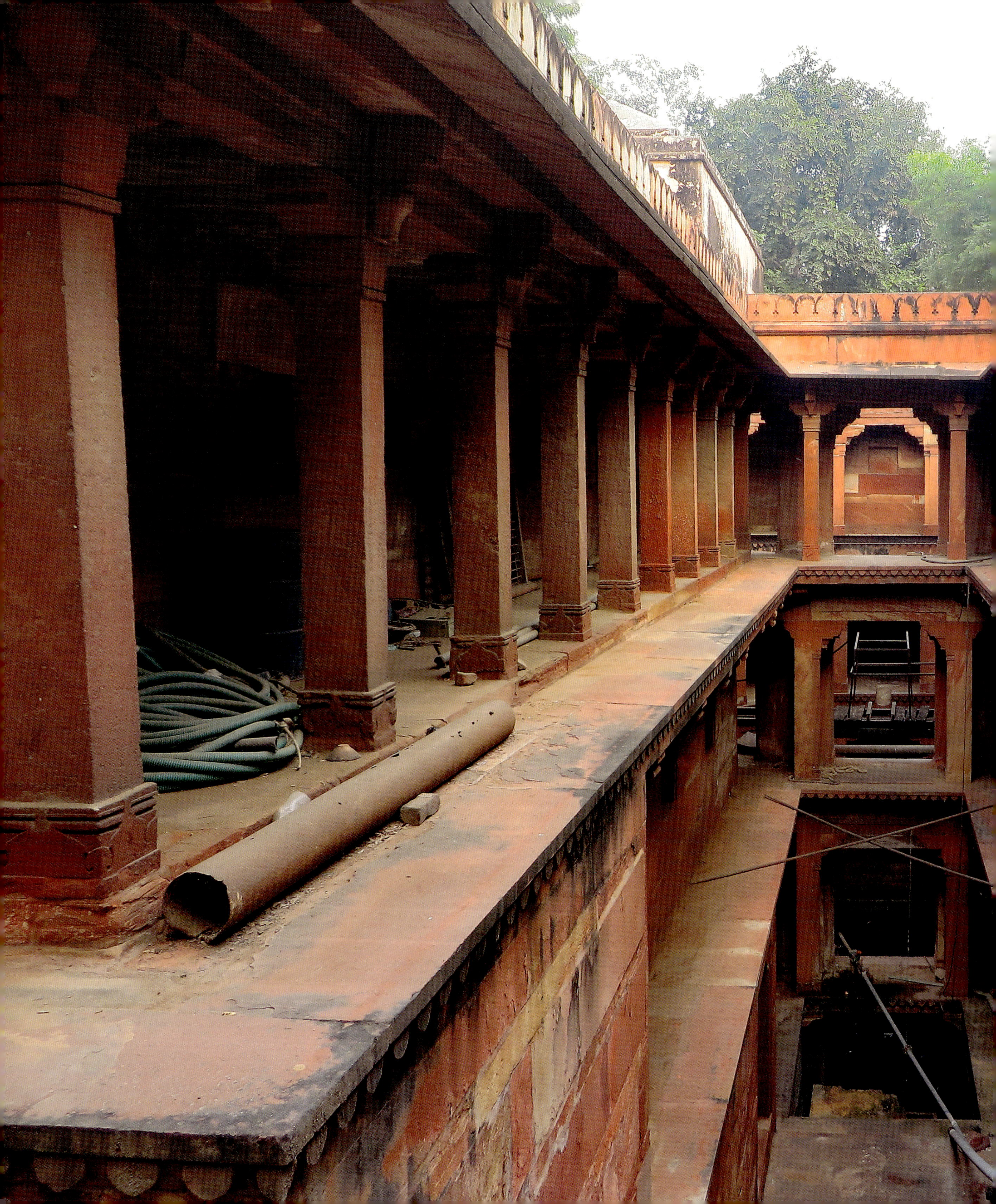

A red sandstone spectacle appears as one turns the corner to face columns, corridors and broad eaves.

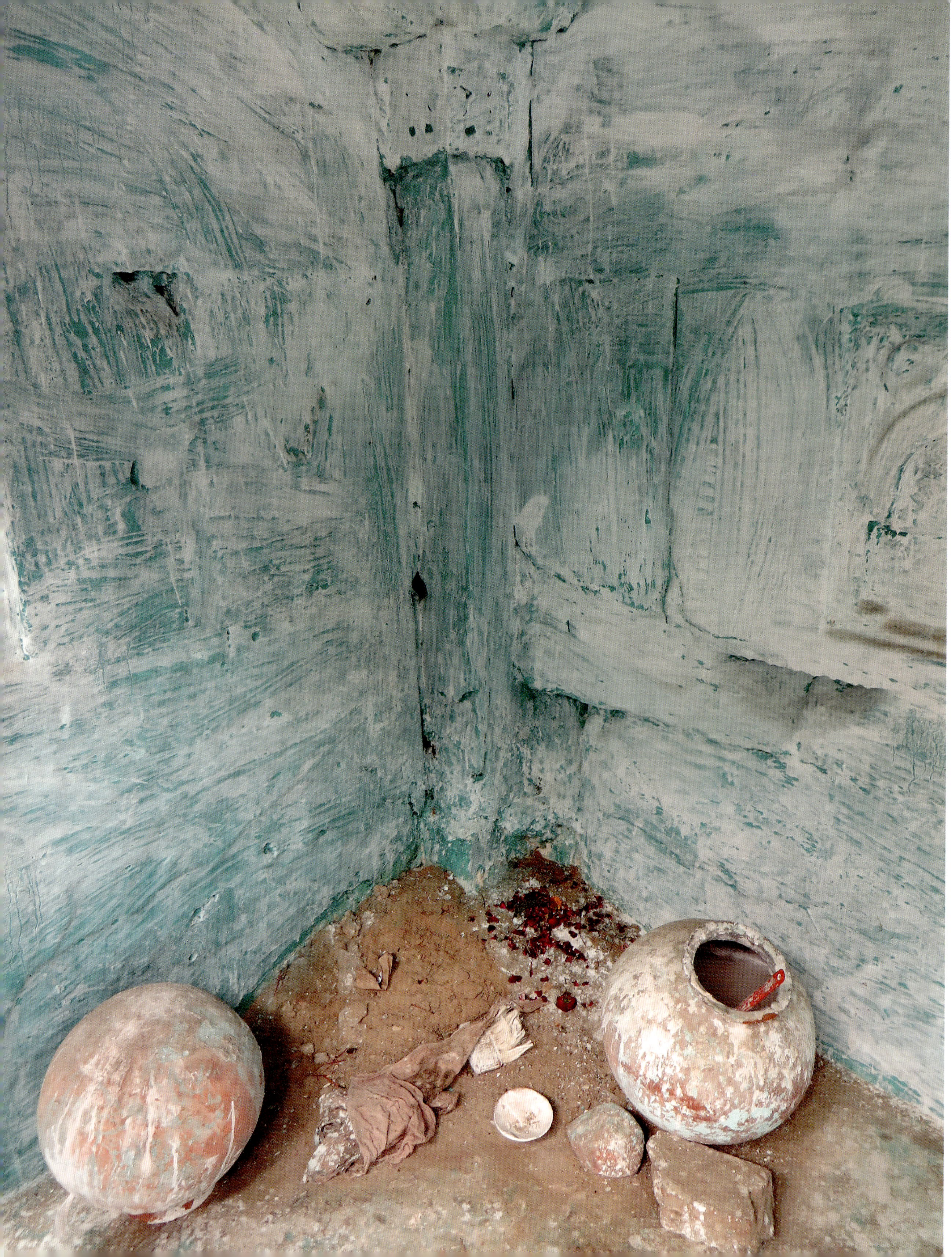

INDARAVALI BAOLI

FATEHPUR SIKRI, UTTAR PRADESH
1570s
27°5'33.83" N
77°39'21.52" E

Indaravali is a good example of the stepwells that were built in and around Emperor Akbar's city of Fatehpur Sikri. It is constructed of the same rich red sandstone that was used for most of Fatehpur Sikri's buildings, and was most probably frequented by travellers on their way to the city. A single, stepped corridor leads directly to the edge of the octagonal cylinder, where a sudden drop awaits. Around the top of the cylinder are multiple supports, used for hauling up buckets of water.

Indaravali has been partly repurposed as a wishing well. Local people beseech the resident *djinns* for help, leaving behind written notes and offerings, as also seen at Feroz Shah Kotla Baoli in Delhi (pp. 76-77). Inside the cylinder stands a simple stone tower of later construction (unfortunately, it obscures a graceful Islamic arch), and each day visitors throw in vibrantly coloured flowers. I believe that any use of a stepwell is preferable to its abandonment, and there is no doubt that Indaravali is respected and cared for by the community.

A beautiful ambulatory passage overlooks the well cylinder. Although such passages can be found at numerous stepwells – for instance, at Ra Khengar Vav (pp. 66-67) – Indaravali's is a rarely seen two-storey version, and there are also separate chambers. Thus, Indaravali is more akin to complex private wells than to simple and utilitarian public baolis. Perhaps the fact that it was built at the same time as Fatehpur Sikri meant that it was afforded extra attention.

Indaravali is a far more modest baoli than Shah Quli's, although it was built during the same period in the same city. Today it fulfils an important community function as a place for petitioning *djinns*.

The array of colour compensates for the fact that much of the stepwell is impassable.

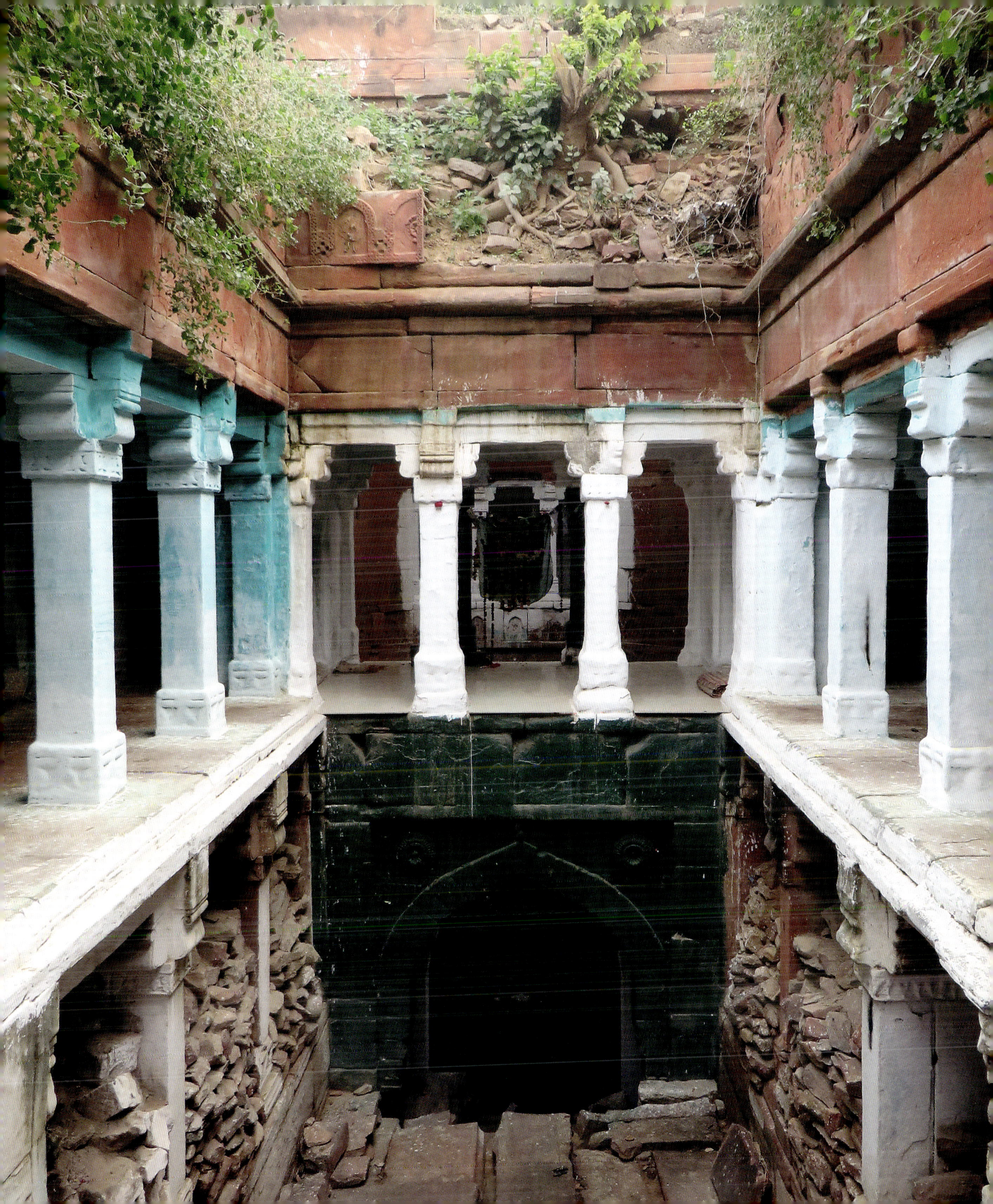

NEEMRANA BAORI

NEEMRANA, RAJASTHAN
c. 1570 (15th CENTURY/1720)
27°59'59.67" N
76°22'57.45" E

The stepwell in the small town of Neemrana is one of India's most impressive by virtue of its sheer majesty; it is an astounding piece of architecture. As in the case of so many baolis, it lies quietly in wait behind a simple wall off a country road. Take a look, and Neemrana's astonishing nine-storey drop will stop you in your tracks.

Information about this behemoth is sketchy at best. The spread of possible dates of construction spans three centuries, which is never a good sign. One theory is that a local landowner built the well as a famine-relief project for villagers in need of work and cash, but it is a story that has not been substantiated. It seems hard to believe that so little can be known about something so vast, but it is not an uncommon situation.

Some years ago there were plans to turn this stepwell into a crafts centre; fortunately, they came to naught. Even though some restoration work was undertaken, the dramatic descent down a few hundred steps would surely have been a deterrent to visitors. I say that everyone should come to see this structure, if possible, but there is no denying that it is unsafe.

Once one is inside the stepwell, the atmosphere is mysterious, even unnerving, thanks to the structure's advanced decay and the overwhelming sense of abandonment. Nesting green parrots provide the only light relief from the eerie ambience. In its heyday, the baoli must have been a wondrous and welcome sight, offering travellers both cool respite in its arched loggia (running down both lengths of the top level) and abundant water – the latter a drastically depleted resource in the area in recent times.

A pair of multi-storeyed buttresses bridge the baoli, narrowing as the descent deepens. They are pierced by arched windows that create disorientating, layered views without equal in Western architectural typologies. To be standing at the bottom of the murky well, staring up at the harsh light while surrounded by the looming walls and the flapping of wings, is an extremely potent experience.

The scale and depth of Neemrana Baori are hard to take in, and the descent to the bottom of the well is not for the faint-hearted.

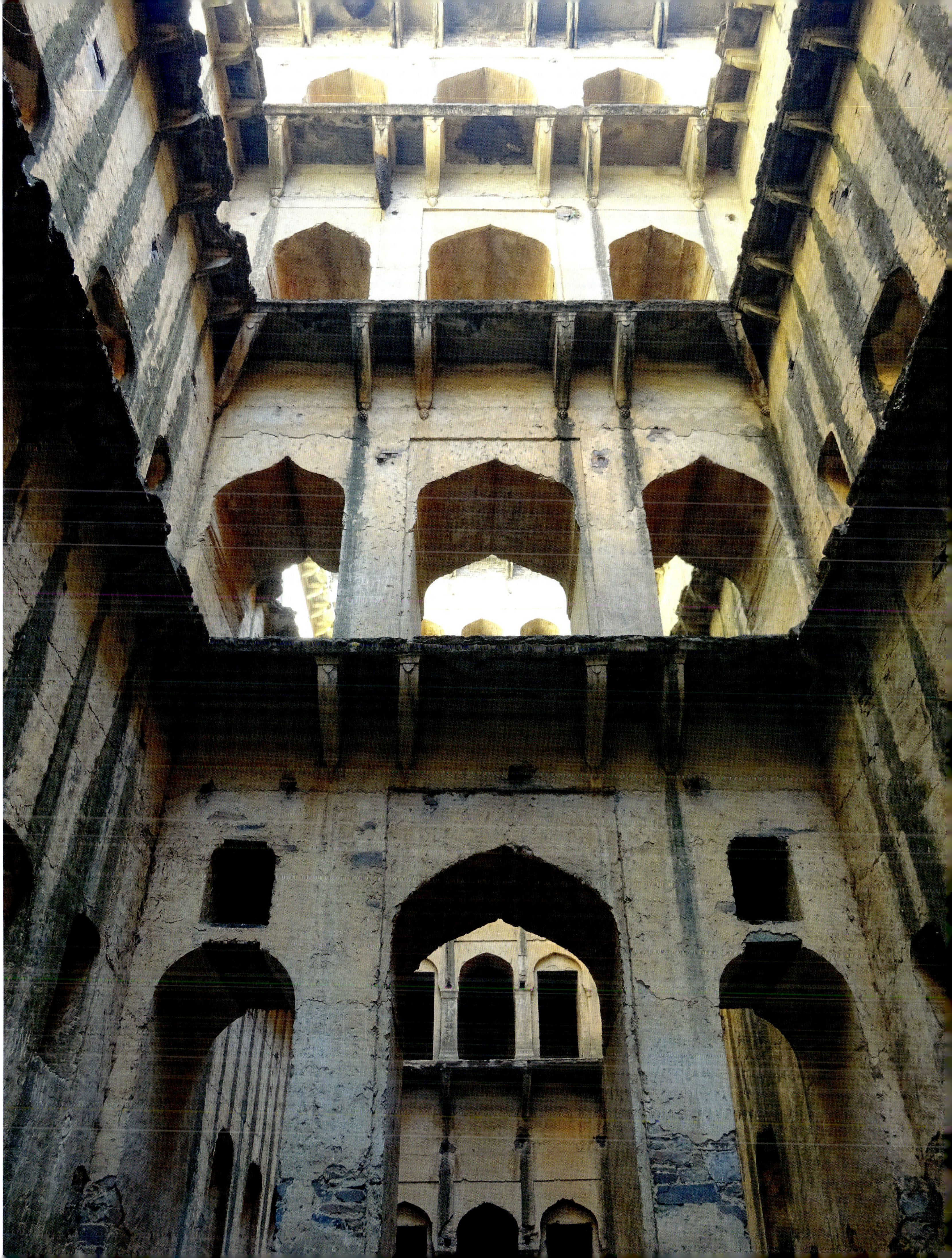

AKBAR'S BAOLI

AGRA, RAJASTHAN
c. 1575
27°10'36.84" N
78°1'24.40" E

The Red Fort at Agra will always get second billing to the Taj Mahal as a tourist destination, but buried within the 38-hectare (94-acre) enclosure is a breathtaking stepwell so complex that the scholar Julia Hegewald describes it as the most elaborate of its kind. Built by Emperor Akbar, it is also extremely discreet, with a profile so minimal as to be nearly invisible to an unaware passer-by. At ground level there is a flat, circular platform with a screen-covered centre; an unremarkable little staircase leads into the well.

This is a perfect example of a private well used solely for pleasure by the wealthy and powerful – in this case, the most powerful ruler in sixteenth-century India. While their public counterparts were usually highly visible, by definition these circular structures turned inwards, as if they were secret bunkers. Generally, they were constructed not for washing or prayers or even for providing drinking water; their dark, cool underground rooms simply offered luxurious escape from the stifling heat.

The design of these private playgrounds makes them very difficult to photograph, especially in this case: Akbar's Baoli plunges six storeys, winding around a central shaft in an elaborate arrangement of stairs, chambers and windows. It is believed that the royal ladies would visit these wells unaccompanied, perhaps taking with them rugs, curtains and all manner of treats. Ventilation shafts were cleverly inserted to draw fresh air into the extraordinary structure, which today houses remnants of Raj-era equipment, plenty of guano and at least one startled mongoose.

Radiating from the central, unembellished cylinder, the rooms relied on lamplight for illumination. At ground level, there is no hint of the depth and complexity of the subterranean building; indeed, that was the point of private wells.

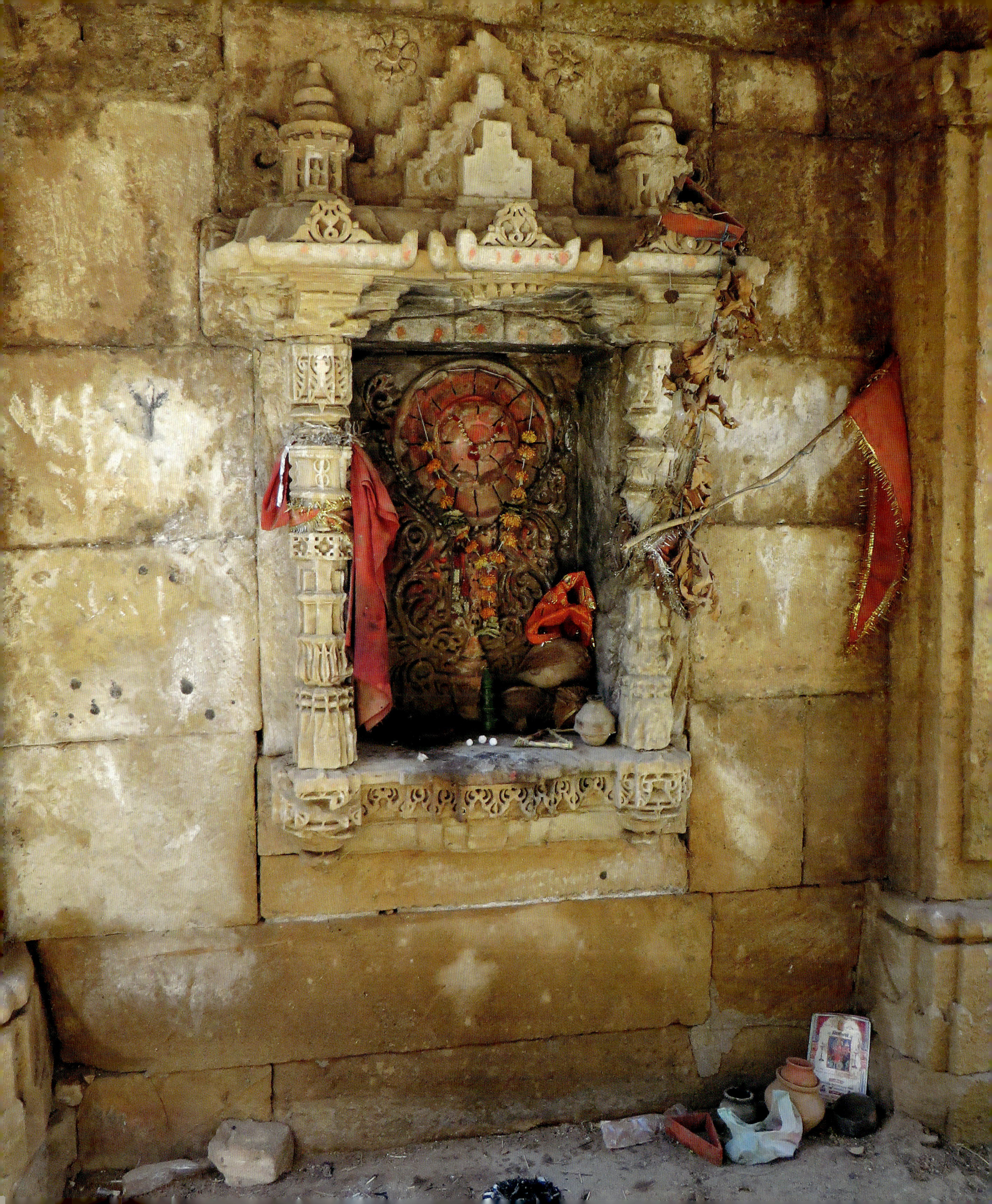

HAMPUR VAV

HAMPUR, GUJARAT
c. 16th–17th CENTURY
22°54'25.83" N
71°34'12.19" E

In common with many stepwells, the once-grand vav at Hampur has lapsed into anonymity over time. On the nearby government protection sign it is referred to simply as 'Ancient Vav'. That the vav is protected at all comes as a shock, given that the town itself is challenging to find and smaller even than Dhank (pp. 30–35). The date of construction, too, is unknown, with the best estimate embracing a 100-year span. What we can be sure of is that any traveller in the medieval Gujarati countryside would have been relieved to arrive at this refuge, six storeys deep, with a welcoming domed pavilion, shady tower pavilions and channels for directing drawn water into adjacent troughs. Sadly, the ghostly remnants of what must have been an outstanding structure are now dangerously unstable. Whatever the previous condition of the vav, the deadly earthquake in 2001 made it much worse. Hampur was not far from the epicentre, and the vav's elegant entrance dome collapsed; today only the base – barely supported by twelve stately columns – is still in place.

Down inside the well, cobwebs and cave-ins notwithstanding, the extravagantly carved niches are still astonishing. Within them, stylized flowers – which replaced the representation of deities under Muslim rule – remain intact, as do the impressive supports above. A large modern shrine, dedicated to Shiva, is a brave but ill-considered addition, built directly on top of the final pavilion and overlooking the entire well. From this perch, the wretchedness of the once steadfast architecture is even more apparent, with a view of cracked and teetering stone blocks. The fact that the local community has integrated the structure into daily life is heartening, considering that far less damaged examples are often ignored completely.

The imposing domed entrance pavilion at Hampur has failed the test of time, but striking details survive within the vav, including the shrine pictured opposite. The modern Shiva temple atop the well sustains the involvement of the community (right).

Although parts of the vav are wrecked, it remains an important – if hazardous – structure.

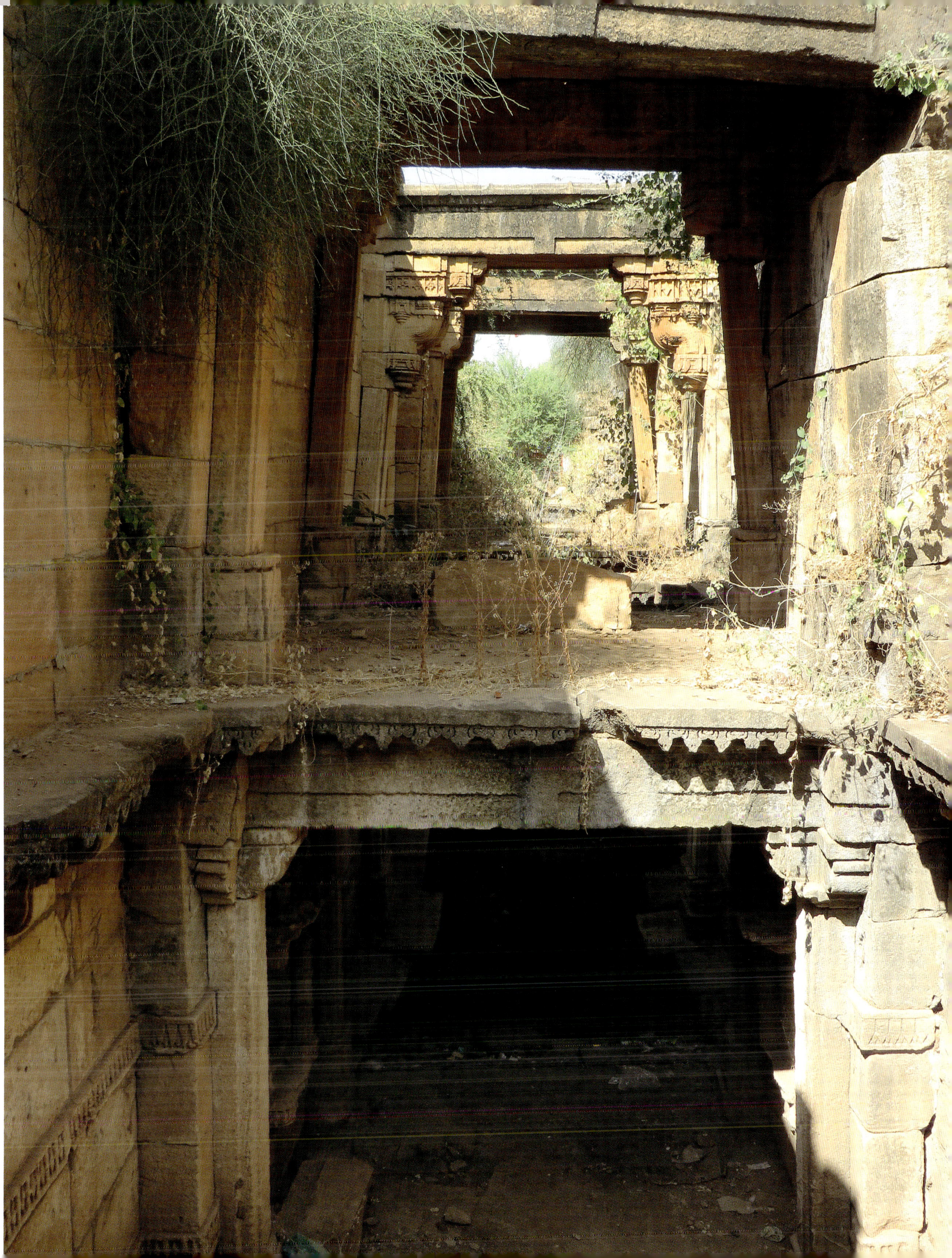

THE CITY OF BAOLIS: BUNDI, RAJASTHAN

Once part of a princely state (of the same name) that was established in the fourteenth century, Bundi has come to be known as 'The City of Baolis' – so anyone with a yen for stepwells should certainly pay a visit. There are well over fifty spread liberally throughout Bundi; little wonder that it is the subject of the only book devoted to the stepwells of a single city. *Baolis of Bundi* was published by the Indian National Trust for Art and Cultural Heritage (INTACH) in 2015. It served as my primary source here, but even INTACH's dedicated and knowledgeable researchers encountered tremendous gaps in information about these largely undocumented, unprotected and crumbling monuments. The book's detailed map is also a first for any city with such significant stepwells.

There is hope for the future of stepwells in Bundi thanks to a handful of local groups that have stepped up to restore baolis in their communities. In the most successful collaboration so far, INTACH worked with The Prince's Charities, London, and local municipal organizations to restore the historically significant Bhawaldi Baoli. Such teamwork is evident across India, albeit on a limited basis, and long may it continue.

Bundi is situated in a relatively water-rich region, and its stepwells are part of an elaborate and efficient system of dams, artificial lakes and tanks that harvest and preserve water (as is also the case in Jodhpur and Jaipur, among other cities). It would be far more difficult to establish such a system today, however, as – according to one expert – the water table in the city is decreasing by some 2–3 metres (6½–9¾ ft) per year.

The baoli-building boom took place mainly during the reign of Rao Raja Anirudh Singh (1682–96) and of his son Rao Raja Budh Singh (1696–1735). The young rani of Anirudh Singh went on a charitable spree that seems to have spurred wealthy citizens to follow suit. The impressive range of styles reflects not only tastes, but also the varying levels of funds committed and the different-sized parcels of land available. In Bundi there are L-shaped, linear and square wells; they may be ornate or modest, shallow or plunging, public or apparently private. Many are in the form of kunds, and those seen here are just a small fraction of the total.

MANOHARI BAOLI
c. 1600
25°26'41.63" N
75°38'33.69" E

Decorative *chhatris* flank the entrance to a number of Bundi's stepwells, lending a dash of pomp to otherwise conventional examples. Manohari Baoli, encroached on three sides by more recent construction, is fading fast.

The Hindi word *manohari* means 'picturesque', and the two large *chhatris* marking the entrance to this baoli on a little side street certainly lend the L-shaped community well a certain grandeur. Such umbrella-like pavilions are a common feature of Bundi stepwells, and are undeniably hard to overlook in bustling neighbourhoods. But here the spindly, decaying columns with their dainty cusped arches now struggle to support the high, fluted domes. The *chhatris* appear unsteady; the left-hand one has had several columns removed and is propped up by an equally crumbling adjoining building.

As one turns the corner in the well, any picturesque quality disappears abruptly. It is possible to gain a decent view of the two remaining arches that span the narrow space, but a lower arch on the bottom level barely peeks above centuries' worth of litter and silt. The neighbourhood children get a big kick out of any visitor's interest in the vanishing monument.

BHAWALDI BAOLI
c. 1677
25°26'47.06" N
75°38'22.06" E

Any time there is a positive, upbeat story in the stepwell world, it deserves to be broadcast far and wide. The recent history of Bhawaldi Baoli provides a breath of fresh air. The well has risen, phoenix-like, from metaphorical ashes, thanks to the combined efforts of INTACH, The Prince's Charities, London, and the local community.

The well was sponsored by Rani Bhawalde, the wife of Rao Raja Bhao Singh (*r*. 1658–82). While Raniji ki Baori (pp. 152–53), built a couple of decades later, may outrank Bhawaldi in scale and grandeur, Bhawaldi holds its own, especially in terms of the success of its restoration and its location in a charming residential neighbourhood. The government of Rajasthan owns the stepwell, but previously, before it became a protected monument, the city was responsible for its care and maintenance. To say that it was in poor condition is an understatement. A comparison of the 'before' and 'after' states – with no sign of vegetation, the crumbling masonry repaired and the rubbish-strewn water cleaned – would be worthy of a museum exhibition.

Bhawaldi is special for several reasons. First, it is strikingly pretty. These images were taken before the restoration work was complete and so cannot fully convey its loveliness. INTACH took great care to analyse and re-create original features while stabilizing, rather than interfering with, others that had survived the centuries. Most notable is the arched entryway, with serpentine brackets (typical of Bundi architecture) and traditional murals painted by local artists. Secondly, the restoration process fully engaged the community. What had formerly been an unappreciated, decaying dumping ground has given the neighbourhood a sense of stewardship and pride, which is essential for the future survival of any stepwell. The laborious clean-up process also provided the locals with new sewers and drains, a regular refuse collection and a steady water supply. Bhawaldi Baoli is back in business.

Sensitive restoration demonstrates that a stepwell can be reconnected to its history, water source and community. The goal at Bhawaldi was to make it a valuable neighbourhood asset, not a pristine showpiece.

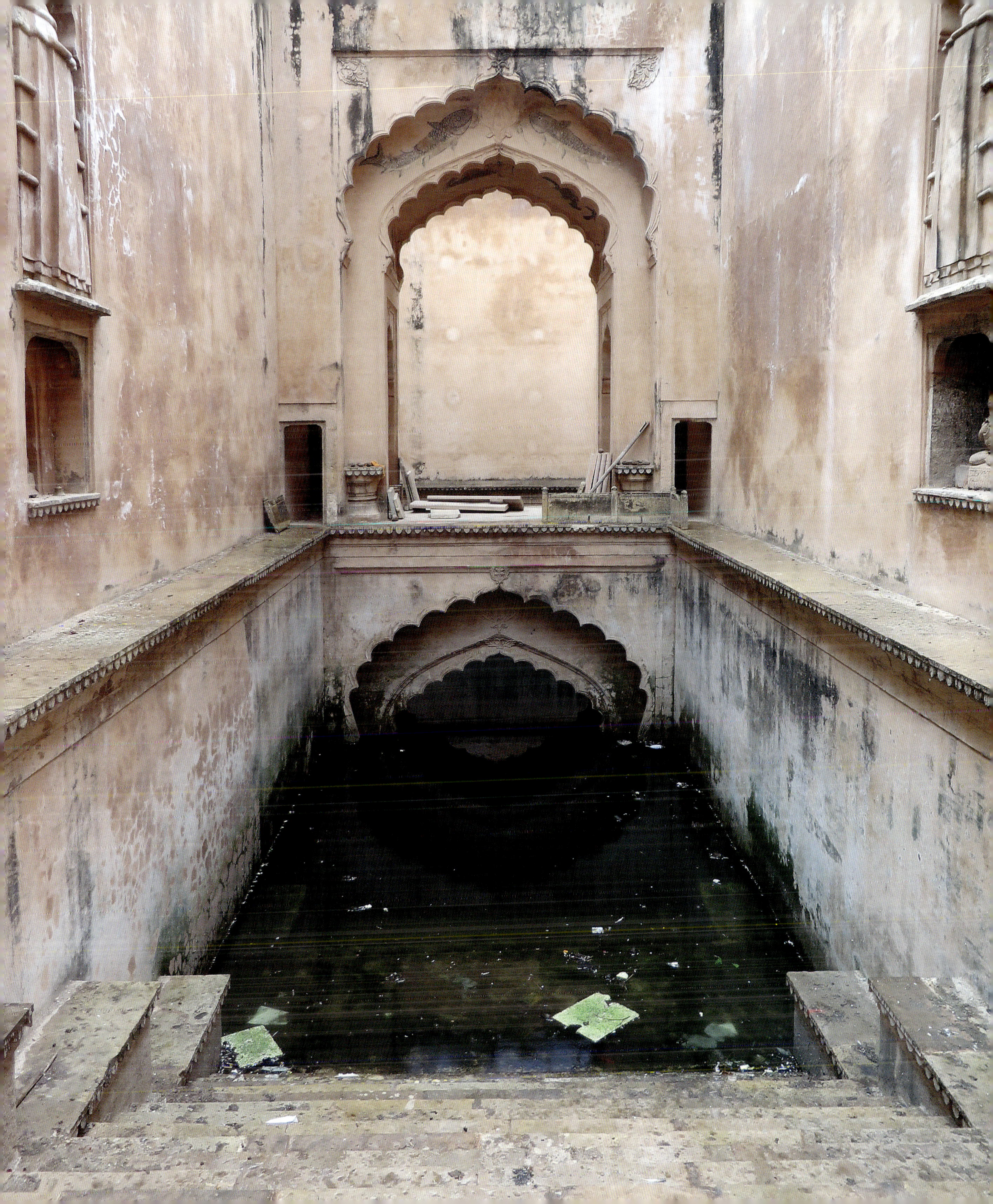

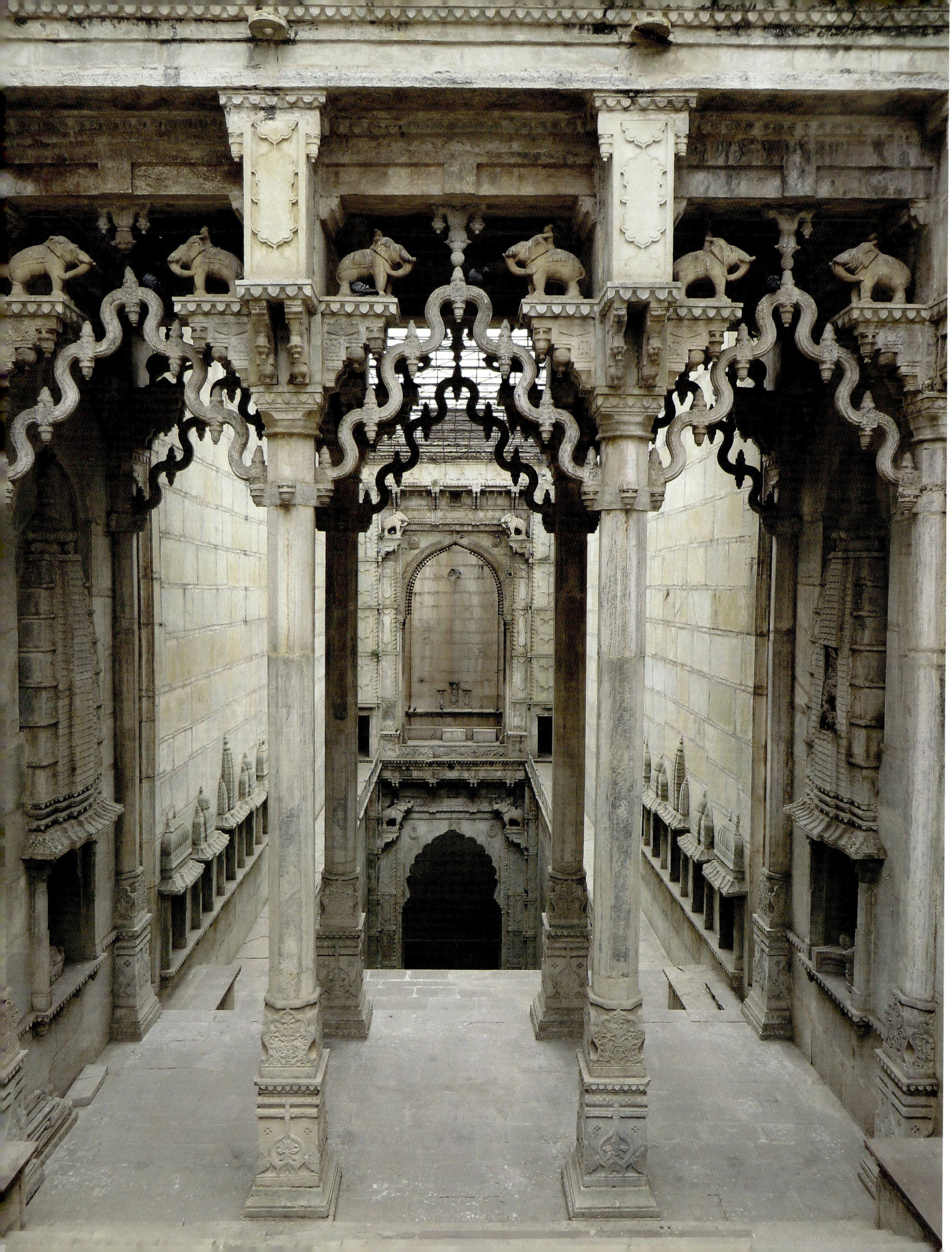

RANIJI KI BAORI
1699
25°26'25.05" N
75°38'21.36" E

When a stepwell is commissioned by a queen, one can expect a few ornamental bells and whistles. Raniji ki Baori does not disappoint. Out of the twenty-plus public wells commissioned by the young Rani Nathawati-ji (wife of Rao Raja Anirudh Singh), this is the most famous, sumptuous and best protected in Bundi; it features in guidebooks as a top tourist attraction. It was built after the raja's death, when rule had passed to his son, and loudly announces itself with a crown of 'cenotaphs' (the term used by the local government on the sign outside the baoli, in reference to the *chhatris*).

Just like Ruda at Rudabai Vav in Gujarat two centuries earlier (pp. 103-105), this queen favoured a well with three entrances. Today, with the main entrance closed, the full dramatic effect is reduced but still powerful. Raniji has a distinctive style that treads a fine line between restrained and ornate. On account of the baoli having been restored, cleaned and fitted with a protective grate roof, the ambience is somewhat sterile compared to that at most stepwells. One could almost be in a museum or library, and there is little sense of being underground. Given the preservation efforts, however, it seems petty to quibble about a change of atmosphere.

Many photographs of this remarkable stepwell include the signature undulating brackets that span the delicate entry columns.

The restoration of Raniji contrasts markedly with that of Bhawaldi, but it both highlights and protects the significant architecture and incomparable details of the stepwell. The four *chhatris* and, inside, the stone walkway are among the outstanding features.

Pairs of elephants and their riders rest on the capitals, and the whole effect is one of such lacy fragility that it is impossible to believe the stone can support anything heavier than a marshmallow. On the first landing are two niches with elaborate *shikharas* (roofs) derived from temple architecture, larger versions of which can be seen on the corner shrines at the tenth-century Gangvo Kund in Gujarat (pp. 44-45). Other exceptional niches line the walls down the steep flight of steps, which passes under an extraordinary double archway. Intricately detailed and sculptural, the arches appear as weightless as the columns. It is not easy to imagine how this demure and dignified space would have looked some 300 years ago, filled with ritual activities and women fetching water, but it still stands as a great testament to the rani's taste and both her generosity and that of the state government.

153

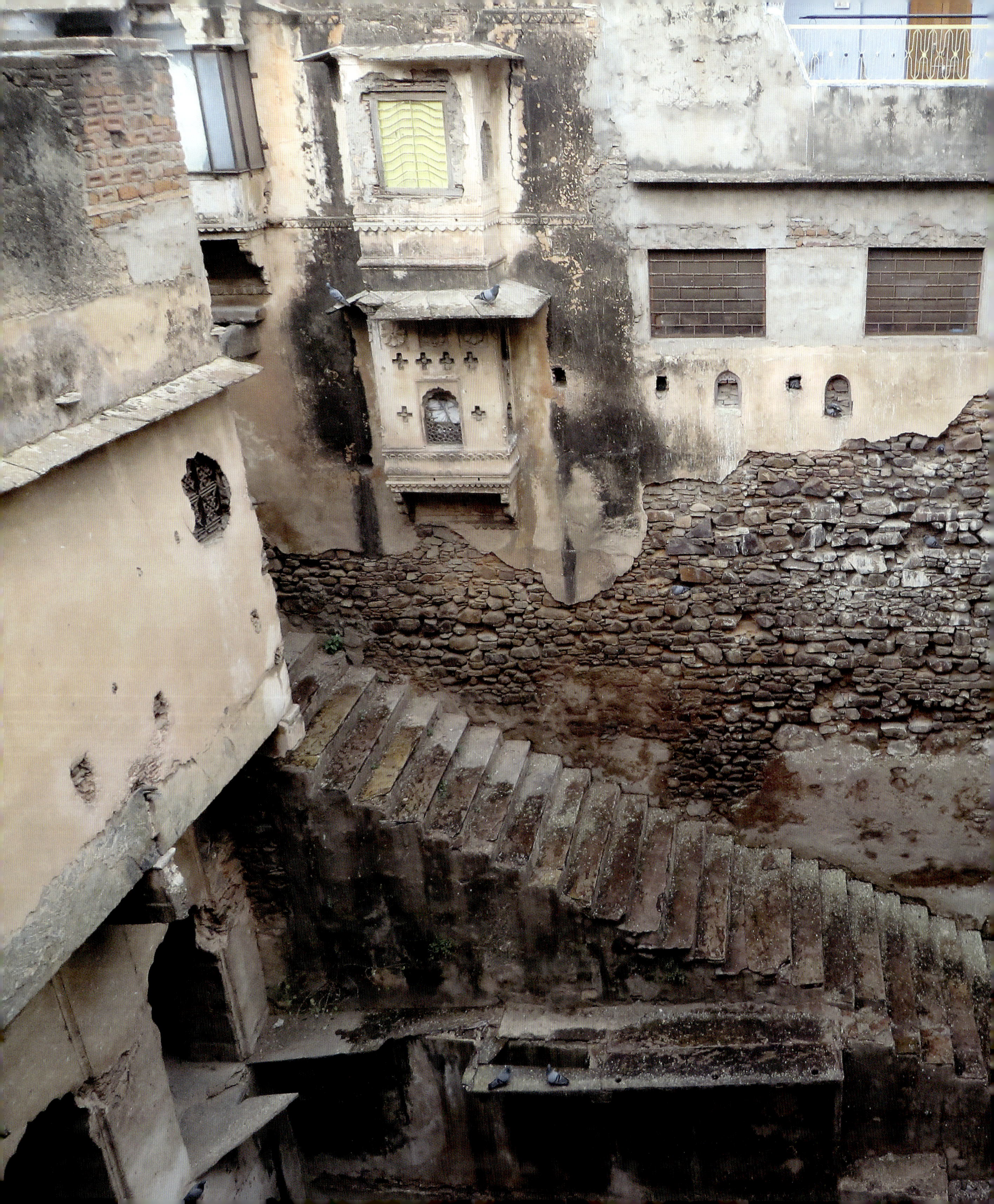

PRADHANJI KA KUND

c. 1700
25°26'37.59" N
75°38'21.03" E

Whereas Ranijl kl Baori is a popular tourist attraction, Pradhanji baoli is a well-kept secret, off-limits to the public. It is surrounded by homes and shops, and is thus very difficult to photograph. It is also something of a stylistic outlier, eccentric and adhering to no particular rule. Since no scholar has attempted to assign a date of construction, the one I give here is simply in accordance with most of the other Bundi wells. The well is thought to have been built by a relative or courtier of an unspecified Bundi maharaja.

Pradhanji was probably a private well, its water used for drinking. It is challenging to describe: square, with a convoluted series of steps that zigzag down the walls, doubling back on themselves, and splitting in two directions at the bottom, perhaps to allow more than one person to access the water. Another eccentricity is a two-storey loggia along one wall, the arches of each floor in a different style (an adjoining balcony is not pictured here); a pair of eaves are set perpendicular to this possibly later addition. Much is crammed into such a tight space. Whoever built this fascinating oddity clearly tried to make the most of a limited footprint.

Inaccessible to the outside world, Pradhanji ka Kund is hemmed in by an architectural collage. Its origin is a mystery, as is the nonconformist design.

SHREE ABHAYNATH MAHADEV KI BAOLI
c. 1700
25°26'50.89" N
75°37'42.60" E

Devi, the mother goddess, is revered in Hinduism and worshipped in many forms under many names that can be unique to a single community or village. She is associated with fertility and birth, and – the life-giving properties of water being a natural connection – many stepwells bear her name. The prefix *maha-* signifies 'great' (as in *maharaja*, 'great ruler'). Shree Abhaynath Mahadev lies close to the sizeable, sixteenth-century Bhora-ji-ka Kund. Comparing these two man-made – and still functioning – bodies of water, one appreciates how efficient Bundi's water-harvesting systems were.

At the entrance to the baoli, a pair of shrines welcome visitors. One houses a foil-adorned sculpture of the elephant-headed Ganesh, the Remover of Obstacles, who is present at many stepwells; the other houses Saraswati, the goddess of knowledge and arts. As is the case at any L-shaped well, there is a sense of anticipation as you turn the corner. Fortunately, Shree Abhaynath Mahadev is no let-down; it is a peaceful well of simple design. On the landing, a pair of large niches are decorated with the pretty, curvilinear brackets that are typical of Bundi. The water in the rectangular pool is clear and blue, so clean that the community still drinks it.

At the far end, a trio of arches lead to an unexpected loggia around the square cylinder. Pumping equipment is the sole distraction at this otherwise serene retreat.

The long, narrow pool is filled to the brim with water that the community continues to rely on. Shrines dedicated to Ganesh and Saraswati mark the simple entrance (above).

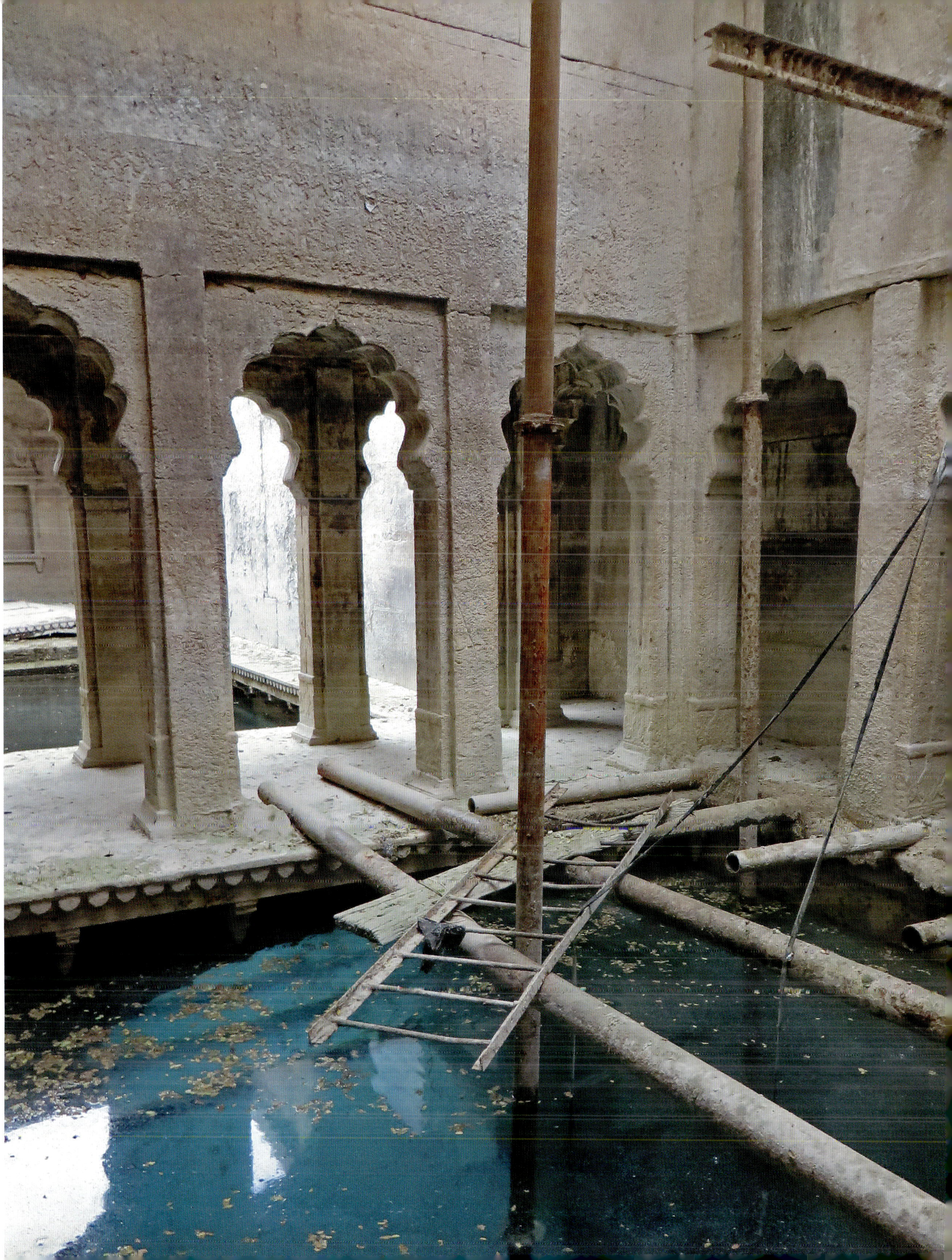

JAIPURIYA KUND
(JEFAR JI KA KUND)
c. 1705
25°26'24.74" N
75°38'26.93" E

Jaipuriya Kund is small but deep. Shiva's *trishula* (trident) can be seen resting on the balcony of the new temple, built above the original structure (below).

The phrase 'small but mighty' comes to mind as you stare into Jaipuriya Kund. At street level, the well is completely hidden from view behind a wall. Once you are through the entrance to the adjacent, salmon-pink Shiva temple, the steep, six-storey drop and the profusion of kund steps come as a surprise. The temple's walkway has been incorporated into the top storey, and brick pilasters support a balcony at the upper level (not pictured).

Jaipuriya has all the classic characteristics of a kund, and proves that, even at a reduced scale, the rhythmic descent of sculptural stairs can still mesmerize. Three sides taper quickly to the small pool at the bottom, while a loggia of arches spans the fourth wall. At some point, perhaps owing to disrepair, several arches were bricked in and shored up with concrete. Most of the stone overhang above the loggia has long since disappeared, and the contemporary temple building was simply plopped on top. Whoever designed this contrasting addition at least made an effort to acknowledge the old structure by aligning the new windows and openings with the originals below.

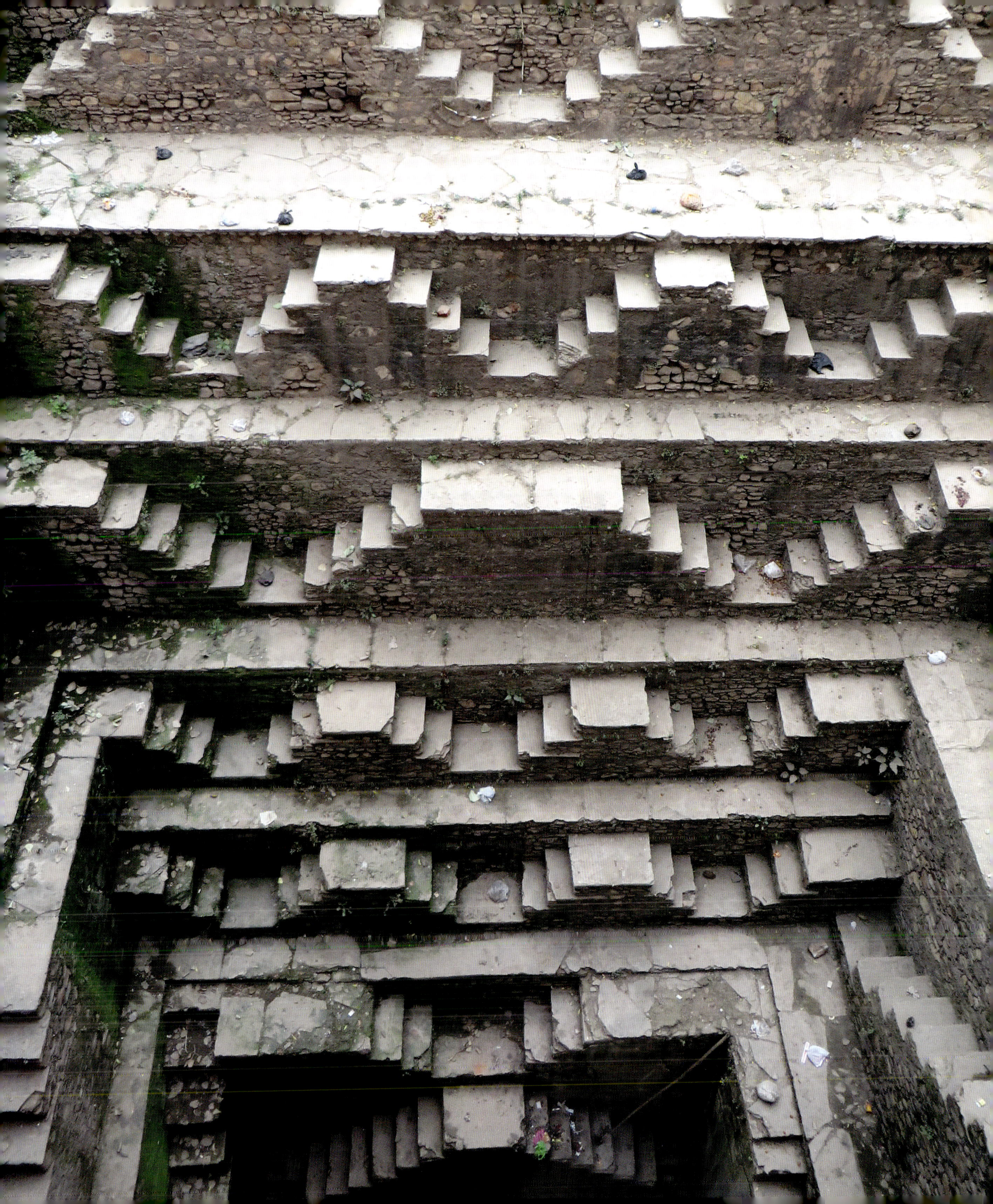

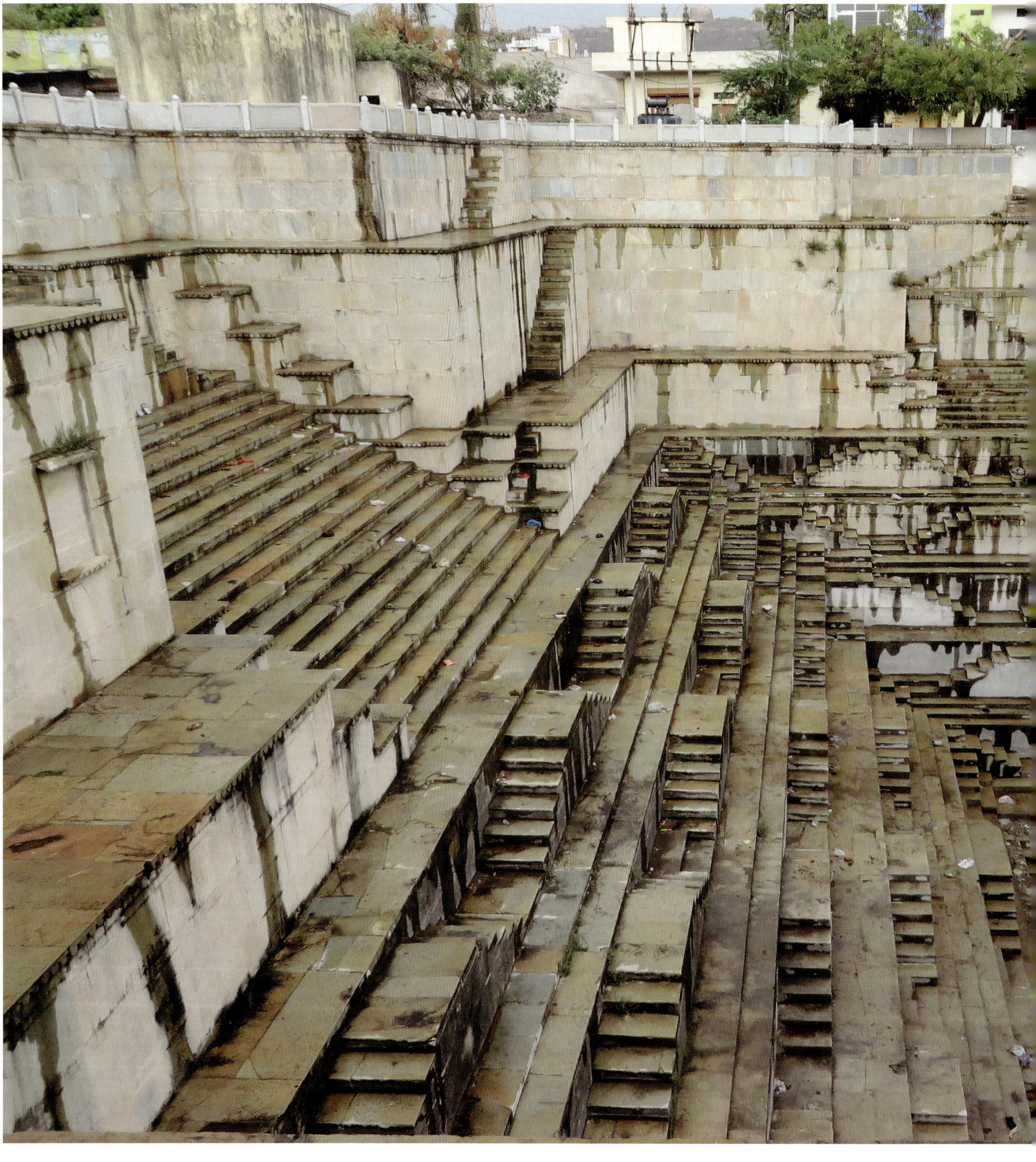

DABHAI KUND

c. 1711
25°26'11.62" N
75°38'17.87" E

Dabhai was a wealthy merchant who donated a water supply to the city, thus securing his name for posterity. At some point the kund underwent restoration, but little information is recorded about the well. It is described as the deepest in Bundi and, according to INTACH, its water was used specifically for bathing and drinking. Today locals bathe there during the monsoon season. At the main entrance, two large *chhatris* (not pictured) are dedicated to the memory of women who died performing the now forbidden Hindu practice of sati, whereby a widow threw herself on her husband's funeral pyre. There are three additional entrances to the kund, including one through a blocky structure of double-decker loggias, balconies and terraces, similar to those seen at Chand Baori (pp. 40–43). A scary, rail-less platform overhangs the pool, accompanied by a pair of large supports that were formerly used to haul up buckets of water.

Dabhai is sometimes referred to as 'Jail Kund' for the simple reason that it is close to the former local prison, but it could legitimately also be named 'Power Kund', owing to the substation built against its rear.

The step configuration at Dabhai Kund, making use of elongated pyramidal forms, is interesting and unusual.

NAGAR SAGAR KUND

c. 1800
25°26'31.63" N
75°38'23.5" E

It is tricky to attribute dates to stepwells; they are speculative and rarely confirmed, and scholarly opinions differ. The date and origin of these twin kunds are still up for debate.

These twin kunds (the singular 'kund' in the name is confusing) are the only ones that contradict the statement that 'no two stepwells are identical'. While there is at least one more pair in Gujarat (the Sasu and Vahu vavs), Nagar Sagar – as they are referenced – are the only exact twins. They lie across the street from each other and have identical descriptions in INTACH's Bundi book. No date of construction is offered by INTACH, but one opinion is that they were built a century later than most other wells in Bundi, which makes them perhaps the latest in the city.

While many water structures can be difficult to locate, Nagar Sagar are known to everyone and are thus easy to find. Their arrangement of steps – in an X-pattern – is simpler than that at Dabhai, where the pyramidal arrangement is more typical of kunds. Deep niches with cusped arches alleviate what would otherwise be a stark descent. There is no structure incorporating rooms or loggias, as at Dabhai and other kunds, but the well shaft projects slightly, with a trio of shallower niches, each distinct, embedded in its wall. The highest one, the most ornate, has curvaceous brackets on top that are similar to those that span the entry columns at Raniji ki Baori.

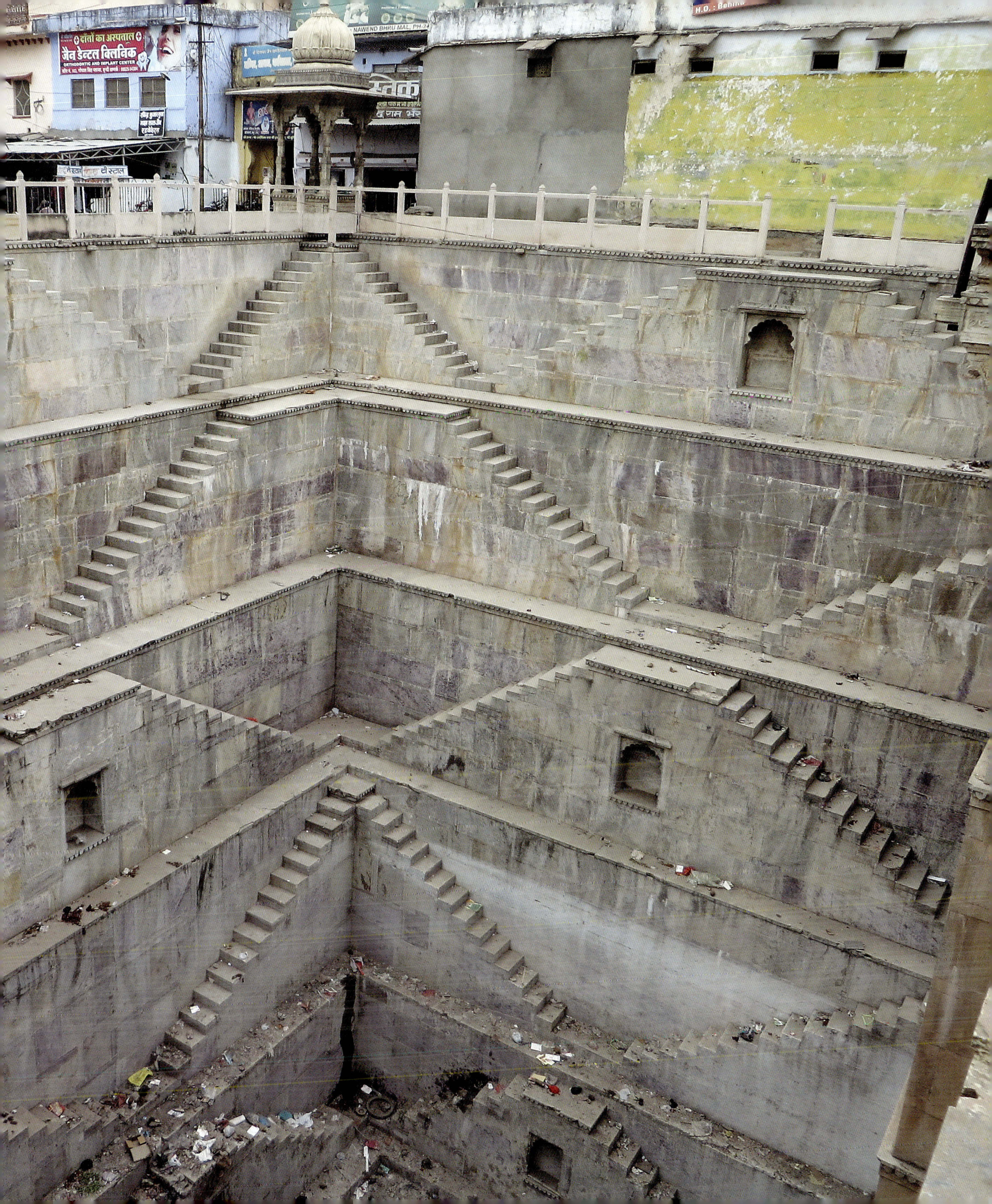
दाँतों का अस्पताल
जैन डेन्टल क्लिनिक
ORTHODONTIC AND IMPLANT CENTER

VAN TALAB BAOLI

AMER, RAJASTHAN
c. 1600/19th CENTURY
26°59'42.69" N
75°52'7.18" E

The overgrown, atmospheric baoli is thought to encompass additions from long after the original date of construction. The carpet of vibrant foliage (pp. 166-67) is inaccessible.

This 'mystery baoli' came to my attention only after a tip-off from another stepwell-lover; it would otherwise have gone unnoticed off a bumpy dirt lane behind the main road in Amer. The name I have assigned to it here is for lack of any other, until more information comes to light; I chose it because the only close landmark is a natural pond, or *talab*, which was without water at the time these photographs were taken.

The baoli is in the same area as the later, restored Maaji ki Bawadi (pp. 190-93), close to Jaipur on what was once part of a network of roads leading to Amer, the former capital of the surrounding Rajput kingdom. At the time that Van Talab is thought to have been constructed, Amer was ruled by Raja Man Singh I (r. 1589-1614), builder of the nearby Amer Fort, and a profusion of travellers would have relied on baolis along the trade routes.

Van Talab Baoli is so obscured by foliage that it is difficult to obtain a clear view. Unprotected and apparently off the radar of local government agencies, it cannot be accessed directly. However, Yash Pratap Singh Shekhawat, a knowledgeable Jaipur conservation architect, examined the images and proposed this spread of dates, based on the original construction. For as long as Amer was the capital, many structures were erected in proximity to the city.

In 1727 Maharaja Sawai Jai Singh II (r. 1699-1743) moved the capital from Amer to his newly founded city of Jaipur. In 1818 Jaipur became a British protectorate. Beginning at that time, Shekhawat told me, earlier constructions were often renovated, which explains the extensive use of mortar facing at Van Talab, perhaps for stability. This probably helped to preserve the basic structure of the baoli, but in the intervening period the well has silted up, begun to collapse and become thick with vegetation. Now a new hotel development adjacent to the baoli may restore it, and it could become a renewed success, much like Toorji ka Jhalra in Jodhpur (p. 22). Or maybe, as in the case of the Rawla Narlai baoli (p. 23), there will be candlelit dinners within.

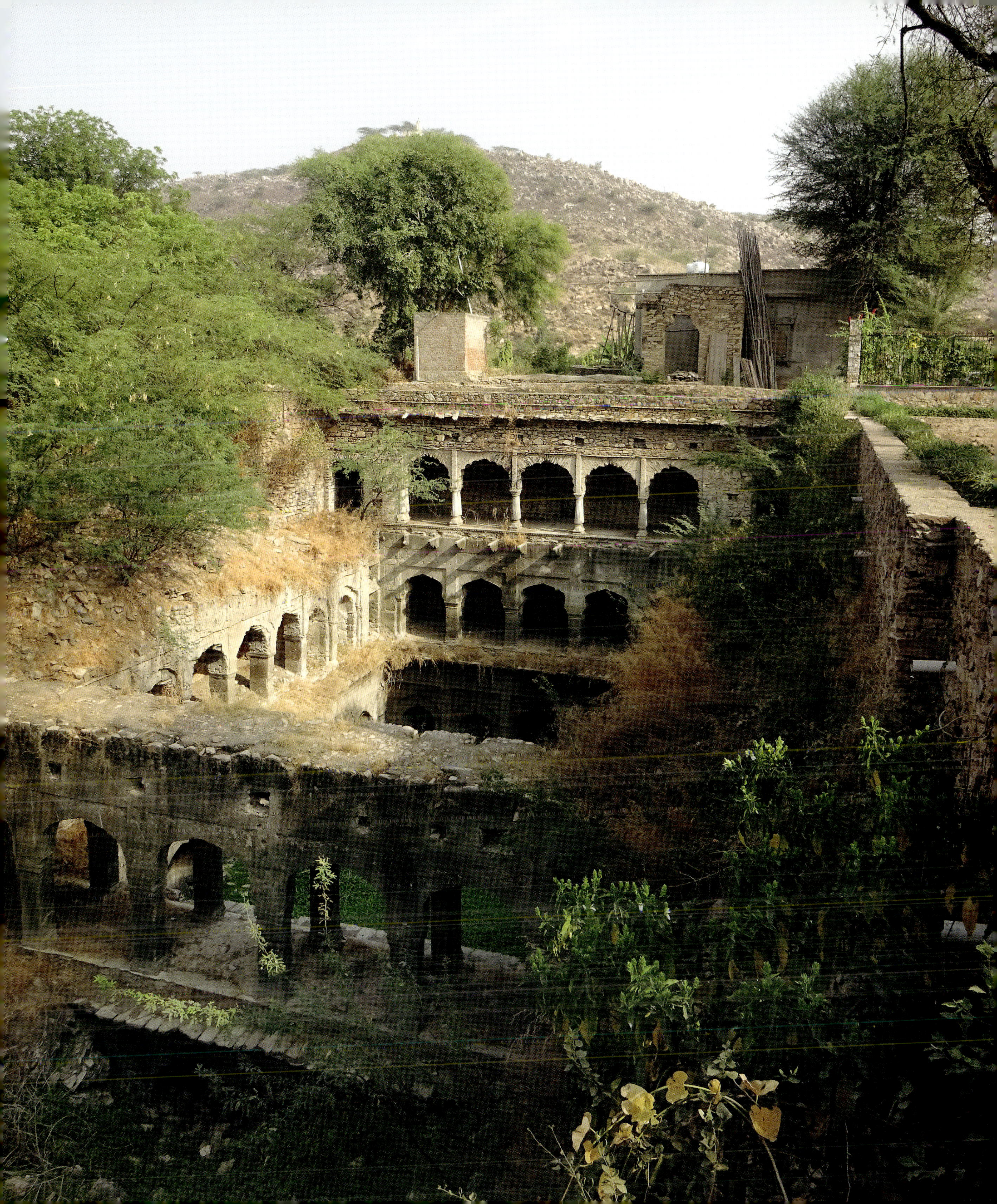

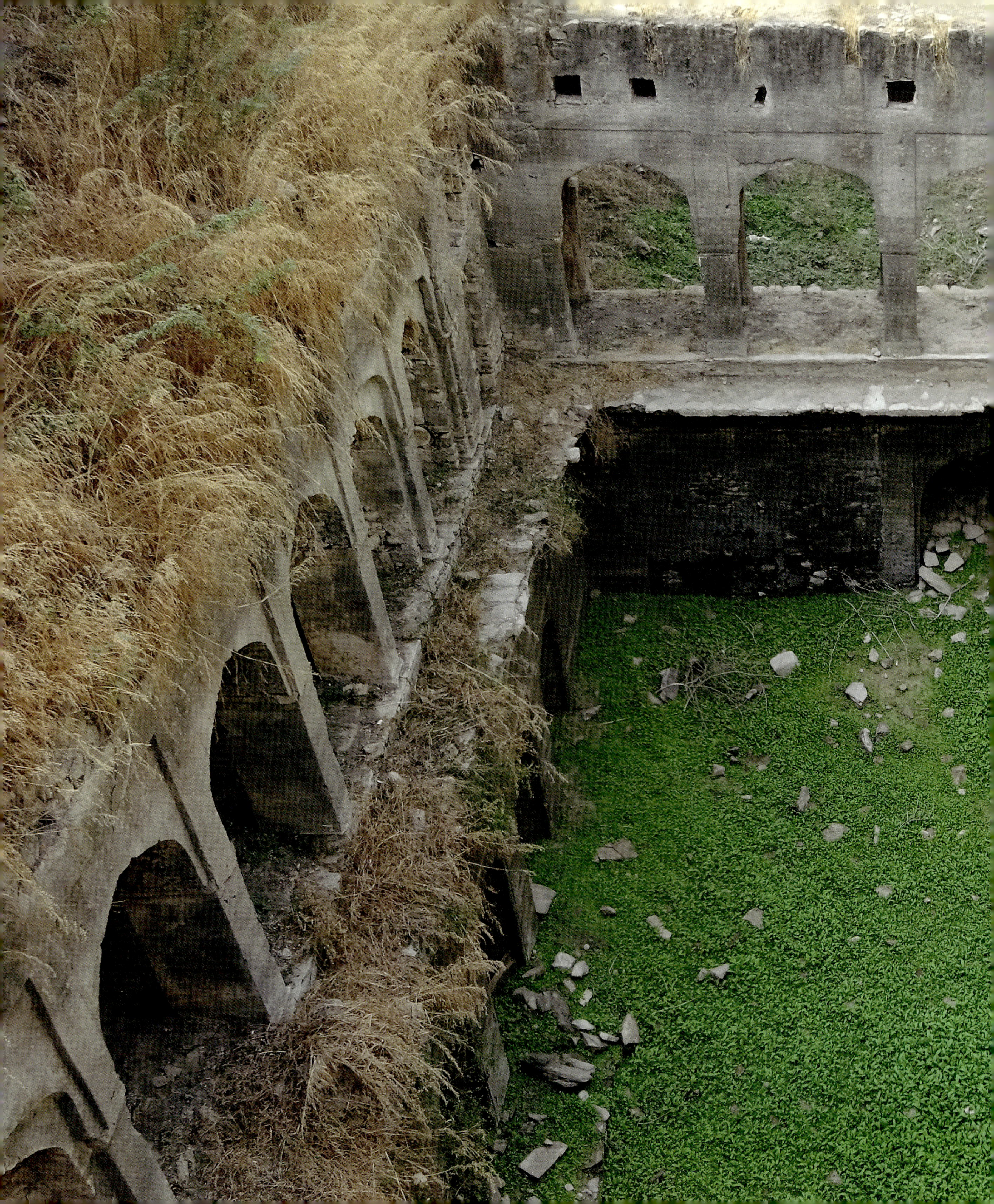

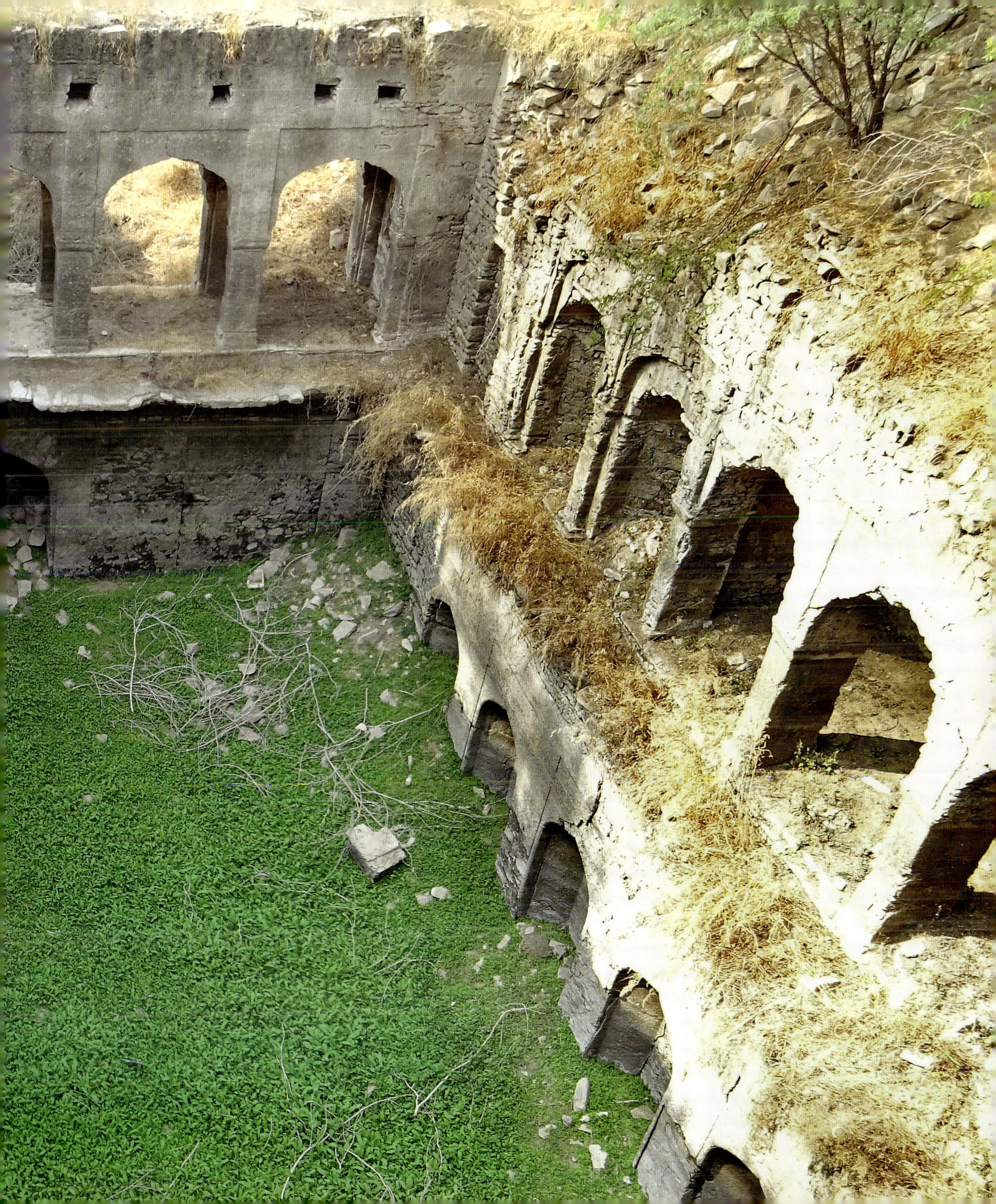

RAJA BIR SINGH DEV BAOLI
SIROL, MADHYA PRADESH
EARLY 17th CENTURY
25°42'55.09" N
78°27'37.04" E

A woman washes clothes in water also used for irrigation (bottom). Particularly striking, the gateway creates an imposing entrance worthy of the exceptional – if small, by comparison – baoli.

Two dome-crowned towers unexpectedly materialize above the trees 7 kilometres (4½ miles) outside the city of Datia, Madhya Pradesh, their decaying majesty breathtaking in the otherwise ordinary countryside. They form the gateway to an extraordinary stepwell, built during the reign of Raja Bir Singh Dev and hence assigned his name, since no other has been identified. Between 1605 and 1626, the raja ruled the historic region known as Bundelkhand. A prolific builder and patron, he developed a unique architectural style that synthesized elements from other regions. His palace in Datia is unlike any other built in India, and was said to be much admired by Sir Edwin Lutyens, the designer of New Delhi. According to one local historian, this elaborate structure is a remnant of the raja's summer enclave.

The ribbed domes, a familiar feature of buildings of this period, make it clear that this is one baoli not shy about announcing itself. High walls surround the structure, which is sited just off a modest country road. The property belongs to a family of farmers whose land grant has passed down through several generations. They use the plentiful water to wash and bathe in, and to irrigate the surrounding fields.

Behind the grandiose gateway, the stepwell itself seems somewhat out of scale, set into a plaza as banal as the entrance is spectacular. As was typical of private pleasure wells, many of the important features are out of sight. A set of narrow steps leads to the long, slim and peaceful pool set between arched corridors. It is a carefully orchestrated architectural procession, with sculptural recesses in the walls and rooms tucked away through thick doorways. Anchored at one end is an octagonal cylinder, encircled by a walkway of elegant arches. The water is so clear and inviting that you cannot help imagining seventeenth-century summer nights, when this was the place to be.

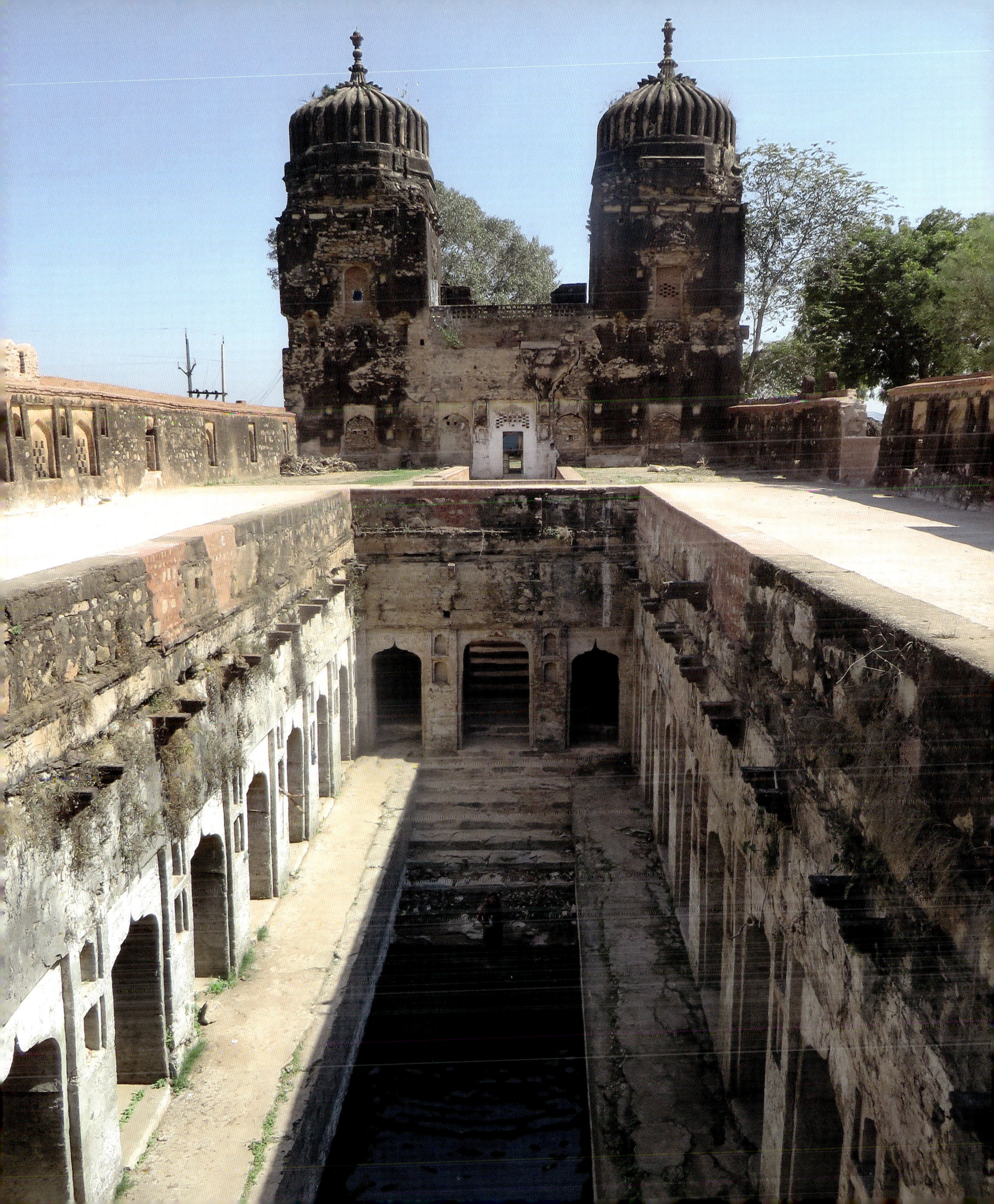

MUKUNDPURA BAOLI

MUKUNDPURA, HARYANA
c. 1650
27°59'12.27" N
76°4'42.9" E

This pretty little baoli is gradually being taken over by the green surrounds of Mukundpura village, 7 kilometres (4½ miles) from Mirza Ali Jaan's baoli (pp. 130-31). 'Mukundpura' refers to Rai Bal Mukund Das, who – according to the historian Ranbir Phaugat – served the treasury of Emperor Shah Jahan (r. 1628–58), mastermind of the Taj Mahal. Shah Jahan gifted Das the revenue from an estate in the area now occupied by Mukundpura village, and Das in turn donated his own gift of this baoli to the villagers. At the same time, he built for himself a sumptuous five-storey palace in Narnaul, and later a large inn (*sarai*) for travellers. It seems that Rai Bal Mukund Das was wealthy and had both good taste and an eye for architecture.

Thanks to its four delicate *chhatris*, the baoli is the tallest thing around, and can be spied easily from the fields and roads near the little agricultural village. It is larger than Ali Jaan's earlier stepwell, and there are two other main differences: first, Mukundpura was a public, not private, well, utilitarian and hard-working. Secondly, whereas Mirza Ali Jaan's showy arched entrance seems ponderous and overdesigned, Mukundpura's is far simpler and welcoming, scaled down for a rural population. It is almost devoid of ornamentation, although, as in the case of many baolis, the plaster that still clings to some walls may have been frescoed in places. Inside the well are two storeys of arched galleries and a few humble niches. The scale and proportions are beautiful, however, and the *chhatris* lend Mukundpura a regal feel. For a country baoli, it is certainly impressive.

There is plenty of water available, judging by a trough standing to one side of the baoli and a pump on the other, but none comes from the stepwell, which no longer has any connection to the community. I made two visits three years apart, and in that time creeping vegetation had made steady progress and more of the graceful structure was crumbling away. Most of the locals turned out on the curious occasion of someone taking an interest in the stepwell; they hoped that the photographs would attract tourists to their village.

Although it is a small stepwell of common design, Mukundpura is still a gem, deteriorating among the fields. Trees and *chhatris* compete for space.

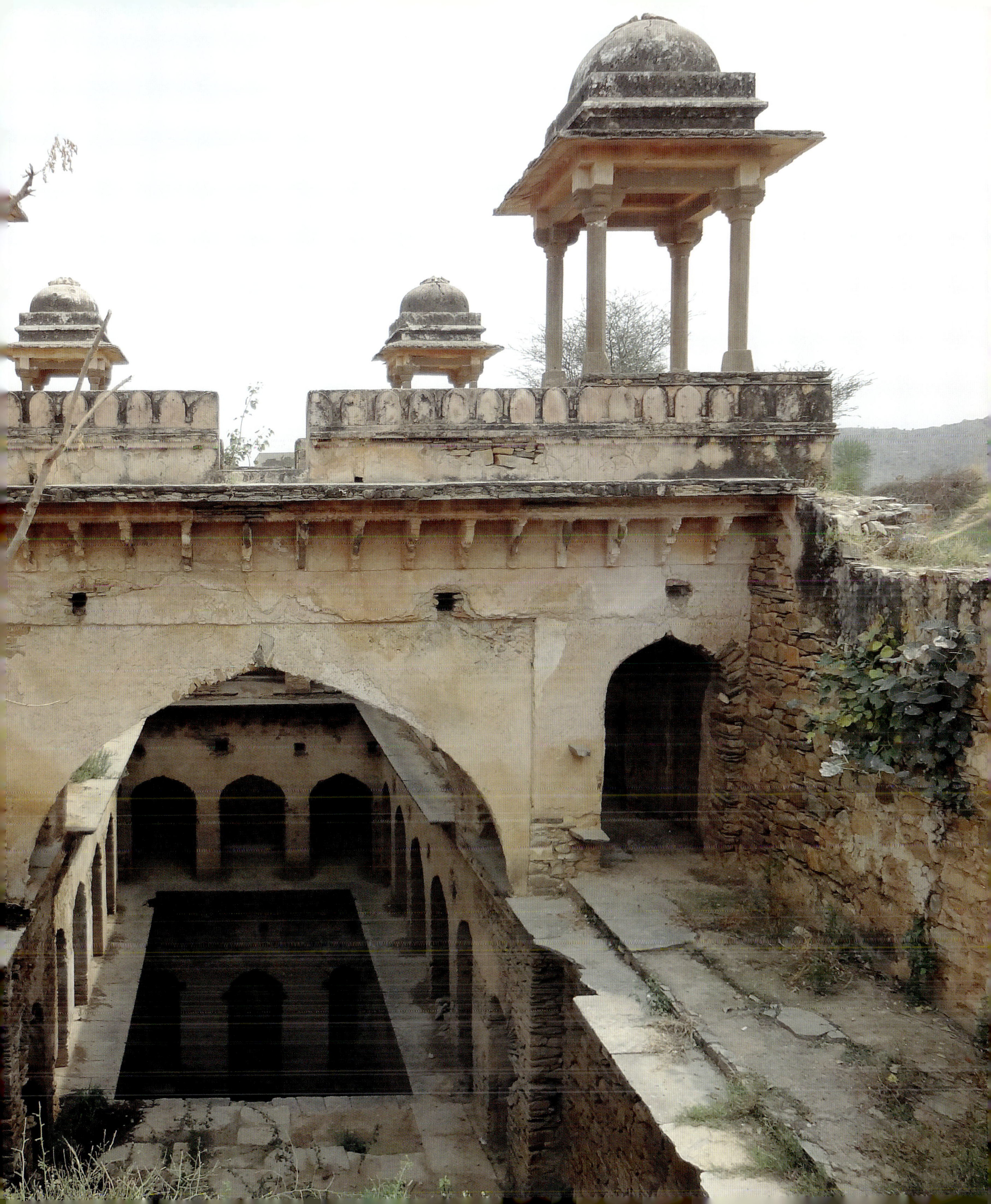

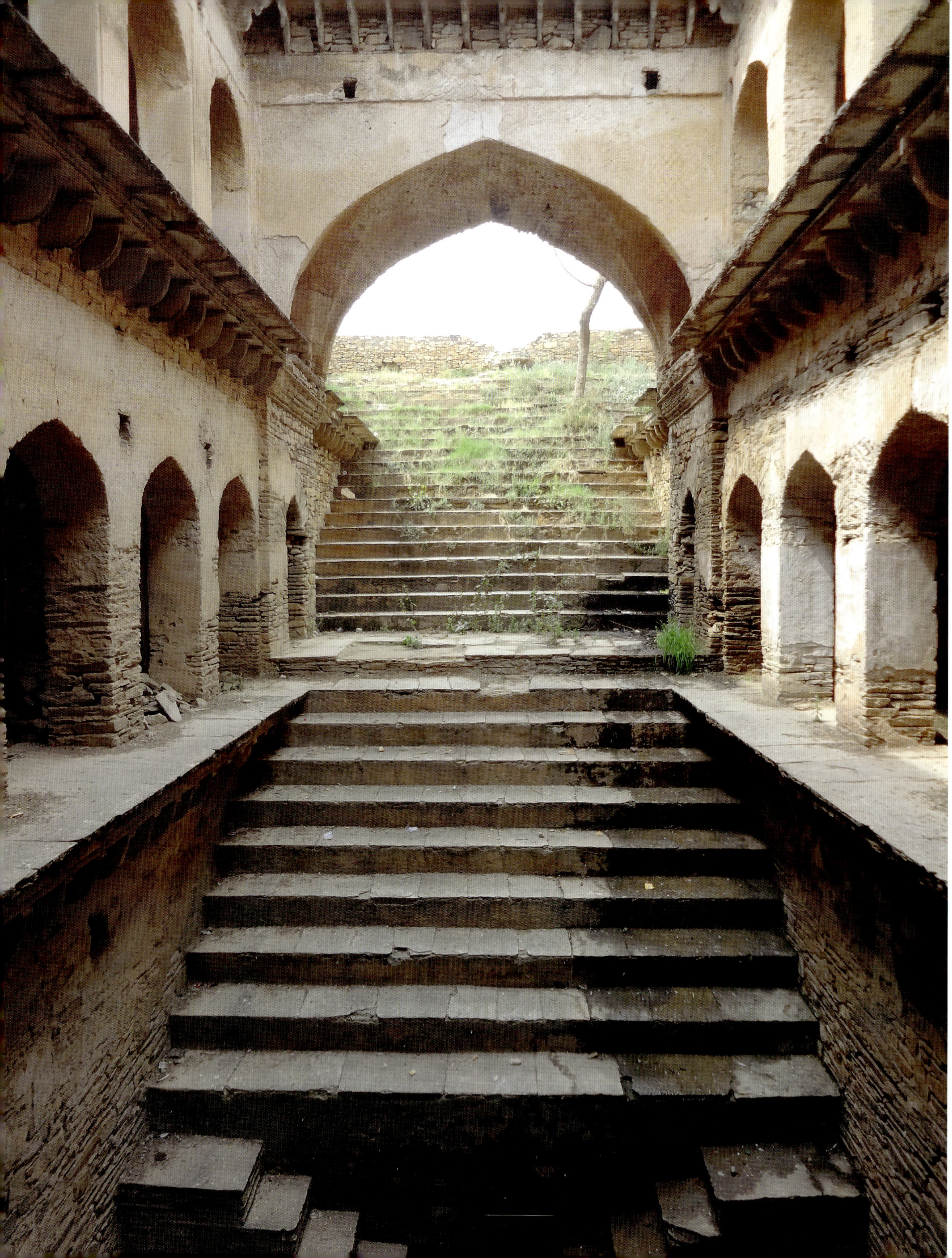

A modern brick building (right) abuts the stepwell, which itself holds little importance to the local community. But the villagers urge more visitors to come and see it.

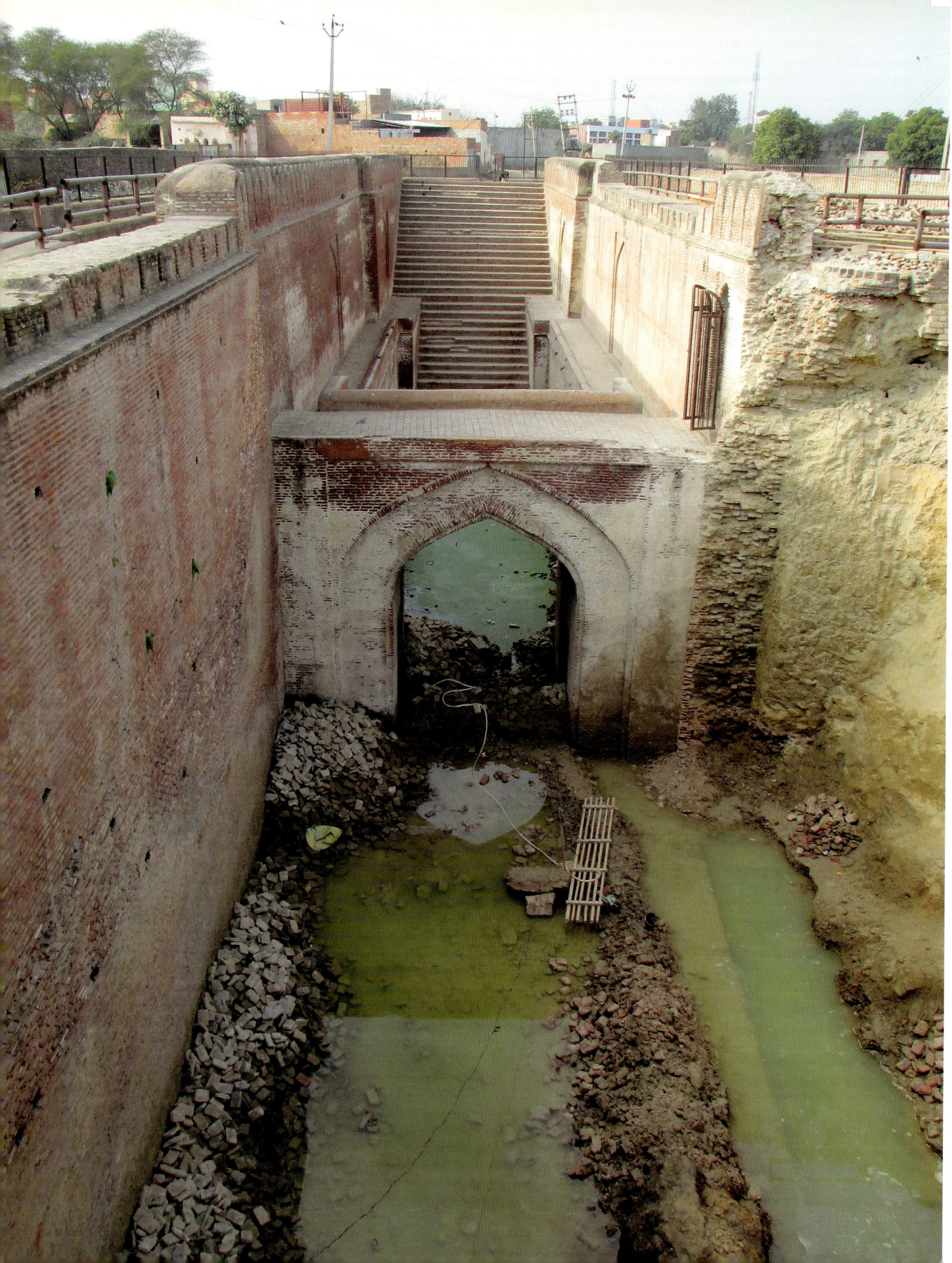

SAIDU KALAL KI BAOLI
(JIYANI CHOR KI BAOLI, SHAH JAHAN KI BAOLI)

MEHAM, HARYANA
c. 1658
28°57'37.46" N
76°17'48.92" E

The fact that this baoli has more than one name adds to its interest, and although it is connected to the illustrious Mughal emperor Shah Jahan, the reference to *chor* (in one of the alternative names) indicates some association, real or mythical, with thieves. Many stepwells in India are reputed to have been hiding places for criminals, which is no stretch of the imagination considering that they were often well hidden in the countryside. The more recent history of this baoli is even more disturbing: during India's First War of Independence in 1857, freedom fighters hid inside the well and were subsequently shot by British soldiers.

Thanks to a handy inscription, visitors can learn a little about the baoli. It was built around 1658 and was generously funded by Saidu Kalal, a mace-bearer for Shah Jahan. He was clearly paid well. While Meham is no thriving metropolis today, in the seventeenth century it was an important city, and there is archaeological evidence of settlers long before then. The city's standing was considerably elevated once the Mughal Empire established a garrison and a now-ruined fort there. This baoli is the largest in the state of Haryana, but in spite of its scale, it is said to be just three storeys deep.

Red brick over sedimentary stone gives the baoli its hue. In comparison to the monolithic masonry of Gujarat, the rubble-and-brick construction does not seem sufficiently powerful for such a behemoth. Because of its size, the structure required reinforcement (as in the case of Neemrana Baori, pp. 140–41), but two supporting arches lost their centuries-old battle to keep the earth at bay when the walls collapsed during floods in 1995. As indicated by the rebuilt arches, the stairs, parts of the main walls and the presence of many stones lying around, the state archaeology department began restoration, but to date the work has not progressed further, and the once imposing baoli, tucked away from view down a dusty lane, is a shadow of its former self.

It is common to have conflicting names and spellings for stepwells, but surprising for one so colossal. Restoration at Saidu Kalal has purportedly been interrupted by further damaging floods.

NAWLAKHI BAOLI

JODHPUR, RAJASTHAN
c. 1700?
26°17'26.78" N
73°2'0.64" E

A great many stepwells may face an unhappy fate for a number of reasons: they lack a name or a recorded date of construction; nothing is known about their patron; they are hard to find; or their general state of ruin pushes them further into obscurity. This well, however, is one of the saddest of the bunch.

Nawlakhi is the name given to dozens of baolis and vavs; the term is spelled differently according to the region, but it refers to nine (*nau*) lakhs being spent on the project. At today's exchange rate (1 lakh = 100,000 rupees), that would be around £10,000 or $13,000 – a fortune in late medieval India. There certainly was no 'going rate' for stepwell construction, but nine seems to be the magic number to apply to otherwise nameless wells, and here it is more noble than the moniker 'Zoo Baoli'.

This particular stepwell is so forlorn not only because, according to the local ASI office, there is no information about its date and origin, but also owing to the fact that it is located rather ignominiously in the middle of a gloomy zoo within the grounds of the otherwise lovely Umaid Garden. Hemmed in by a fence on one side and animal cages on the other three, it can be accessed only by traipsing through a storage area adjoining the goose enclosure.

Once one has descended via a covered stepped passage, a landscape of broken and submerged columns – and the odd tree or shrub – awaits. The baoli would be wonderful if it were not in such a dilapidated state. Long and apparently four storeys deep, it is built of rich red sandstone reminiscent of that at Fatehpur Sikri (pp. 132–39). There are cusped wall niches along the well's length, and apparatus used to haul up buckets of water is visible to one side. Water is still pumped from the well cylinder, supplying the zoo and the well-ordered gardens. As far as the date of construction goes, one can assume the seventeenth or eighteenth century (I have opted for a date in the middle), based on similar nearby baolis, but perhaps it will eventually be clarified.

Unknown and undated, this mystery baoli was constructed earlier than the surrounding zoo. It was left in place when the zoo was built, even though it is now almost inaccessible.

177

CHHARDWARI BAOLI

ORCHHA, MADHYA PRADESH
c. 1700
25°20'41.62" N
78°36'13.27" E

Chhardwari Baoli, in the Bundelkhand region of Madhya Pradesh, is not far from Sirol and Raja Bir Singh Dev's summer enclave (pp. 168-69), and even though it was not built for cavorting, it shares many stylistic, if necessarily muted, similarities. For one, a massive entryway leaves no doubt as to the baoli's presence. Although functional rather than grandiose, it is not without charm. The heavy slab of a façade is enlivened by the same thick, distinctive archways as at Sirol, looking here as if they have been carved from cream cheese.

Once one is inside the baoli, the resemblance continues. A similar long, arched corridor runs down both lengths, narrow steps descend to the water, and there are shallow approximations of the deep lamp niches at Sirol. But at Chhardwari (which means 'four entrances', although only one is to be seen), these details have moved above ground, into public space, instead of unfolding below ground level and out of view. The steps do not terminate at a rectangular pool, but lead directly to the well's octagonal cylinder, here lacking an expensive arched gallery all the way around. Nonetheless, for a utilitarian baoli, this would have been a spacious, pleasant place in which to take refuge and, with no way to compare it to the raja's supersized version, those using it might still have felt like royalty.

Tucked behind the well cylinder is a Shiva shrine, tended by the local holy man, who also watches over the baoli and the water.

Chhardwari Baoli is unpretentious compared to the nearby, grandiose Raja Bir Singh Dev. But there are enlivening details, such as multi-cusped blind arches in the cylinder (left) and decorative passages.

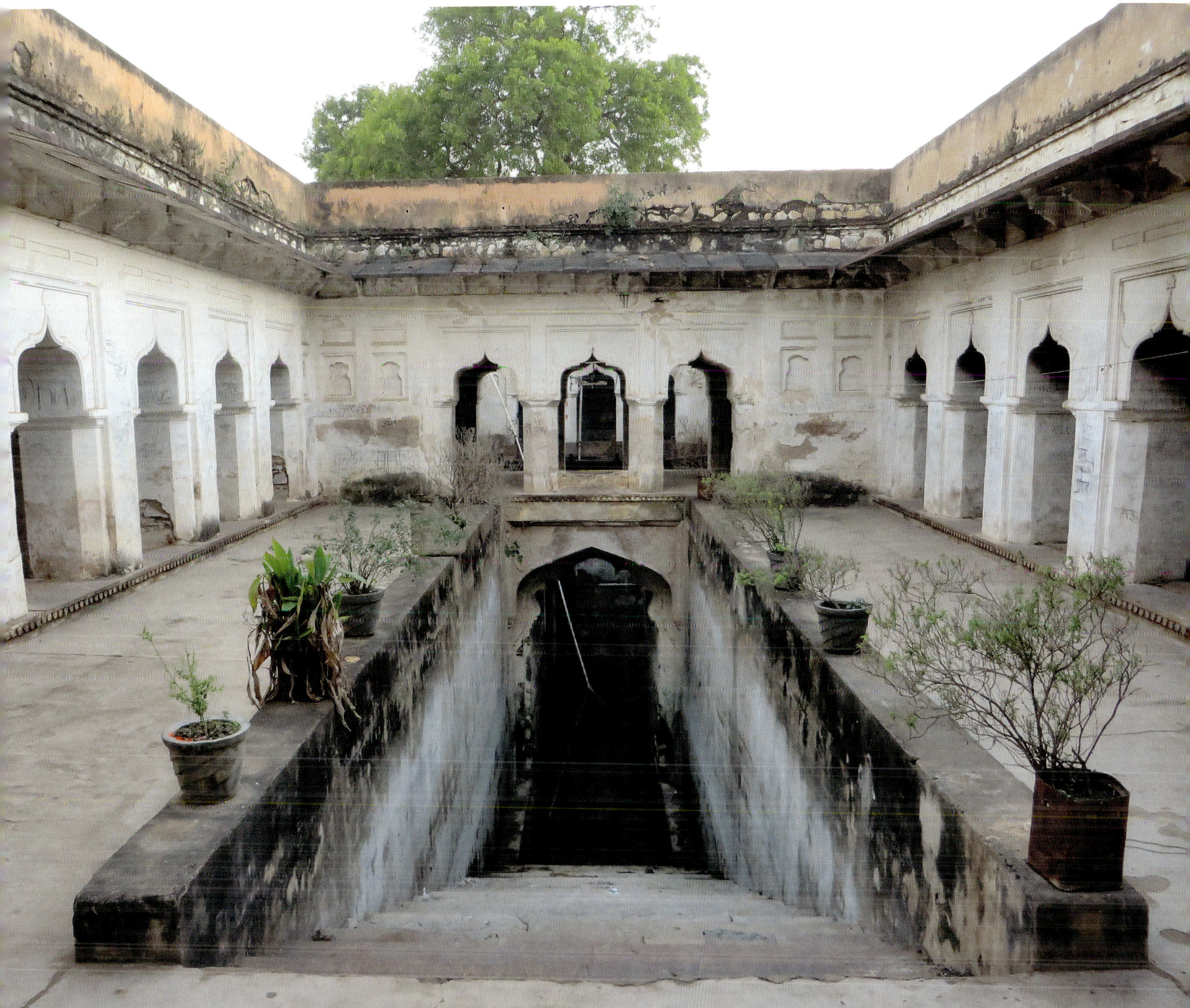

TORAN BAORI

UDAIPUR, RAJASTHAN
c. 1700
24°34'41.41" N
73°41'54.53" E

The approach to Toran Baori, along a busy, dusty road, is not particularly pleasant. The diminutive stepwell is hemmed in by various shopfronts and a slew of motorcycles, and it is only once one is inside the enclosure – in what seems like another world – that one finds quiet reprieve. And, it has to be said, the well is kept remarkably clean and protected. A metal grate over the tank prevents detritus from falling into the water, and a modern balustrade forestalls any accidents. To descend the steps, one must negotiate a concrete barrier with just a chunk removed; but, on a positive note, it probably also prevents animals from straying in. Unfortunately, new construction has not only enclosed the stepwell, but also, in places, sits directly on the original carved-stone edges.

According to the Indira Gandhi National Centre for the Arts, the two-storey baoli dates from the sixteenth century. The conservation architect Manas Sharma believes the early eighteenth century is closer to the mark, and this is the date I have used. The well's name derives from the monumental carved archway, or *toran* (smaller than the one at Kundvav; pp. 56–57). This arch, once a prominent signpost to welcome the public to the well, is now in such a penned-in position that it is difficult to appreciate fully. The sinuous brackets on top are decorated with birds and flower motifs, and there are also lion-faced *kirtimukha*, which are said to provide protection.

Another noteworthy feature of Toran Baori are the niches that completely line the well, two registers stacked in the cylinder itself, where some would have been submerged when the water level was high. Most of the carved deities survive intact. On the short descent to the water's edge, another pair of niches house the deities Ganesh and Shiva, who are encased in gleaming foil. Even if the centuries-old haven has lost its lustre, these two gods, in their lovingly embellished homes, have retained theirs.

The baoli may be boxed in on all sides, but the well shaft (above) is protected and in good condition. The stepwell is named after its *toran* (arch), which can now barely be seen from the street.

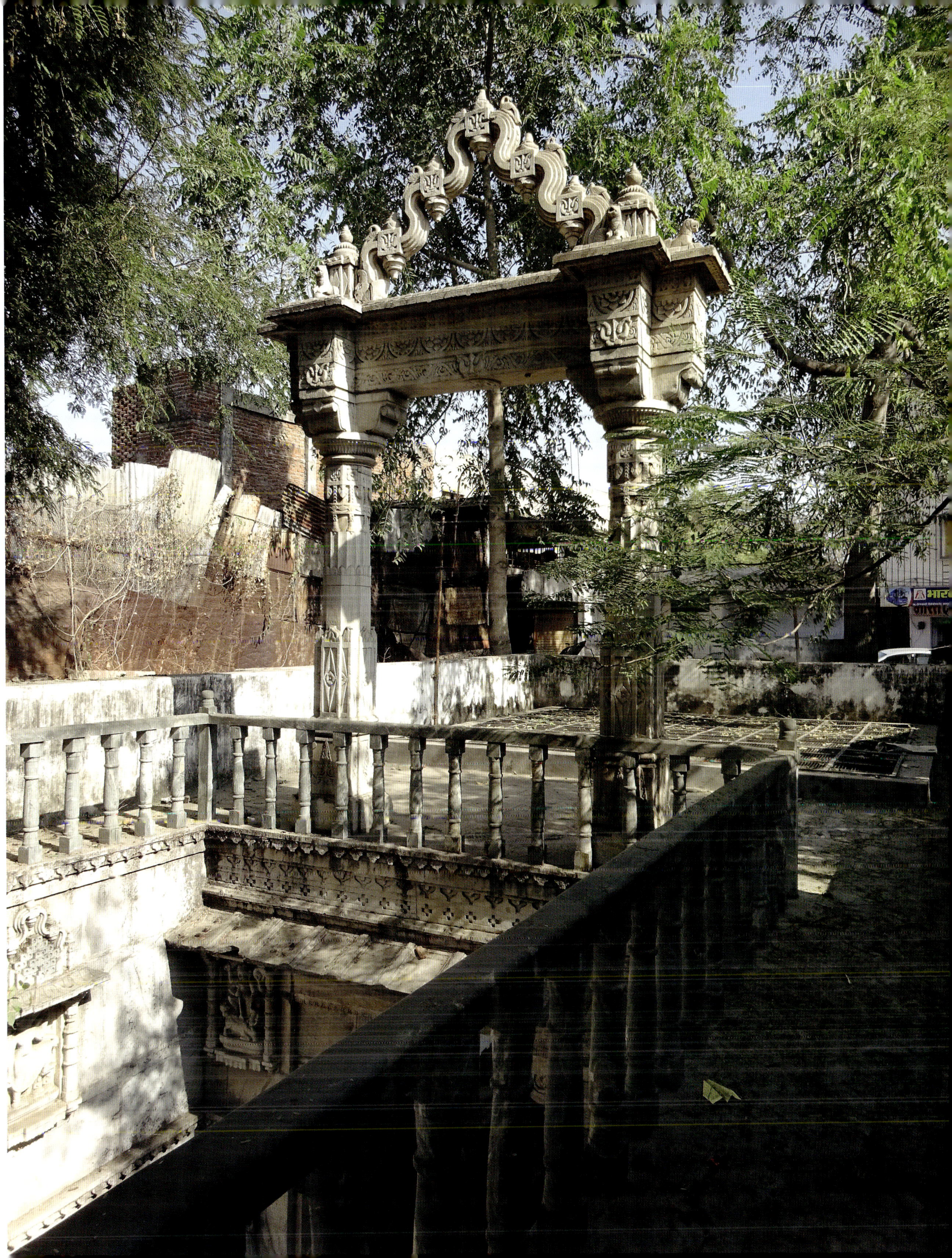

AMRITVARSHINI VAV

AHMEDABAD, GUJARAT
c. 1722
23°1'29.82" N
72°35'49.92" E

A modern structure has been built into the tight corner (below, left), but does not detract from the interior of the vav. Below, the view up through the well cylinder.

The dedication plaque inside this small, L-shaped stepwell declares that it was built by Ragunhathdas, a treasury official working for the nawab (governor) of Ahmedabad, Haider Quli Khan. By the early eighteenth century the Mughal Empire was on the wane, as were patrons of stepwells, so this was a particularly benevolent act on the part of Ragunhathdas. The area of the old city where the well was constructed, Panchkuva, derives its name from the five wells that existed there. This one adjoins a small neighbourhood temple devoted to Shiva.

The three-storey vav is stately and subdued, but inventive nonetheless. It is completely open to the sky, the narrow interior spanned by a series of elegant Islamic arches that meet at the corner of the 'L' with surprisingly dramatic flair. The parade of arches is subtly nonconformist, with each arch being slightly different – a little architectural surprise. The entrance to the well cylinder is also unusual, rejecting arches in favour of a tall, trabeated doorway that harks back to traditional Hindu construction; it is impossible to know if the reference was intentional. Today the vav wraps tightly around a later structure, which was built right up to the edge of the well and in fact eliminates the low perimeter wall. Fortunately, this arrangement does not detract from the corner treatment of Amritvarshini's arches, which, when viewed from below, frame the sky in a particularly uncommon way.

The local government restored the vav in 2004, a laudable project considering how modest the structure is, particularly in comparison to the city's far showier Rudabai and Dada Harir stepwells (pp. 103–107). Furthermore, the community's connection to the well endures, as local women perform rituals here in the hope of conceiving sons.

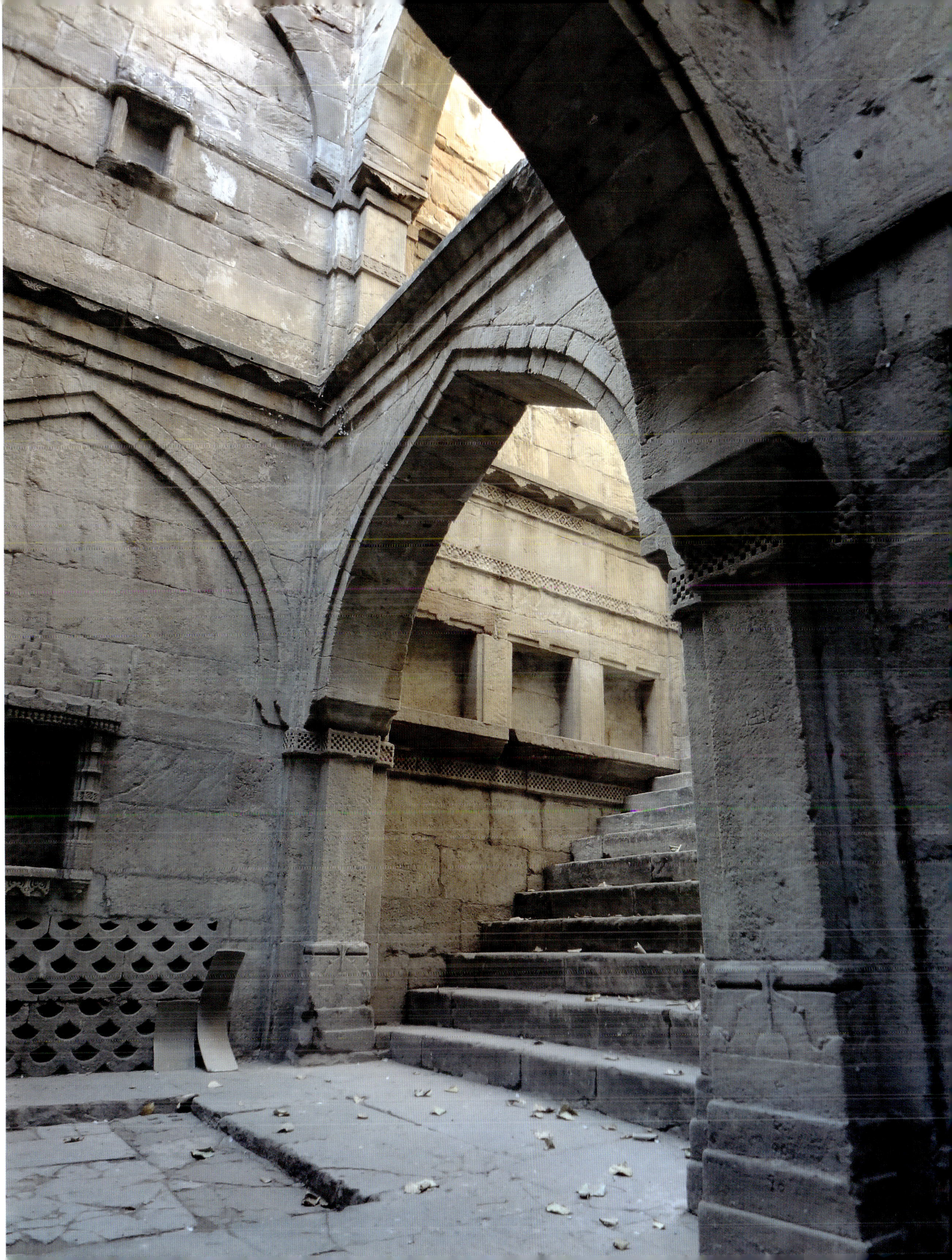

KALE HANUMAN BAOLI

JAIPUR, RAJASTHAN
1727
26°57'7.92" N
75°50'20.95" E

The history of the stately Kale Hanuman Baoli is entwined with that of the famous temple across the street, which is renowned for its unique black icon (or *murti*, meaning 'sculptural embodiment') of the revered deity. One story is that the temple, situated between two of the old gates that led into the city, has been there a thousand years. It is more likely that the founder of Jaipur, Sawai Jai Singh II, acquired the sacred icon and built the temple to house it. Then, in the same year that he moved the capital from Amer, he constructed the baoli to fulfil the water requirements of the temple, which still uses and maintains the well.

It is doubtful that you would stumble across Kale Hanuman if you were not looking for it. It is hidden, like a secret garden, behind a high wall and can be reached only via an arched entrance. Once you are through the gate, steps lead directly from the street to the pool, and a vista of water and arcades unfolds. This three-storey baoli is one of several in and around Jaipur that were restored in 2008 through a public-private initiative partly funded by Hindustan Coca-Cola (see also Sarai Bawadi, pp. 82-83). Nearly a decade on, the climate of Rajasthan has taken its toll, and Kale Hanuman would benefit from some weeding and new plasterwork at the very least.

There is supposedly a second, fascinating reason why Sawai Jai Singh constructed the well; a sign in Hindi outside the baoli explains that he did so in order to perform the ancient Vedic rite known as Ashvamedha Yagna. This ceremony entailed the sacrifice of a horse, and was used by kings to prove their absolute authority. Jai Singh is believed to be the last ruler in India to have undertaken the powerful ritual.

A discreet entrance (right) opens on to the historic stepwell, constructed by the founder of Jaipur. Modern plumbing has been installed alongside original water-hauling supports (opposite).

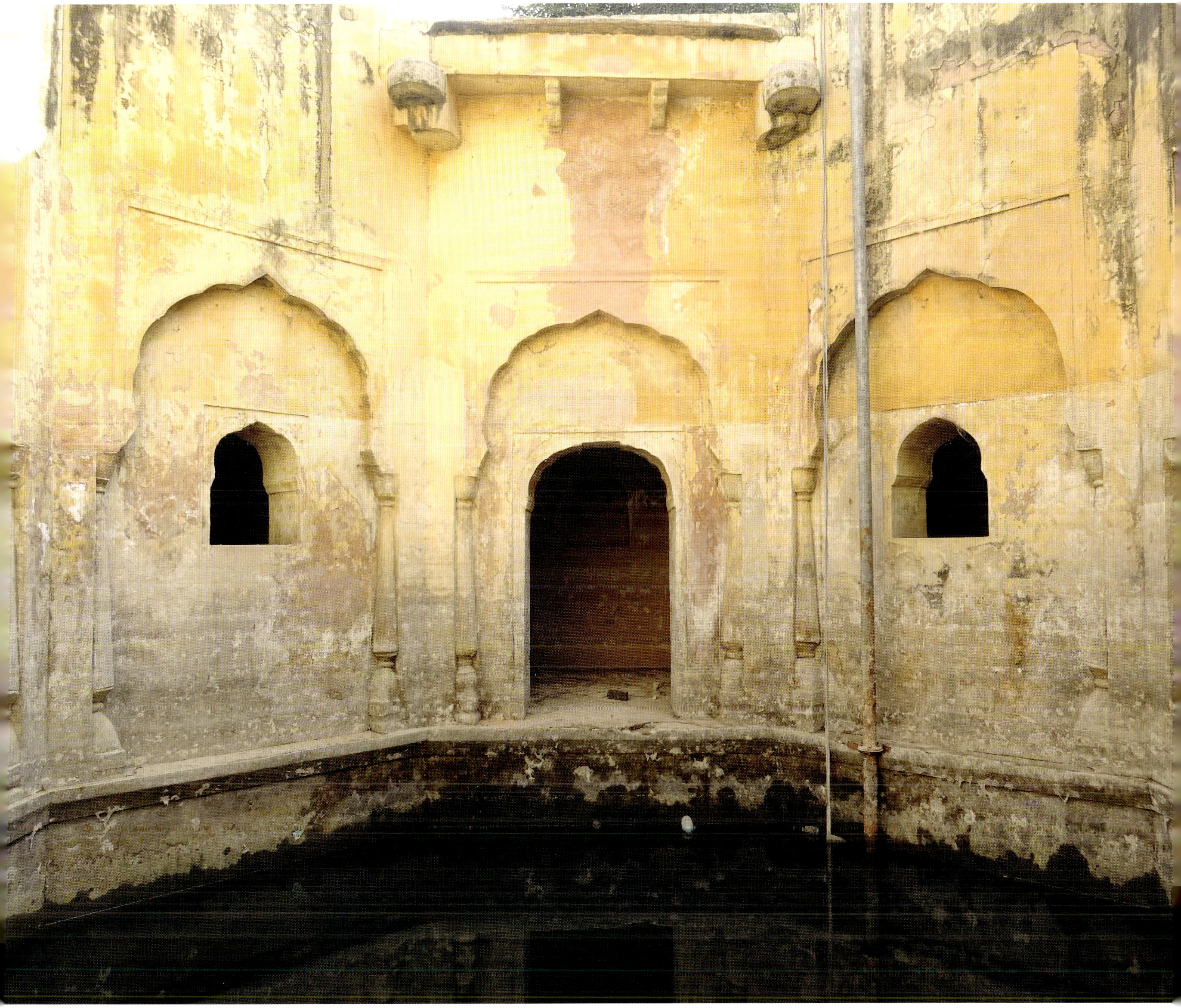

ALI GHAUS KHAN BAOLI
(ALI GHOSH KHAN BAOLI)

FARRUKHNAGAR, HARYANA
c. 1730
28°27'00.6" N
76°49'33.4" E

The city of Farrukhnagar, about 60 kilometres (37 miles) outside Delhi, was founded in 1732 by Faujdar Khan, who was appointed nawab (governor) by the Mughal emperor Farrukhsiyar (r. 1713-19, hence the city's name). Khan and his architects conceived an unusual urban plan: to design Farrukhnagar – that is, the outline of the city – in the form of an octagon, the geometric building block of Islamic art and architecture, derived from the all-important eight-pointed star and seen in everything from tilework to minarets.

Apart from the lovely houses once inhabited by Jain traders, the ruins of a palace and a beautifully restored gateway, little remains of the old city. The baoli was restored some years ago. According to the Haryana historian Ranbir Phaugat, Ali Ghaus Khan was one of the nawab's senior officers, and he commissioned the well at the same time the outer walls of the city were being constructed.

An unusual feature is the baoli's octagonal shape, which nicely reflects Farrukhnagar's plan, but is an uncommon form for a stepwell. In fact, this is the only octagonal baoli I have encountered, even though I have seen numerous octagonal cylinders. The well has been compared to a Turkish hammam (steam bath). A graceful loggia encircles the lower level, its arches framing views across the pool. The general assumption is that this was a private well for the wealthy ruling family. There are interior rooms and an extraordinary 'secret' corridor that leads beneath the city's gate – an easy way not only to protect women from view, but also to beat a quick retreat if necessary. Perhaps on account of the violent, uncertain times, Ali Ghaus Khan built the walls of his baoli so high above the ground that, from a distance, the well appears more like a fortification than a pleasure retreat. The parapet of the top level could be used to keep an eye out for unwelcome visitors.

Unlike most stepwells, the well shaft is not adjacent to the pool but in its centre (opposite). A protective wall along the top of the baoli contrasts with the alluring, peaceful haven below.

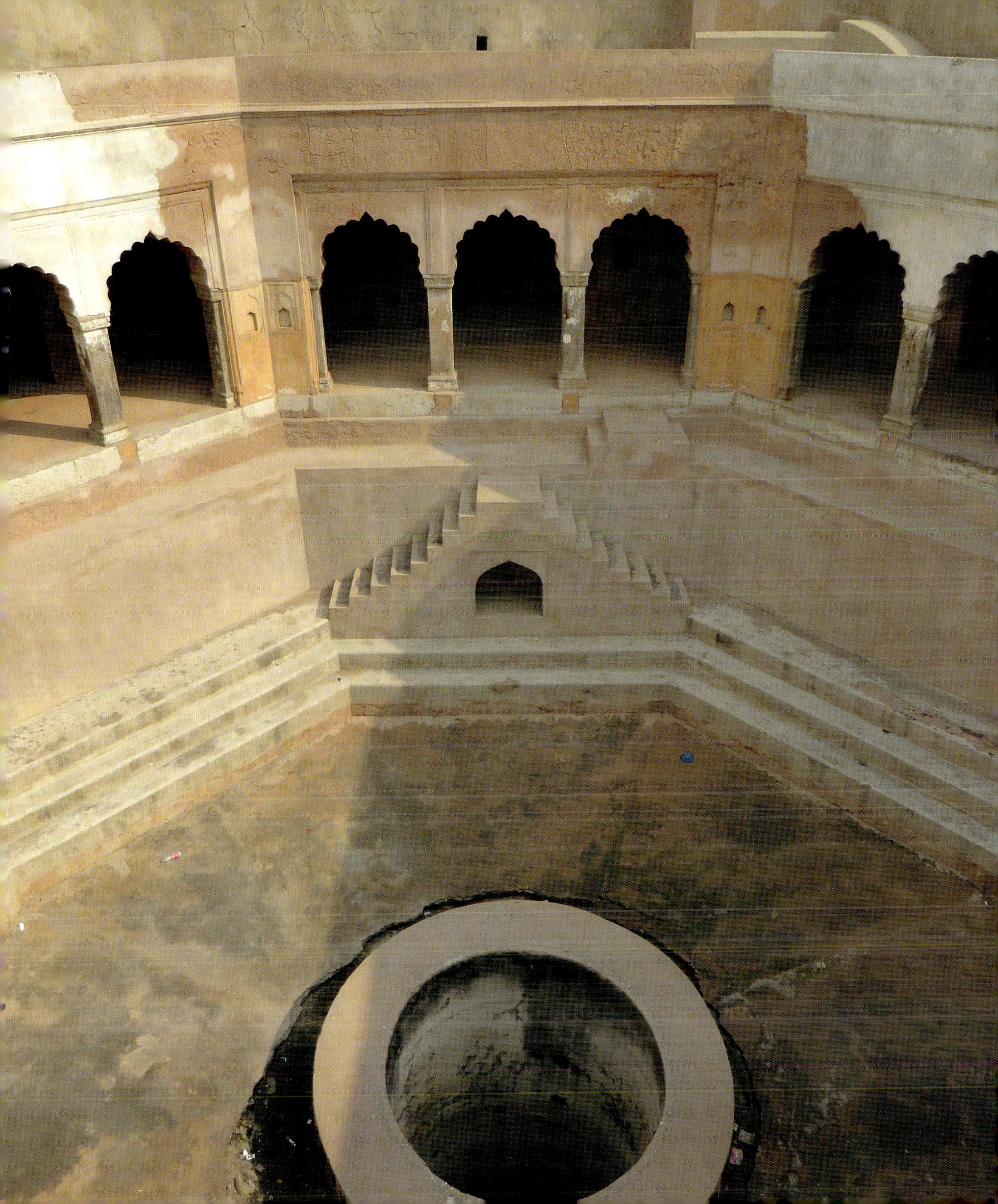

RAMKUND

BHUJ, GUJARAT
MID-18th CENTURY (c. 700 CE)
23°14'51.02" N
69°39'52.9" E

The city of Bhuj, founded in the early sixteenth century, was close to the epicentre of the disastrous earthquake in January 2001 that killed roughly 20,000 people across Gujarat. The city was levelled and most of its historic monuments destroyed or badly damaged – although many have undergone restoration in the past decade.

The lovely little Ramkund, situated behind a small Ram temple, either was a miraculous survivor of the devastation or, more likely, is one of the recently restored structures. Either way, it is in remarkably pristine condition, which makes the apparent lack of information about its origins all the more mysterious. While it appears on lists of 'things to do in Bhuj', there are no detailed references to its history, and the only two possible dates of construction that are mentioned are more than a thousand years apart. It is frustrating, but the later date seems probable.

At the time I visited, the water level had risen to the second storey – a good sign in the arid region of Kutch – but the kund's celebrated stonework was still accessible. There are tiny carved niches for oil lamps, several of which are set into a wall of solid rock – a curious feature considering that the other walls are masonry. Hovering above the water line, a narrow frieze is adorned with a procession of deities from the ancient Sanskrit epic the *Ramayana*, juxtaposed with beautiful carved flowers. Unusually in the case of a kund, the steps that lead down to the frieze are not terrifyingly steep.

By day, the placid water in the kund reflects its surroundings. Lamps in the recesses (left) created a glittering display at night.

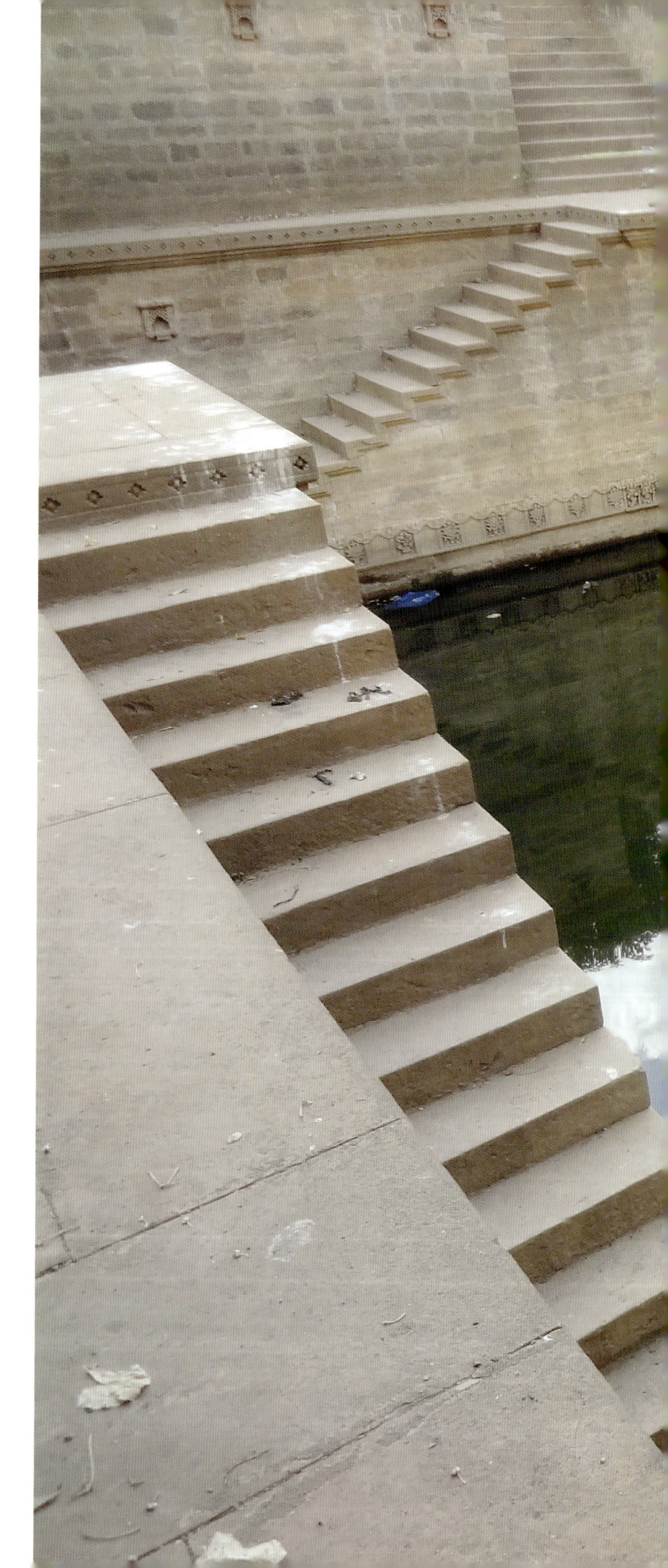

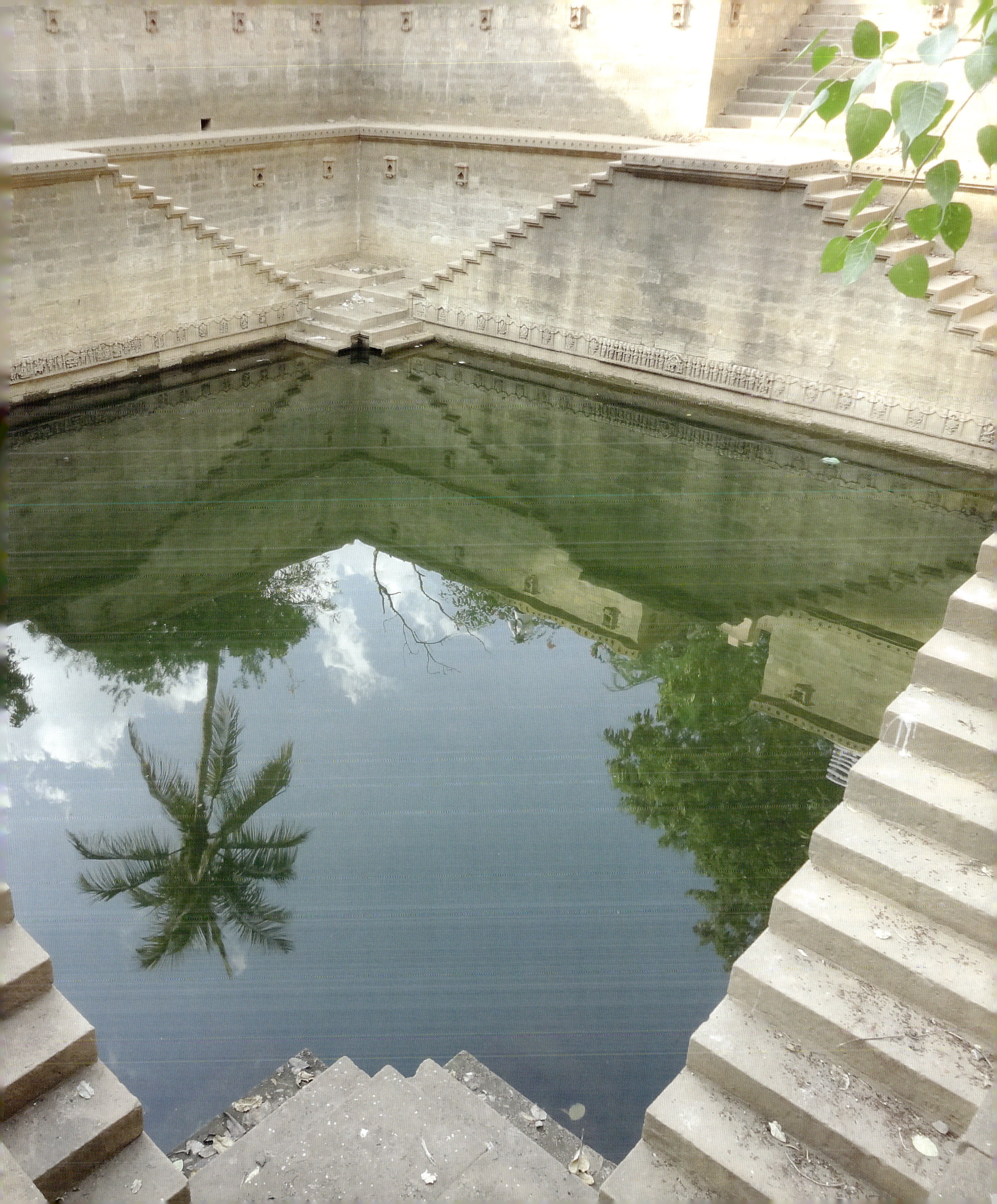

MAAJI KI BAWADI

AMER, RAJASTHAN
MID-18th CENTURY
27°0'29.70" N
75°52'21.11" E

Of the many 'mystery baolis' in India, Maaji ki Bawadi is one of the most intriguing by reason of its size, beauty and location. Amer was the ancient capital of the region until 1727, when the forward-thinking Maharaja Sawai Jai Singh II founded the new capital bearing his name. Many monuments in and around Jaipur, including numerous stepwells, date from Jai Singh's reign or later.

The Jaipur-based conservation architect Yash Pratap Singh Shekhawat explained that, at some stepwells, the term 'Maaji' refers to the mother goddess, Devi, but it can also connote the widow of a former king. Sadly, we do not know who was the 'dowager' patroness of this well. The baoli is situated at the end of a winding, unpaved road off the main highway that slices through downtown Amer (as opposed to Amer village, which spills down the road from Amer Fort), between a small group of houses and the entrance to a wild animal sanctuary, with tigers pacing behind fences just a few feet away. It makes for a peaceful, bucolic setting; on the day I visited, there were no curious crowds, just one intrepid cow on the steps.

The beauty and scale of Maaji are impressive, especially considering its secluded position. The *bangaldar* (or Bengali-style) roof – a shallow arc flanked by two small domes – is a familiar feature of architecture in Jaipur and other cities throughout Rajasthan. Four neat storeys of arched galleries, windows and stairs stand proud, but it is not until one has descended the wide flight of steps that the rock-hewn well reveals itself: a frightening stone maw with an arched opening to the cylinder, where a limited supply of water is still present. Narrow steps lead all the way into this lower level.

The original hue of the structure is unknown, but restoration work some years ago left it pale yellow, a similar hue to Panna Meena ka Kund (pp. 114–17). Earlier photographs show that the baoli was neglected; its current state is a great improvement. Maaji has obviously been cared for by its neighbours, one of which is a small temple of unknown origin.

At Maaji ki Bawadi, airy construction is juxtaposed with a fearsome rock pit and, as at Rajon ki Baoli, the builders incorporated stone outcroppings into the walls (opposite). The hilly setting (pp. 192–93) further enhances the pretty stepwell.

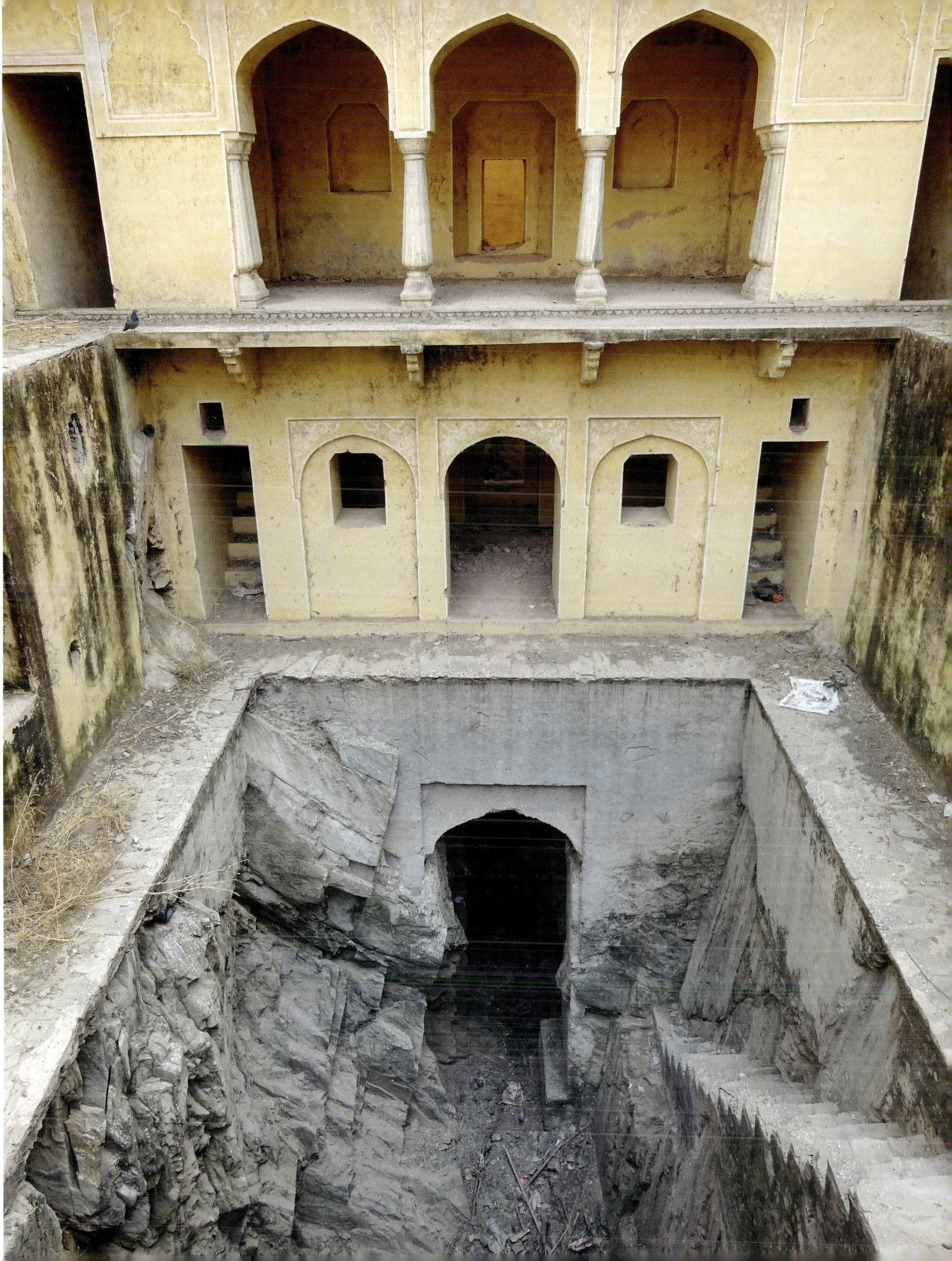

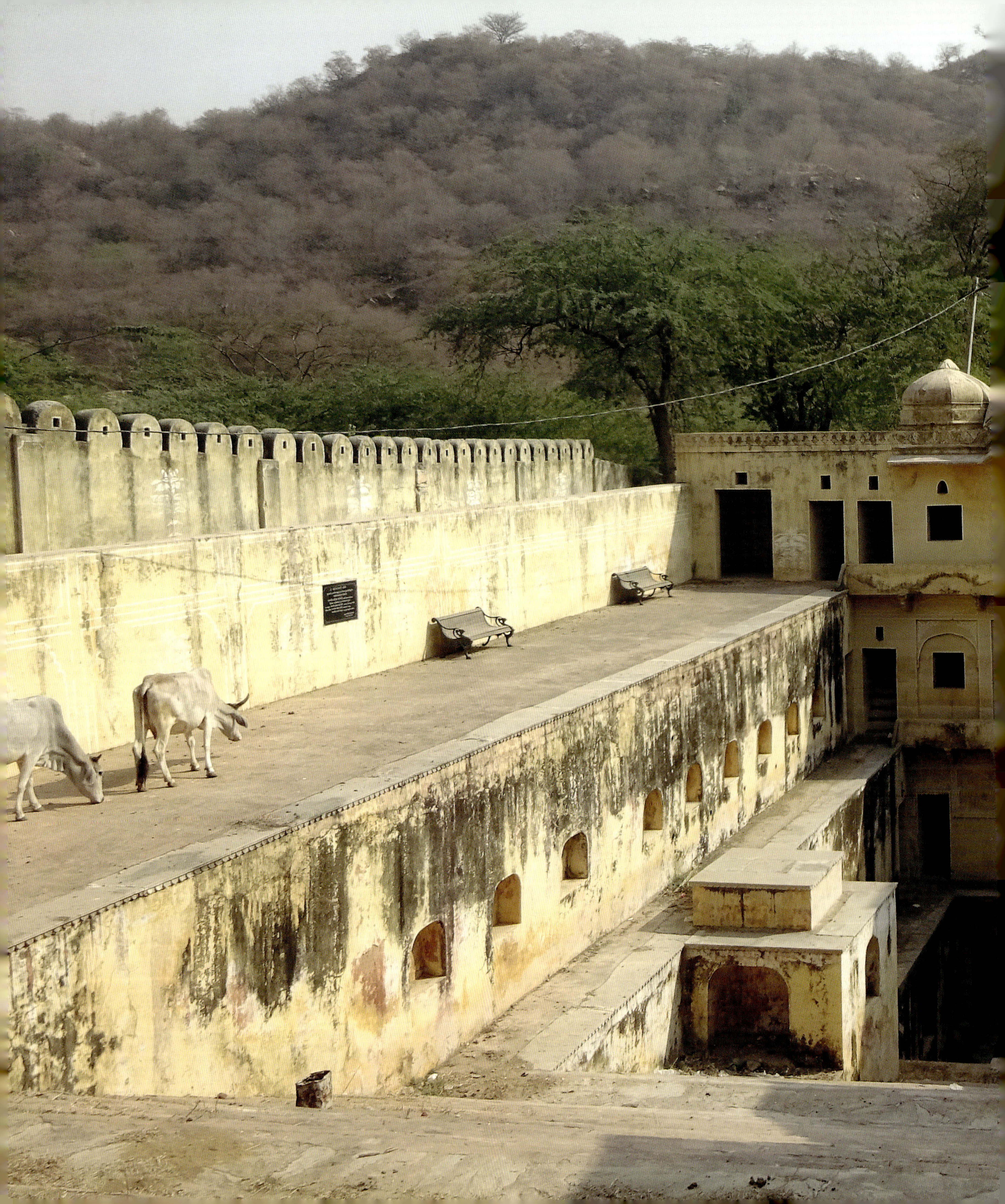

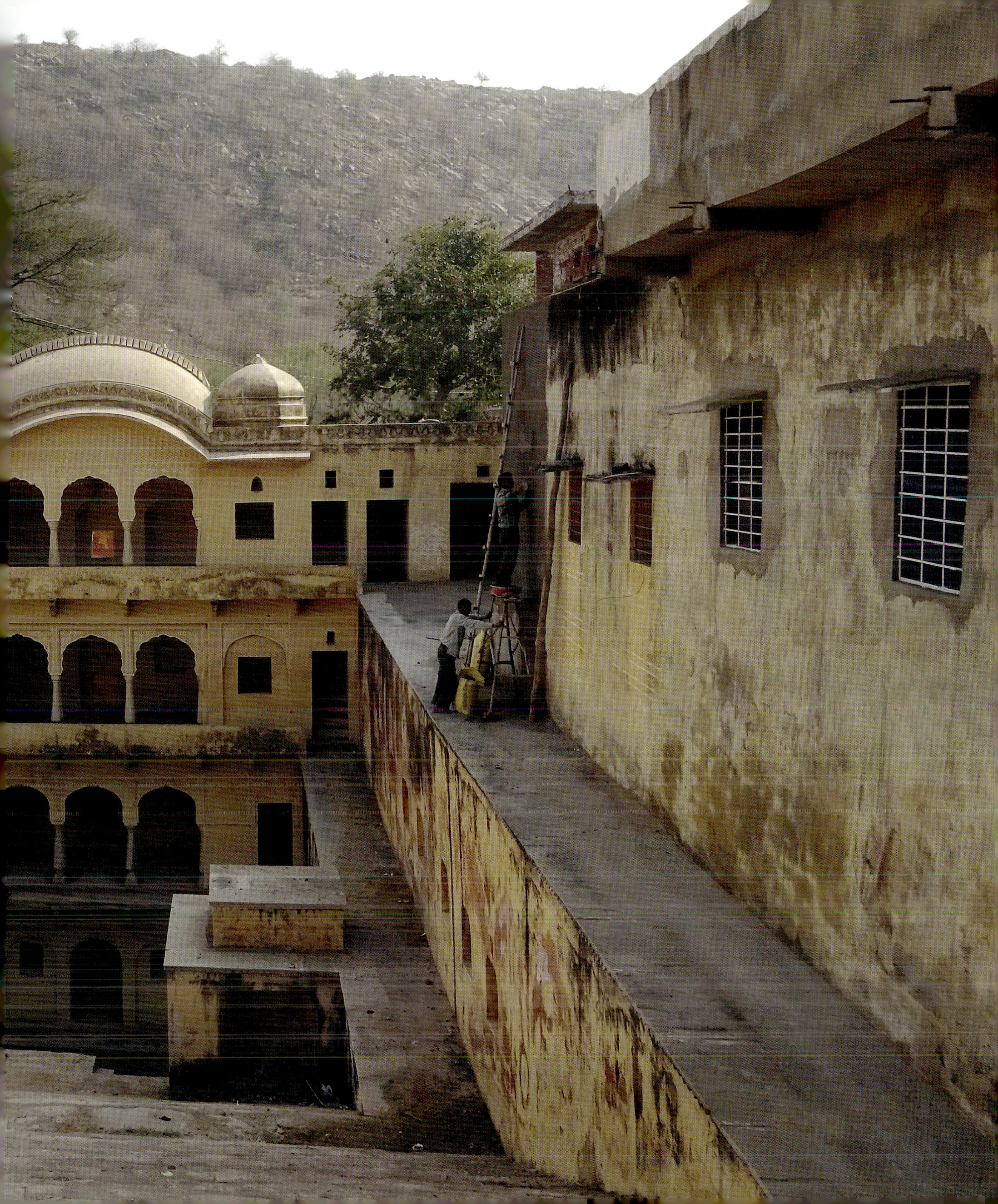

MAHILA BAAG JHALRA

JODHPUR, RAJASTHAN
c. 1780
26°17'47.6" N
73°1'31.27" E

Maharaja Vijay Singh of Jodhpur ascended the throne twice, his first reign lasting an unimpressive four months. During his second, longer reign (1772–93), his beautiful and apparently wealthy concubine Gulab Rai built Mayla Baag Jhalra amid a garden and orchard (*baag*). Over the centuries, the term *Mayla* evolved into *Mahila*, meaning 'female'. The baoli's other name is Chamukhi Ghat, which translates as 'stairways leading to water'. What pedestrian names for such an exquisite well.

Mahila is easy to find in the old city, because it lies directly across the road from another of Gulab Rai's beautiful water projects, the Gulab Sagar, a large tank that feeds the baoli year-round. Each year a water festival takes place at the well, within sight of Jodhpur's magnificent Mehrangarh Fort.

Jodhpur sits at the edge of India's brutally hot Thar Desert, and the city has always marshalled its water resources skilfully. A system of man-made lakes, tanks and baolis has ensured a steady supply of water; even in the driest months the most neglected stepwells are amply supplied. Mahila's water is pumped out for various neighbourhood purposes, and it is the plentiful supply that has created perhaps the most beautiful feature of the baoli: the covering of algae, causing a change of hue across the structure from green to white to pink. It is the most colourfully pleasing of all the wells I have seen, and among my very favourites.

Each corner of the baoli is enhanced by two dainty features: freestanding *chhatris* on the steps, with larger pavilions above. The latter, duplexes of sorts, offered shade under their arches and views from their rooftop balconies. The niches set into the perimeter of Mahila have long since been stripped of deities, and the carved sandstone balustrades are a modern addition – as are the many encroaching buildings.

Since these images were taken, Rajesh Joshi, a local environmental activist, has 'adopted' several of Jodhpur's stepwells; he started with this one after noticing a dead fish in it. He has almost single-handedly cleaned the baoli, and it now holds twice as much water. Sadly, a local business has tried to co-opt Mahila, sanding the steps and removing the centuries-old surface.

A covering of algae enhances the vibrant appearance of Mahila Baag Jhalra, where centuries of calcium scale have whitened the stone.

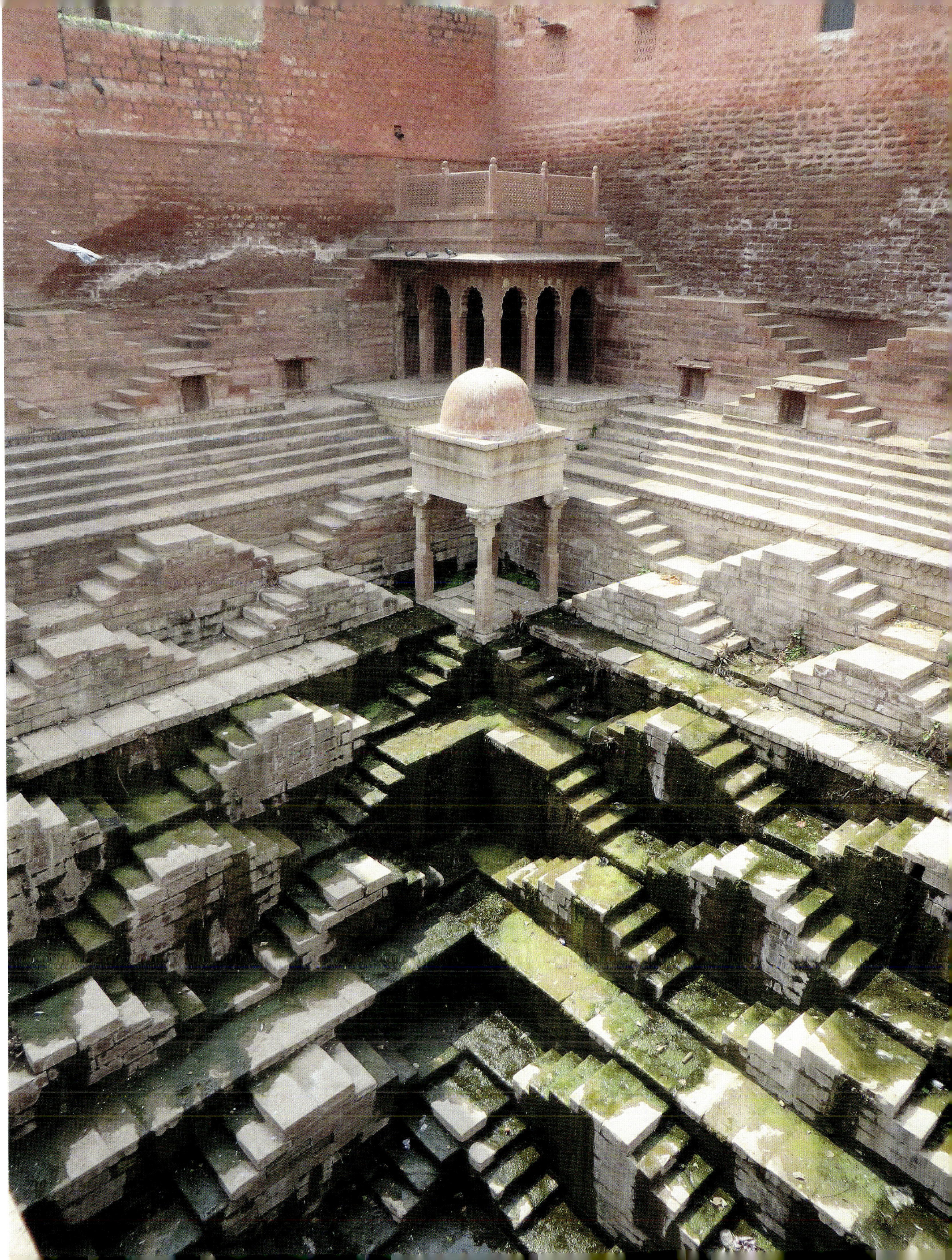

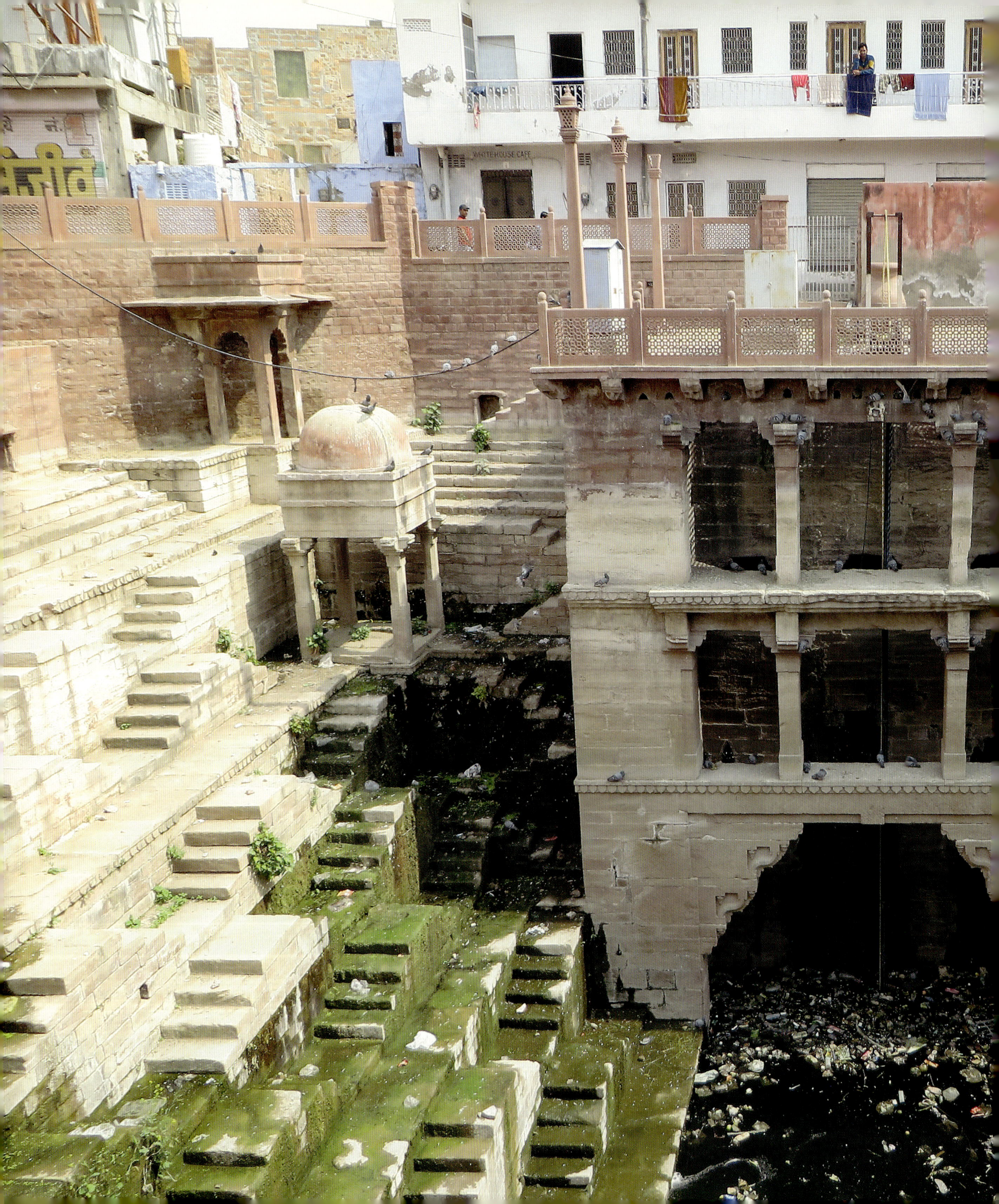
WHITEHOUSE CAFE

Since this photograph was taken, a devoted local activist has removed rubbish and increased the fresh water supply to the picturesque kund.

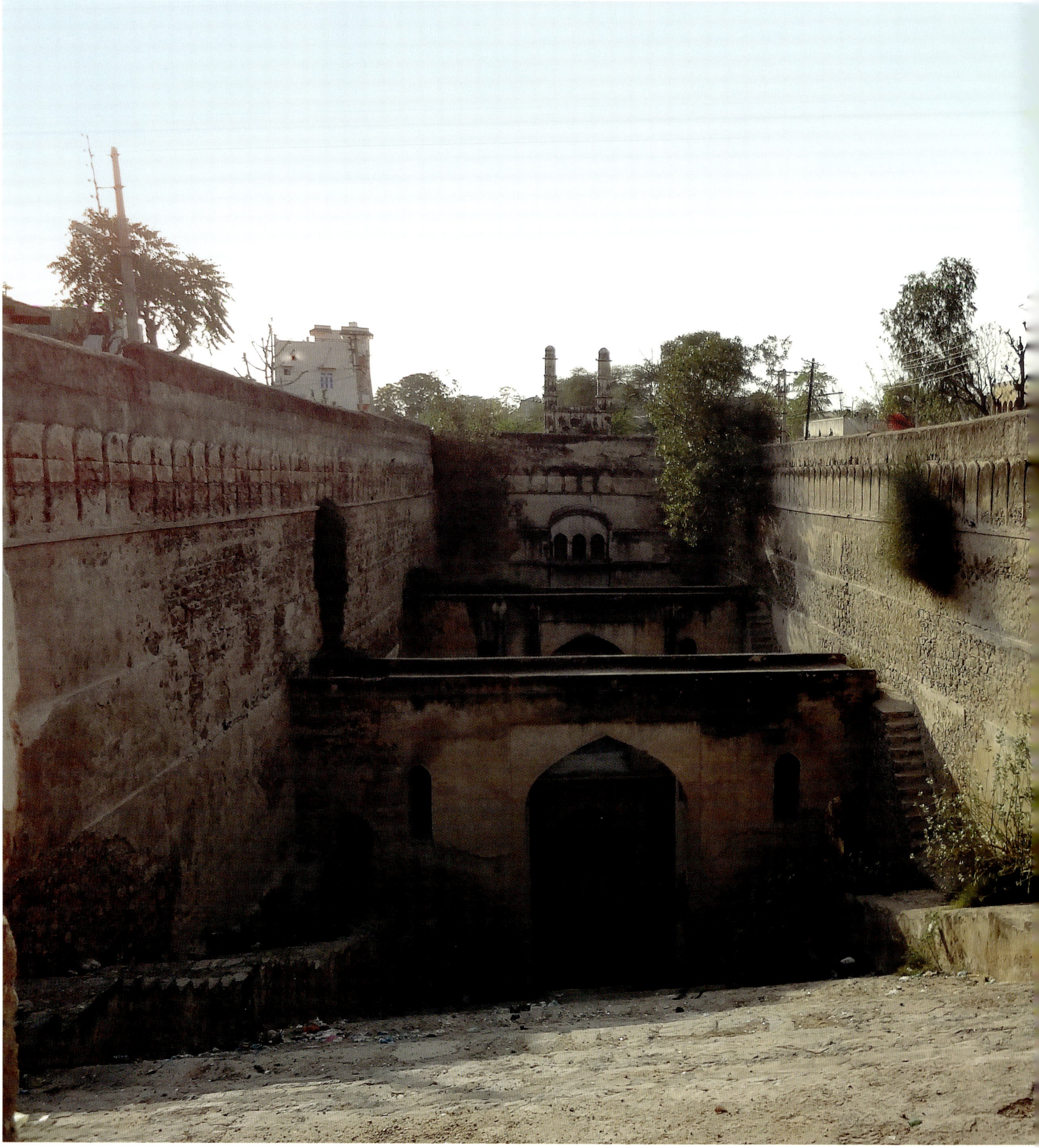

MERTANIJI KI BAWARI

JHUNJHUNU, RAJASTHAN
1783
28°8'1" N
75°23'43" E

As explained in beautiful script on a sign outside this enormous stepwell, it was commissioned by Queen Mertani following the death of her husband, Maharao Sardul Singh Shekhawat. While this was a suitable means by which to honour the former ruler, it is also a conundrum: it is believed that he died in 1742, so it is rather puzzling that it took some forty years to build this supersized but sculpture-free baoli. Mertaniji's waters were said to have curative properties, but in 1831 a British official allegedly circulated a statement warning that the water was so poisonous that those who drank it 'perished within two hours'. Bad publicity indeed.

Ultimately, there is little point in fixating on a date of construction or other aspects of a troubled history. No matter when it was built, Mertaniji is an impressive feat of engineering. Nothing can prepare you for the scale of the well or the dizzying number of steps that await. At the start of the descent, the two buttresses seem very far away. By the time you reach the first one, the top of the baoli is barely visible.

Mertaniji is similar to Neemrana Baori (pp. 140–41; built two centuries earlier and two hours' drive away) in that the combination of bridges, arches, blind niches and small windows serves to enliven the entire structure, making a massive form appear less weighty and ponderous. As you look from the silt-filled bottom to the walls soaring nine storeys up, you notice a dainty little *jharokha* (balcony) that slightly humanizes the baoli's jaw-dropping size. Mertaniji was restored some time ago, but what look like rivulets of dirty tears seem to fall from its rain spouts.

Two pillars mark the distant well shaft at the far end of the immense baoli (far left). The enclosed *jharokha* (balcony, seen beneath the pillars and on p. 201) is typical of Rajasthani architecture, but seems oddly out of scale.

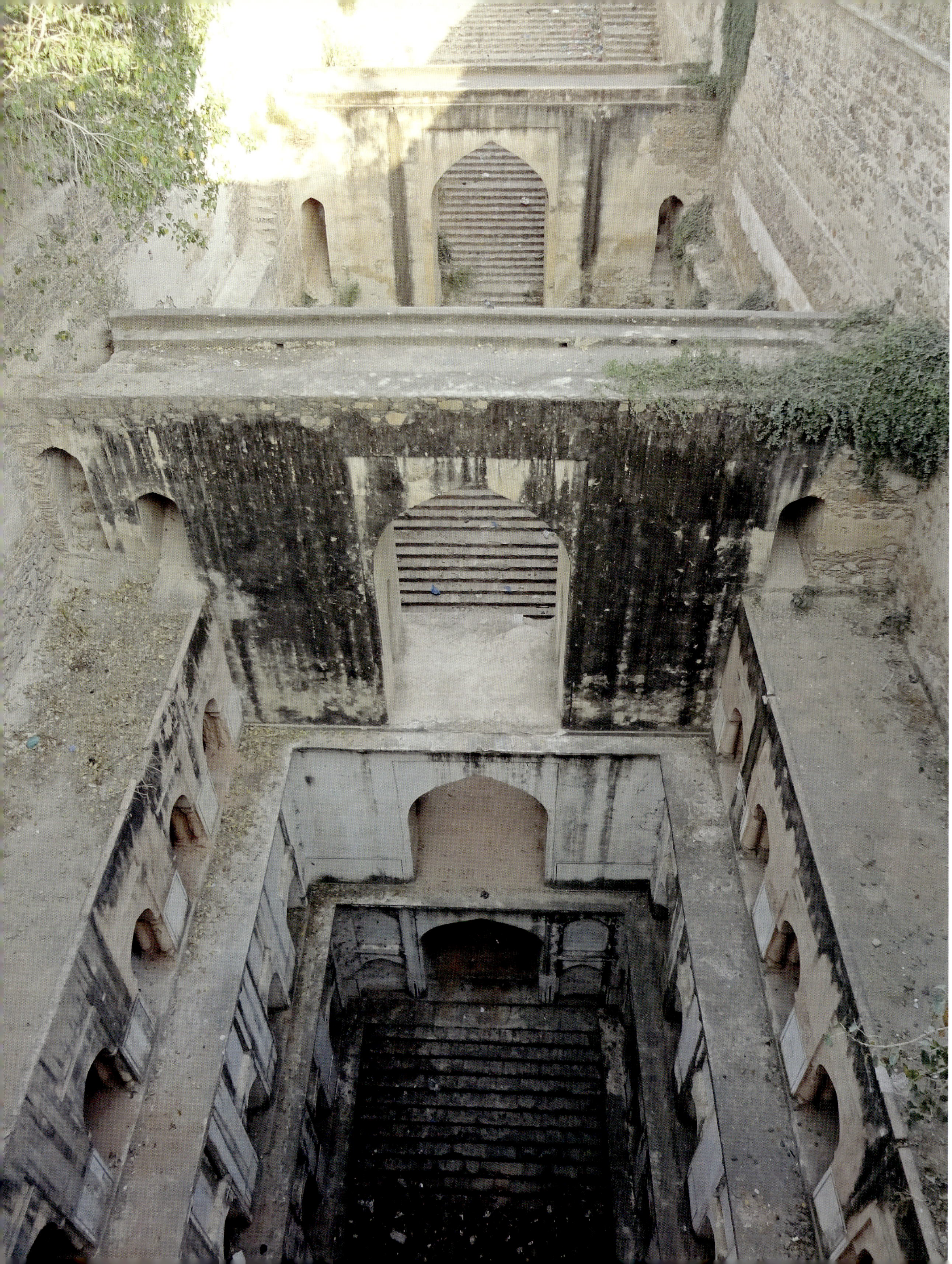

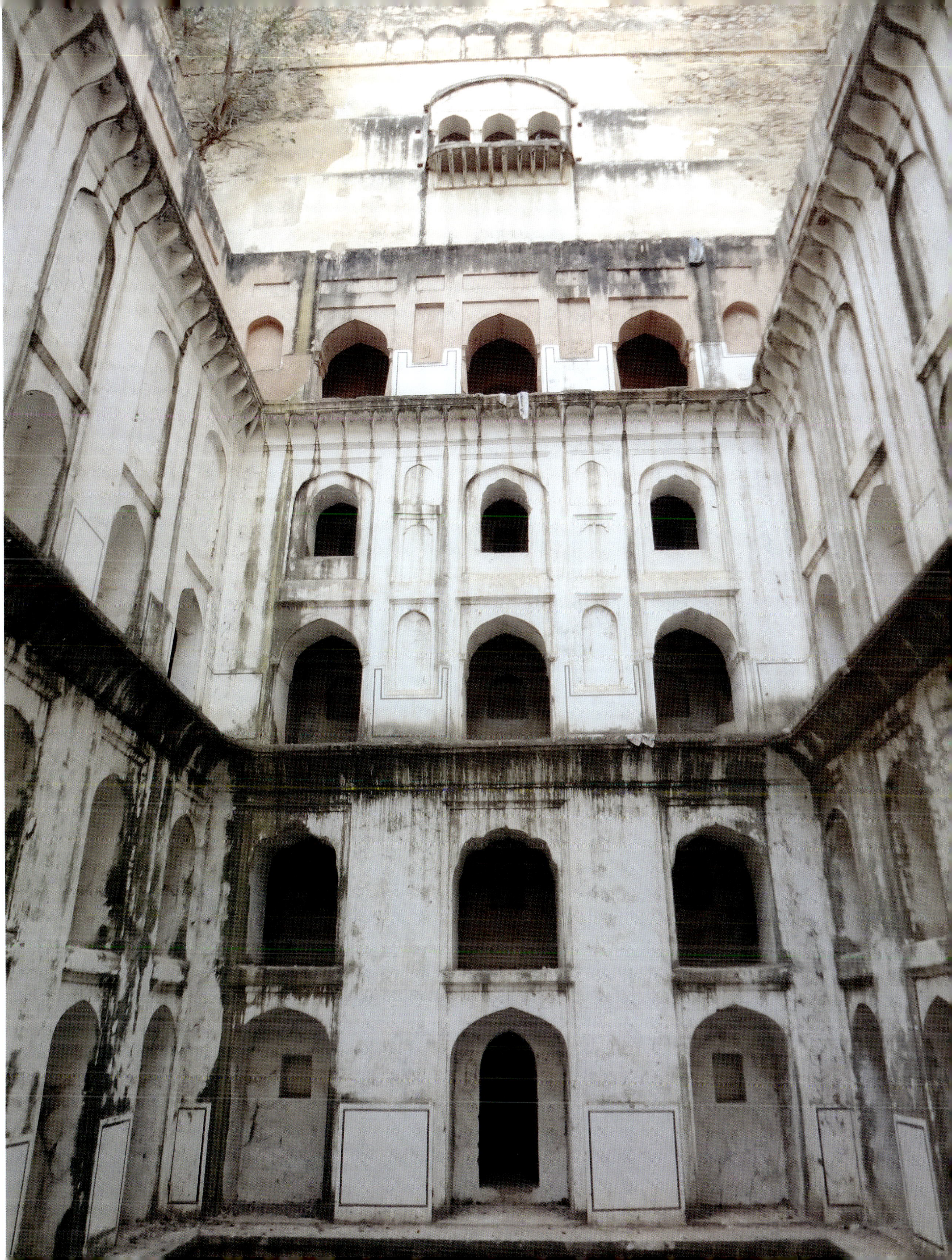

NAWABI BAOLI
(SINGH SAHEB KI BAOLI)
MAHENDRAGARH, HARYANA
c. 1800
28°16'22.58" N
76°9'27.54" E

Mahendragarh is a town with an exciting, though not atypical, history of warring families, dynasties and even countries, the last arising because the district played a dramatic role in the First War of Independence, the rebellion against British rule in India, in 1857. There are still historic buildings in the city, including – so I heard – a baoli. It finally materialized off a dirt road, amid a group of arched pavilions that were once elegant but are now disintegrating. The pavilions originally flanked the entrance to the well; it is believed that they were constructed at the same time. They have fared poorly, and are now used for storing hay or tools, or are bricked up completely. The baoli itself supports a bridge of more recent construction. Modern buildings at each end of the bridge hem in the well, their high walls and even the baoli providing a canvas for graffiti.

Even though the site is overgrown, crumbling, silted up and generally inaccessible, the baoli retains a certain elegance. It is three storeys high and crafted with care. Decorative plasterwork is still visible in places, along with – miraculously – some painted details. Naghpuria Baoli in nearby Narnaul (pp. 210-13) was built later in the century, but has similarities: a graceful bridge, plasterwork and painted remnants.

The well's alternative name at first appears curious. *Singh* means 'lion', and it is a common surname among the Sikh community and the Hindu Rajputs, both originally warrior clans. The baoli is part of a Sikh family compound, hence the name given to it by the owner, who explained that his family has lived there for generations and that his forebears built the stepwell. The family also maintains a small Sikh temple on the property. The baoli is not actively maintained, however; its use is limited to holding up the bridge.

The Haryana scholar Ranbir Phaugat disagrees with the name and the history, believing that the baoli was built before any Sikh compound. In the absence of an actual name, his more general name, Nawabi Baoli, references a nawab (governor) who may have had a direct hand in its conception. Such is the confounding nature of stepwell history.

A modern bridge was built atop the original structure (right), where traces of paintings are visible. Access to the stepwell is gained between two ruined pavilions (right, top).

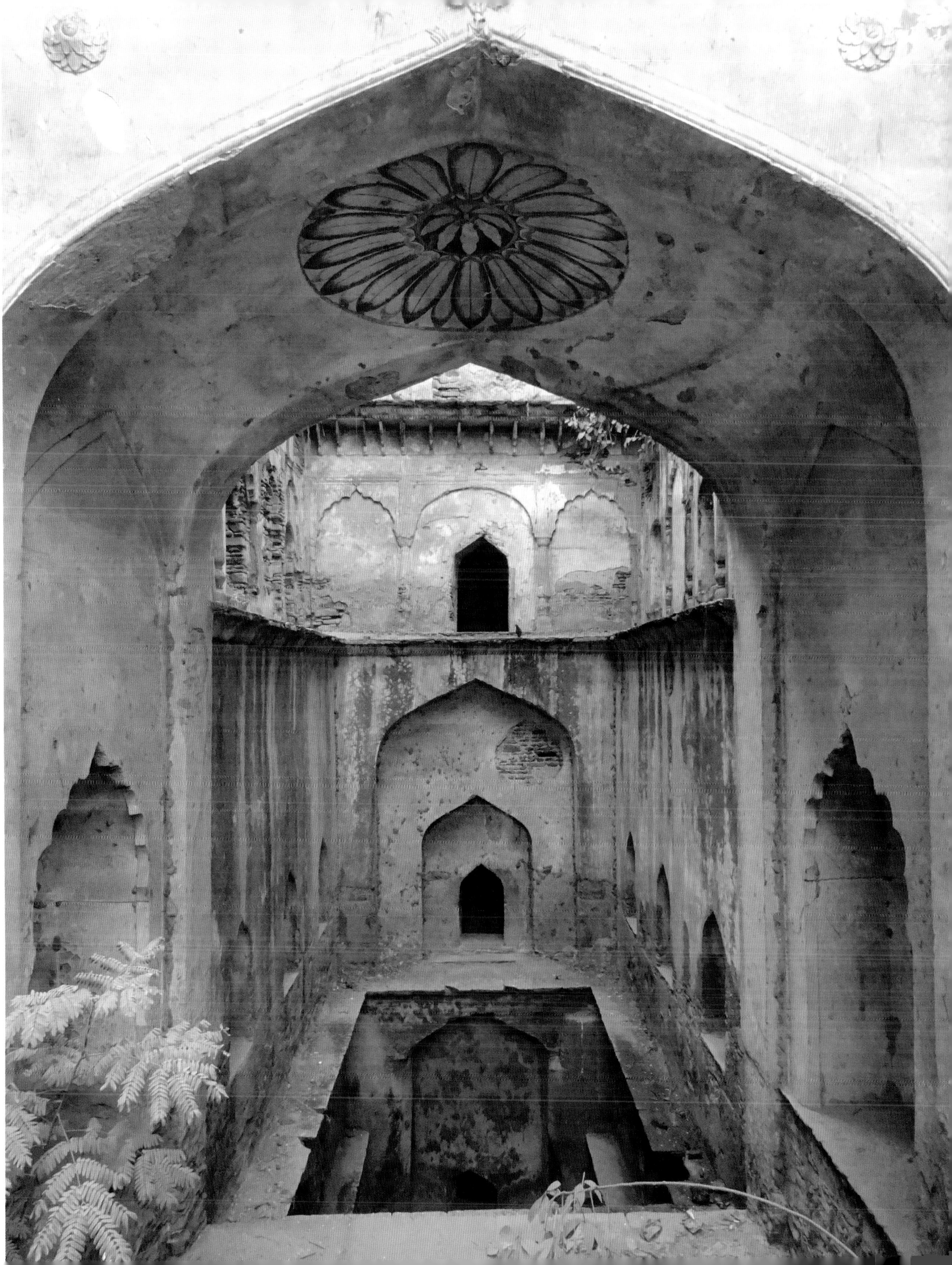

BAHADUR SINGH BAROT KI VAV
(TRIKAMBAROT VAV)
PATAN, GUJARAT
1811
23°51'17.32" N
72°7'5.9" E

A few kilometres from the enormous and elaborate Rani ki Vav (pp. 52-55), a smaller stepwell appeared some 800 years later. Its patron was Bahadur Singh Barot, a landowner whose property included the area around the queen's well; he did not have to look far for construction material. An inscription announces that he began the well in 1805, but it was completed by his son in 1811 for the benefit of the community. Now the community has grown to the extent that it surrounds the five-storey structure, which is sandwiched tightly between dwellings.

While mud and silt obscured the full glory of Rani ki Vav, it was possible for anyone in need of building supplies to cart away columns, stone blocks and sculpture at the uppermost level. The cannibalization of monuments was common in many cultures, particularly where edifices had been destroyed by invaders. Nagaur Fort Baoli (pp. 128-29) and Jethabhai Vav near Ahmedabad (pp. 208-209) are other examples of stepwells that appropriated remnants of older buildings. Bahadur Singh Vav, however, is essentially an eleventh-century jewel stuffed into a nineteenth-century shell. It is beautiful but ersatz, and Rani's sublime Solanki-era craftsmanship outdid anything that could have been created in Singh's time. Every column, capital, deity and frieze bears the signature of Rani ki Vav.

Singh's vav has one advantage over Rani's: any visitor is fully aware that they are descending into the earth, which is crucial to experiencing the magic of a stepwell. This vav is deep and narrow, intimate, more physically and psychologically accessible, while Rani's is canyon-esque in comparison, and completely transcends human scale. Moreover, there is far less visual excess at Bahadur Singh Vav, with fewer columns, sculptures and steps. In an odd way, it is easier to appreciate Rani ki Vav by not being in it.

Singh had no scruples about adapting Rani's bounty to his own project, as the bases of many columns reveal. If a column was too short to fit into a desired slot (as was the case in many instances), an extra piece of stone was shoved in at the bottom. Above ground, at the far end of the vav, Singh made a contribution of his own: a trio of little Islamic domes projecting above the last pavilion, serving as punctuation marks to keep the eye from straying.

Unlike most of the vav, the three domes atop the final pavilion are probably original (right). Exquisite columns were appropriated from Rani ki Vav and then lengthened as necessary (opposite).

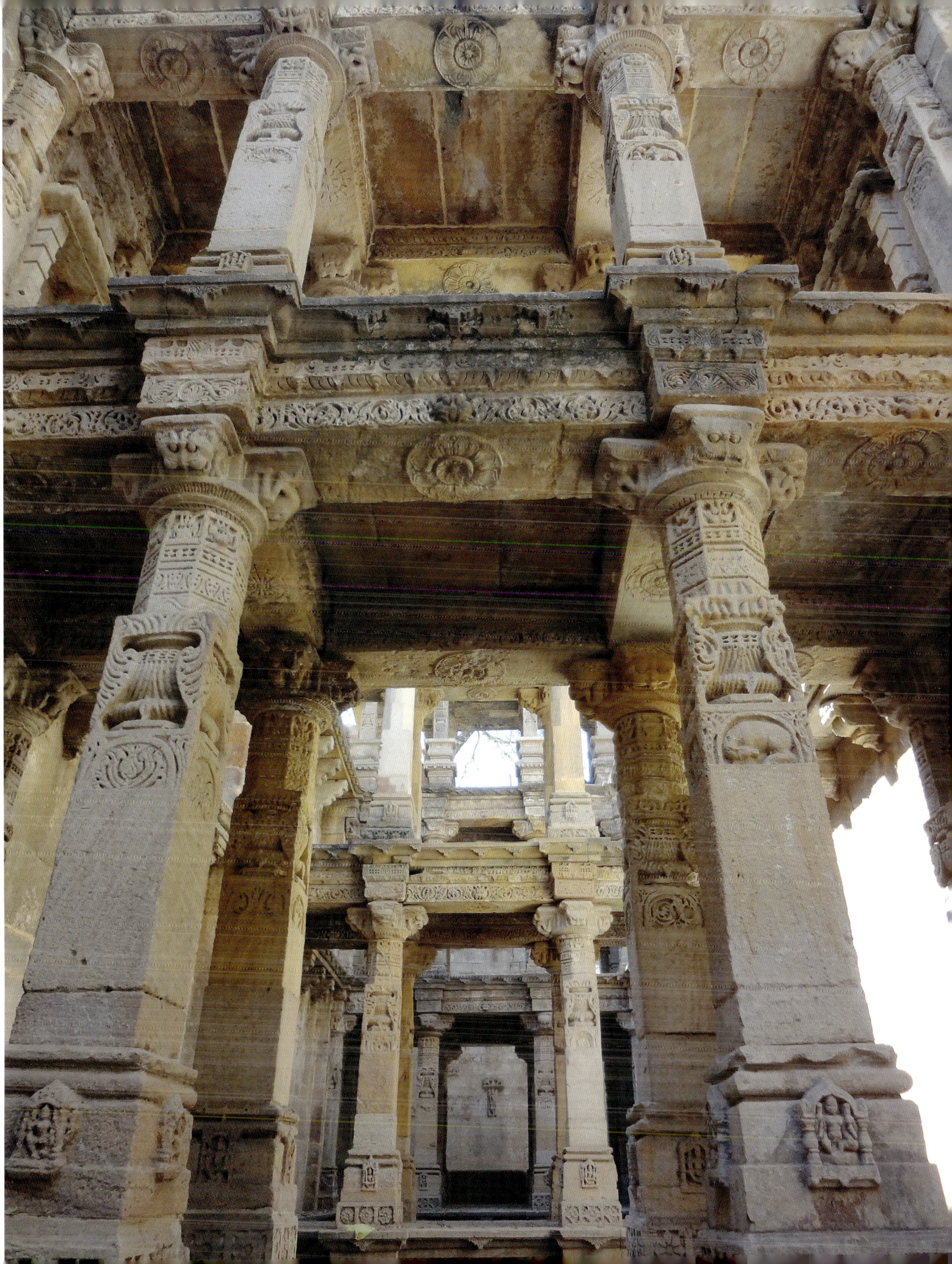

Narrow walls and soaring towers close in, heightening the visitor's awareness of descending underground.

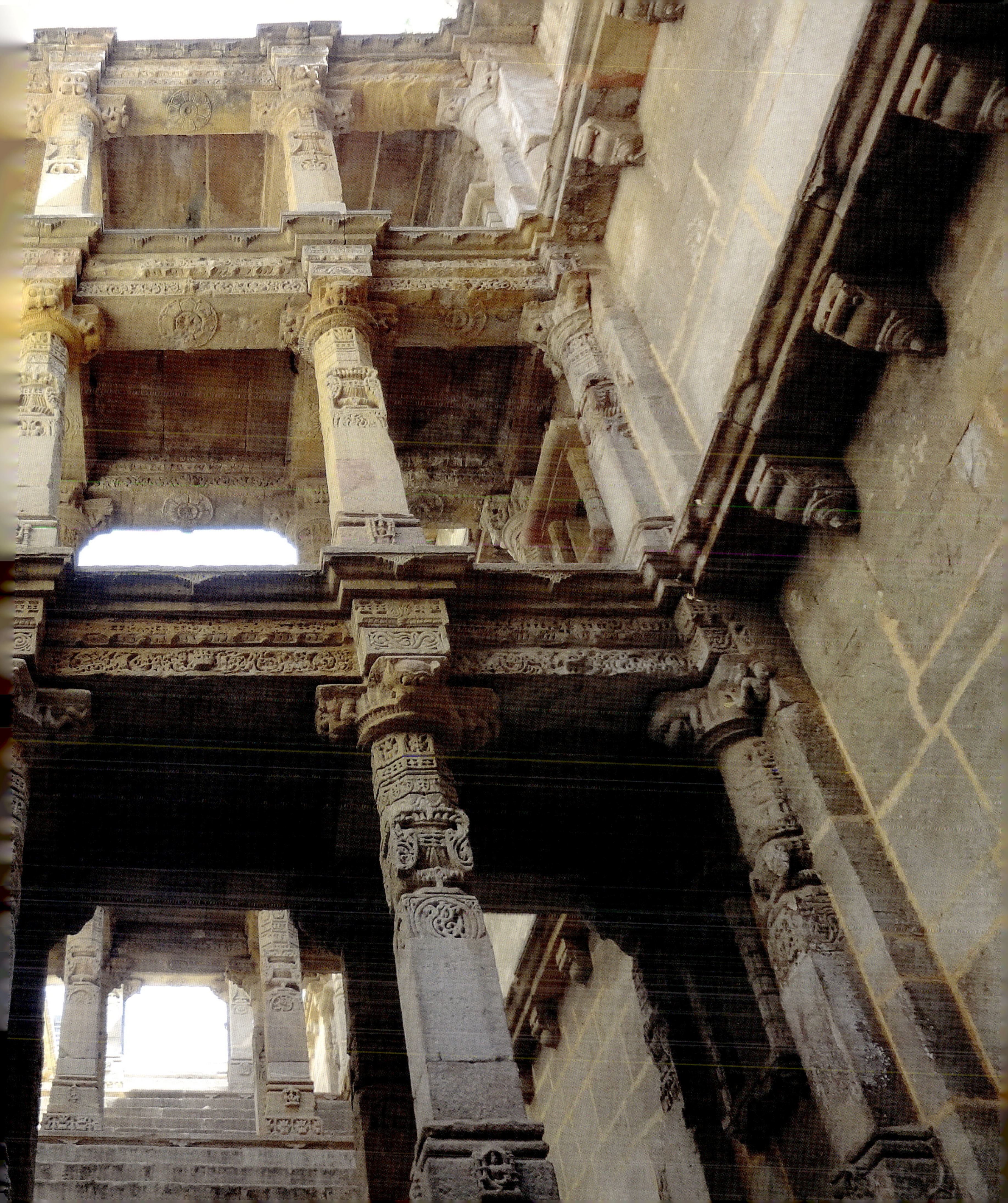

JETHABHAI VAV

ISANPUR, GUJARAT
c. 1860
22°58'28.1" N
72°36'12.34" E

The entrance dome gives no hint of the incongruities to come, including piecemeal columns and a masonry melange. Niches adorn the inside of the cylinder (opposite).

Today Isanpur is a suburb to the south of Ahmedabad, but it was a rural, agricultural village in 1860, when Jivanlal Nagjibhai constructed his eccentric edifice to irrigate the land. Somewhat miraculously, given that it is situated in a noisy, crowded area, the vav is still surrounded by lush green space. Unlike Singh, who appropriated materials for his stepwell from one magnificent source (Rani ki Vav; pp. 52–55), Nagjibhai took from several sources, including the remnants of a mosque and a Muslim tomb, and also incorporated an array of Hindu artefacts. The overall effect is one of approximation, as if a complex structure has been built from memory, the blueprint destroyed.

The mixture of building materials must account for the bizarre interpretations of spindly columns, pieced together using different components that have nothing to do with one another and do not correspond in colour. Proportions are distorted, patterns do not match up. It is a genuine architectural patchwork with an Indo-Islamic twist all its own. The mismatching even extends to the well cylinder, where there are two niches, one with an Islamic lotus flower, the other with a crudely carved, unknown deity.

Even though Nagjibhai was recycling older structures, he also added something new: a huge domed entry platform that marks the presence of the stepwell when seen from afar. This stately entrance is something of a facsimile of Dada Harir Vav (pp. 106–107), built more than 350 years earlier, but just 9 kilometres (5½ miles) away.

The construction of a stepwell in the mid-nineteenth century was anachronistic from the outset, and the building methods employed at Jethabhai Vav made the venture even more extraordinary. While Bahadur Singh raided the most elaborate stepwell of all time (pp. 204–207), at Jethabhai the builders created an architectural melange.

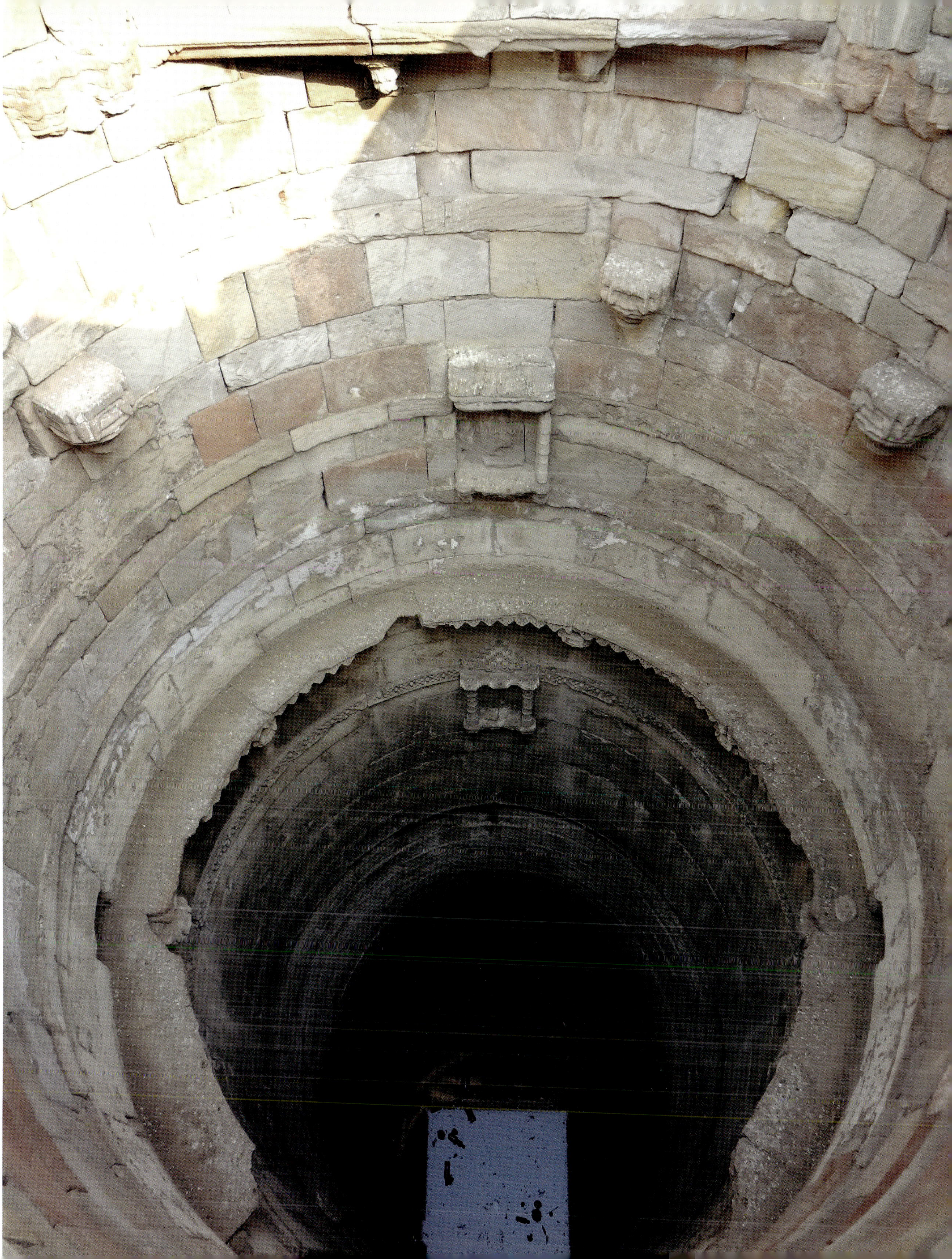

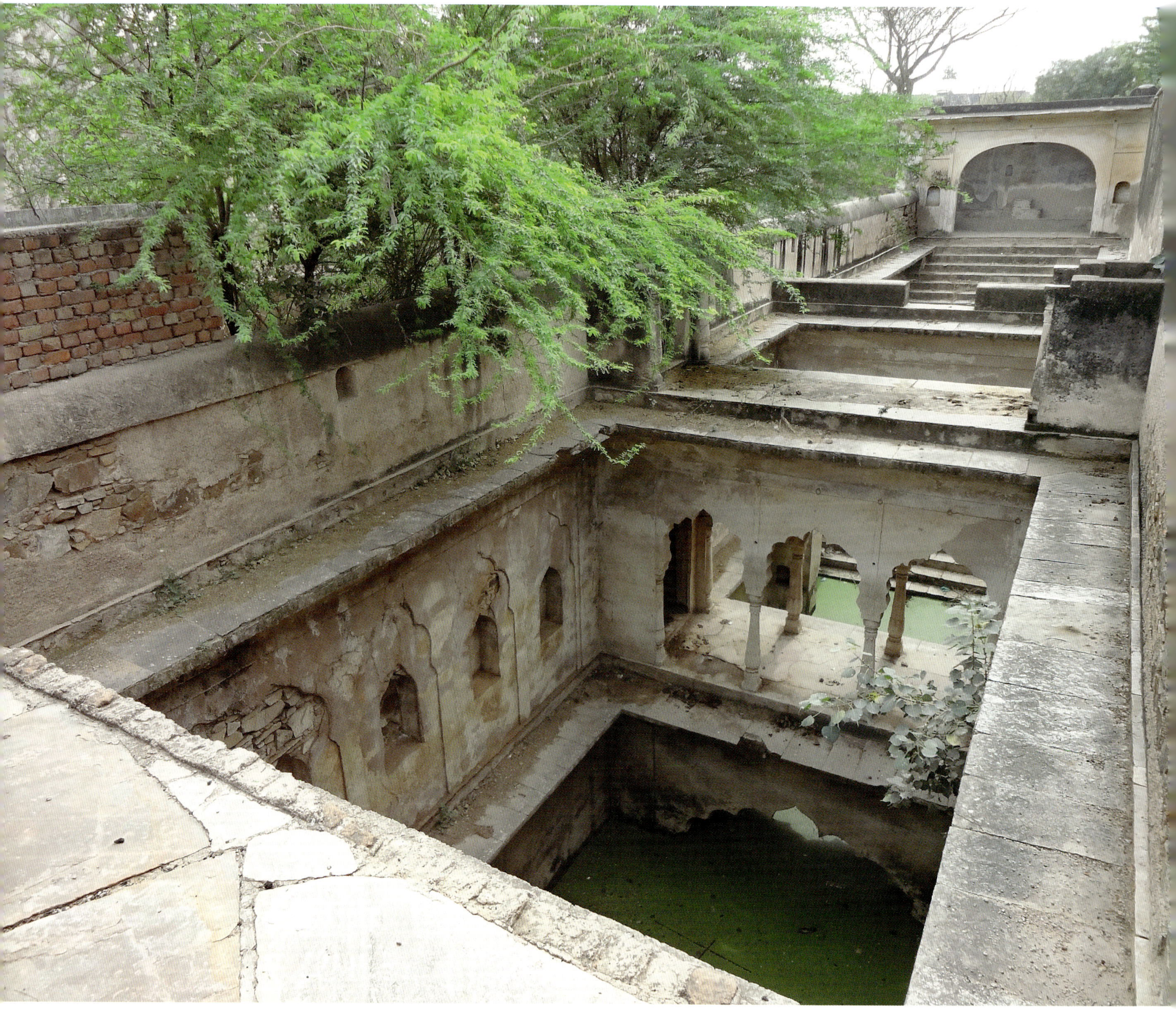

NAGHPURIA BAOLI
(NAGPUR BAOLI, NAGPURION BAOLI)
NARNAUL, HARYANA
c. 1880
28°2'50.79" N
76°6'2.09" E

This long, rectangular baoli in the monument-rich city of Narnaul is a short walk from Mirza Ali Jaan's much more imposing and showy structure from three centuries earlier (pp. 130–31). Here, there is no fancy setting. At ground level, Naghpuria Baoli is rather inconspicuous, with a canal on one side and a blank wall on the other. With nothing of substance known about its origins, the name of its patron has been lost to time. The only, somewhat flimsy piece of information I have gleaned is that it was commissioned in the nineteenth century by a gentleman who was born in Narnaul but moved to the distant city of Nagpur (hence the well's name) to seek his fortune. If the story is true, the fellow fared so well that, on a return trip, he commissioned the baoli as a gift for his home town.

Whoever the patron was, he (or she) built an appealing well, but it is difficult to explore owing to the high water level, narrow ledges and inaccessible side entrances. The submerged archway obscures the depth, but suggests that the steps descend remarkably far. Certainly, the delicate bridge, the wide cusped arch and other details, such as a faded, Mughal-inspired flower above the same arch, elevate this baoli beyond the ordinary. On the other hand, although it was built as a philanthropic gesture, it was surprisingly late in the game. By the end of the nineteenth century, the construction of stepwells was decidedly outmoded. Few were commissioned at the time.

In the past few years Naghpuria has fared poorly, as I discovered on a second visit. A local man explained that it was no longer maintained or used for swimming. The water level has lowered drastically, plants have taken over the steps, and what used to be a jaunty little stepwell now seems sad, even perhaps a little malevolent.

Within a period of three years, the derelict baoli (opposite) became further degraded and developed a rather sinister ambience (right).

Decorative arches and columns are mirrored in low relief on the far wall – a subtle detail.

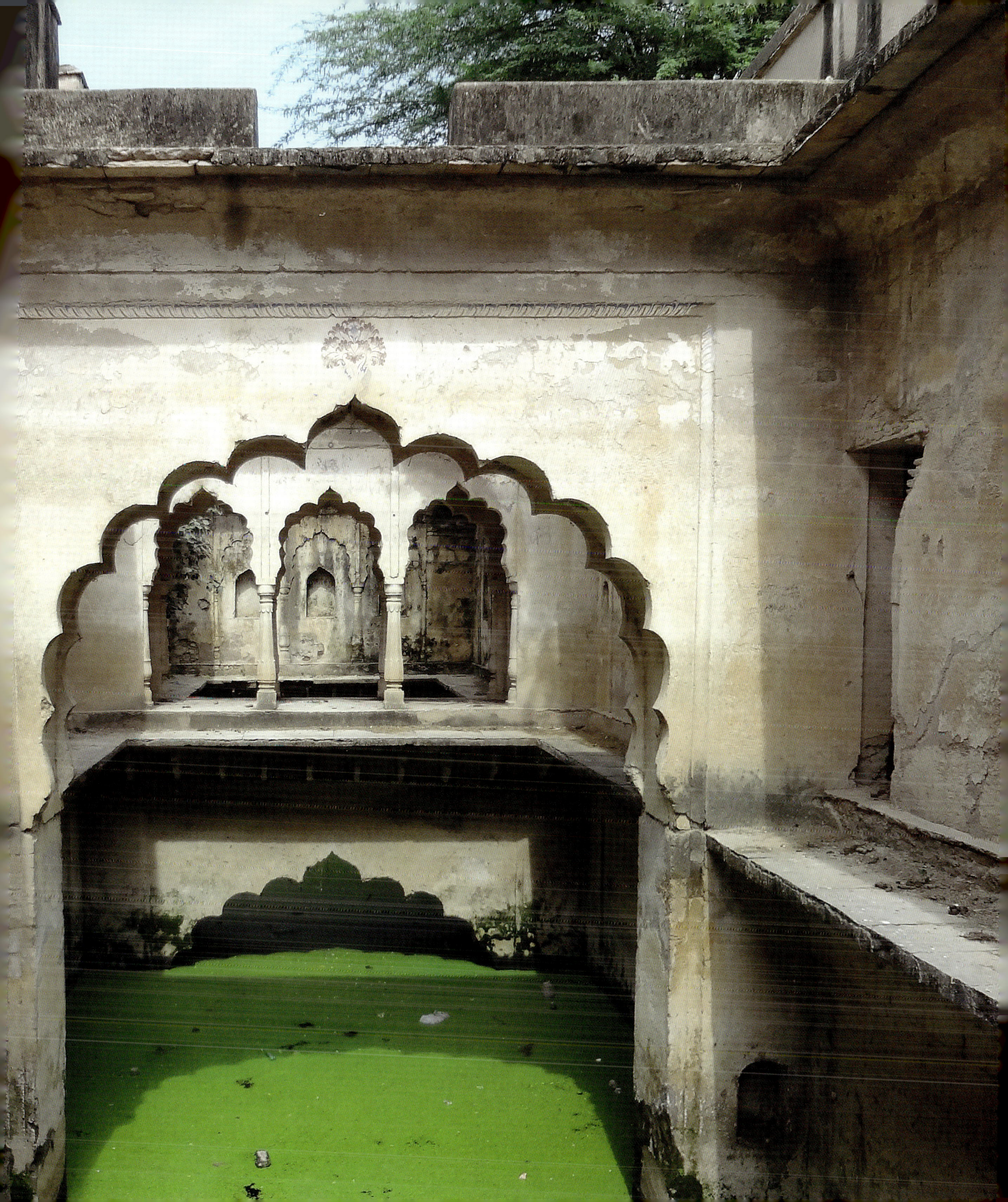

BADSHAHPUR BAOLI

BADSHAHPUR, HARYANA
c. 1900
28°23'19.92" N
77°3'5.84" E

This colossal baoli in Badshahpur is a mystery in many ways, and while it is obviously not the most photogenic of stepwells, it should be acknowledged, if only for its strangeness. Badshahpur is an agricultural village 34 kilometres (21 miles) from Delhi and a short distance outside the chaotically overbuilt city of Gurgaon. A palace was constructed there in the eighteenth century, when Badshahpur was a rural Mughal outpost. Today the palace is in ruins, decimated by the local population for its stone. Reportedly, a baoli was excavated at the same time as the palace, and it was while I was in pursuit of that stepwell that I was made aware of a pair of more modern wells. Apparently both date from around the turn of the twentieth century, which makes them among the most recent of Indian stepwells. Sadly, both are also in a deplorable state, abandoned within school grounds. This one is hemmed in by buildings on three sides and on the fourth side by a terrible slum. At the time it was built, it probably irrigated the surrounding farmland, of which there is today far less.

Even though this stepwell is right in the centre of Badshahpur, I had to make many enquiries before I found it (and I never found the Mughal one). Residents who live mere blocks away were unaware of its existence, which is not atypical of many baoli hunts.

A local official had no information about this inaccessible baoli, except for the date. But its arcade, cusped arches and niches pay homage – intentional or otherwise – to the long history of stepwells in India.

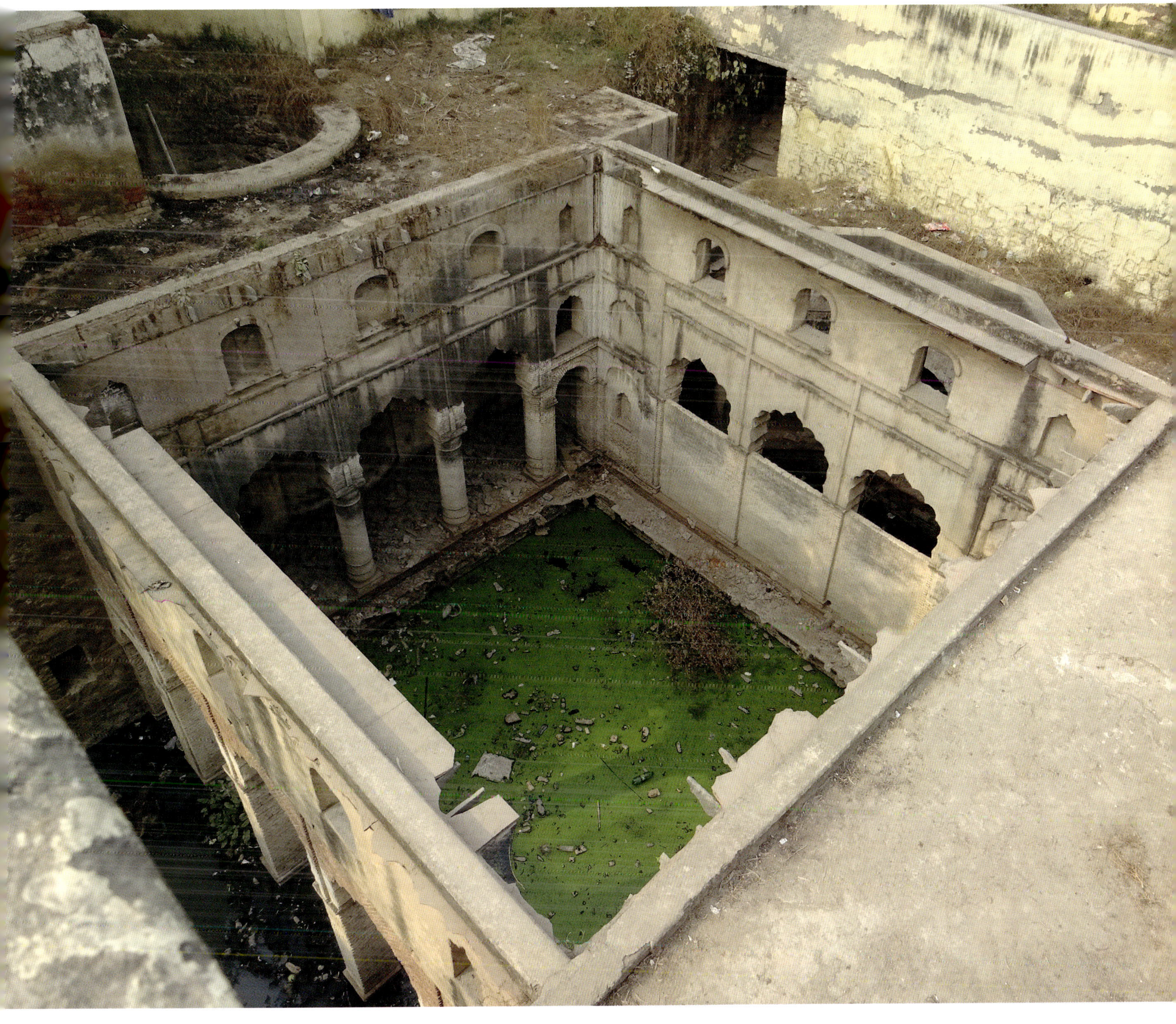

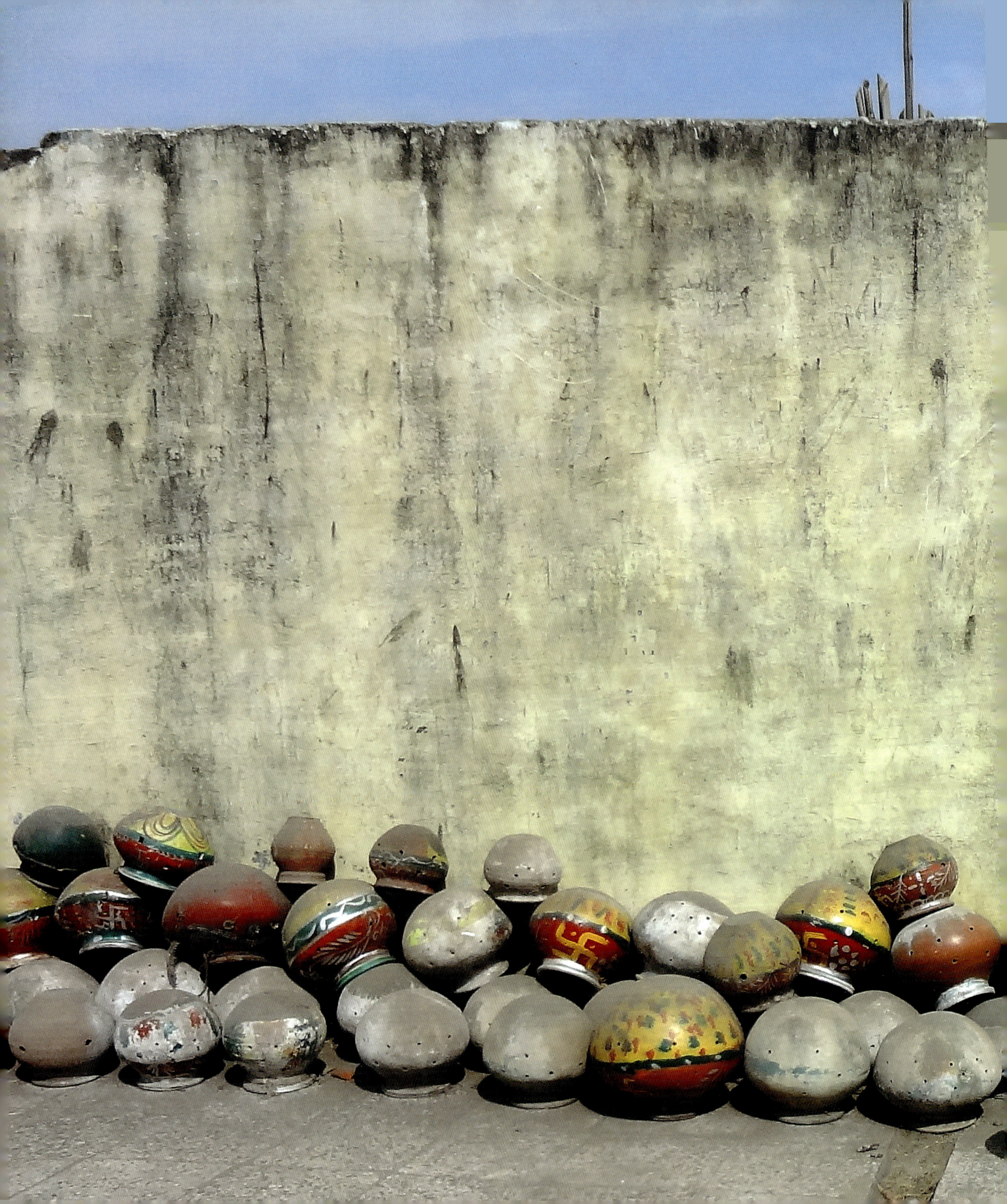

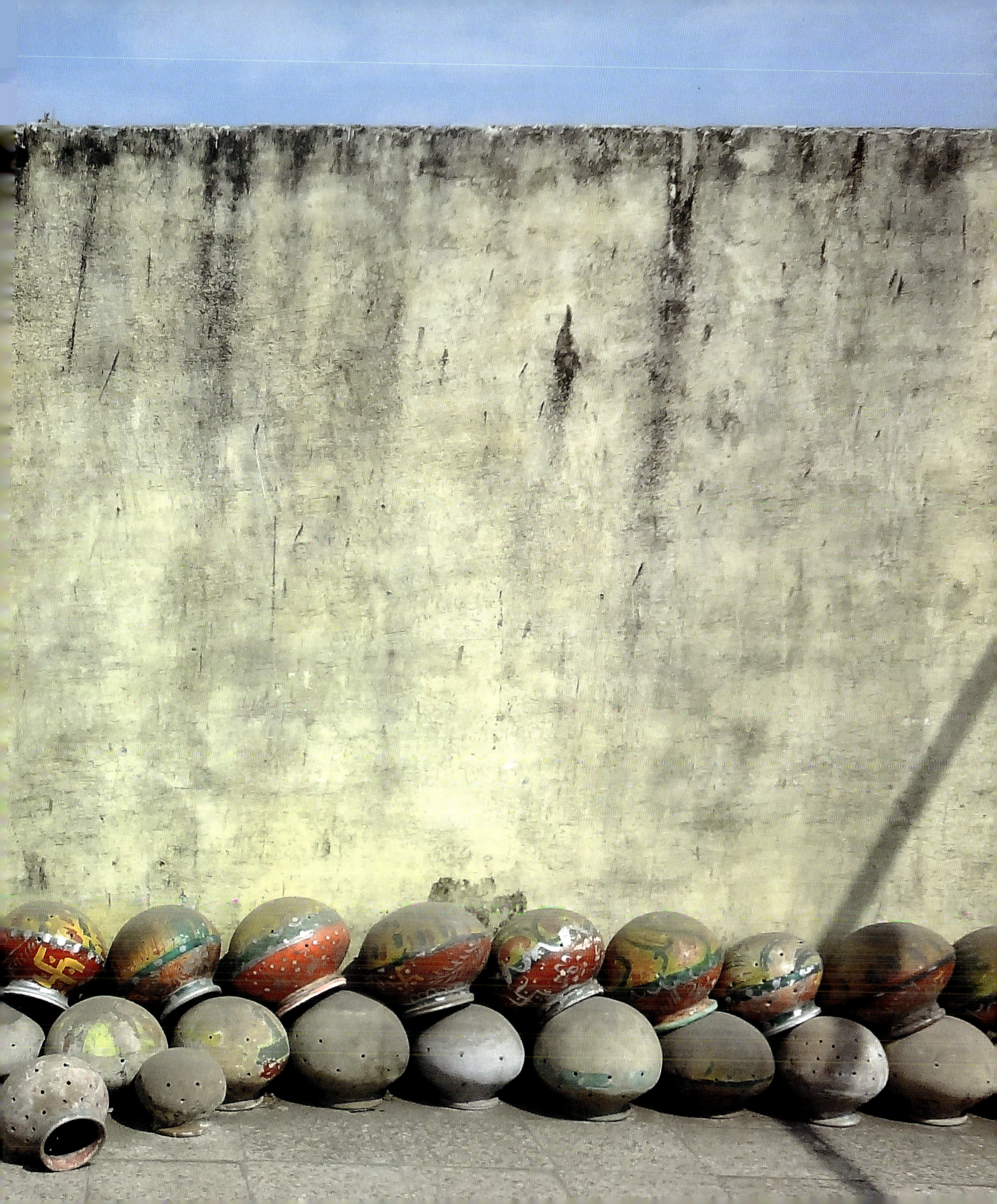

BIBLIOGRAPHY

Agarwal, Anil, and Narain, Sunita (eds.), *Dying Wisdom: Rise, Fall and Potential of India's Traditional Water Harvesting Systems*, New Delhi (Centre for Science and Environment) 1997

Burgess, James, and Cousens, Henry, *The Architectural Antiquities of Northern Gujarat*, London (The India Society) 1926

Cooper, Ilay, *The Painted Towns of Shekhawati*, Middletown, NJ, and Ahmedabad (Grantha Corporation in association with Mapin Publishing) 1994

Cousens, Henry, *The Architectural Antiquities of Western India*, London (The India Society) 1926

Davies, Philip H., *The Penguin Guide to the Monuments of India. Vol. 2: Islamic, Rajput, European*, London (Viking) 1989

Gulia, Yashpal, *Heritage of Haryana*, New Delhi (Rolleract Press Services) 2012

Hegewald, Julia A.B., *Water Architecture in South Asia: A Study of Types, Development and Meanings*, Leiden and Boston (Brill) 2002

Herdeg, Klaus, *Formal Structure in Indian Architecture*, New York (Rizzoli) 1990

India Guide Gujarat, Ahmedabad (India Guide Publications) 2011

INTACH (Indian National Trust for Art and Cultural Heritage), *Baolis of Bundi: The Ancient Stepwells*, New Delhi (Architectural Heritage Division, INTACH) 2015

Jain, Shikha, and Dandona, Bhawna (eds.), *Haryana Cultural Heritage Guide*, New Delhi (INTACH with Aryan Books International) 2012

Jain-Neubauer, Jutta, *The Stepwells of Gujarat in Art-Historical Perspective*, New Delhi (Abhinav Publications) 1981

Juneja, Monica (ed.), *Architecture in Medieval India: Forms, Contexts, Histories*, New Delhi (Permanent Black) 2001

Kamiya, Takeo, *The Guide to the Architecture of the Indian Subcontinent*, rev. English edn, Goa (Architecture Autonomous) 2004

Livingston, Morna, *Steps to Water: The Ancient Stepwells of India*, New York (Princeton Architectural Press) 2002

Mankodi, Kirit, *The Queen's Stepwell at Patan*, Bombay (Franco-Indian Research) 1991

Michell, George, *The Penguin Guide to the Monuments of India. Vol. 1: Buddhist, Jain, Hindu*, London (Viking) 1989

Nath, R., *The History of Mughal Architecture, Vol. 3*, New Delhi (Abhinav Publications) 1994

Pandya, Yatin, *Concepts of Space in Traditional Indian Architecture*, Ahmedabad (Mapin Publishing) 2005

Peck, Lucy, *Delhi: A Thousand Years of Building*, New Delhi (Roli Books) 2005

—, *Agra: The Architectural Heritage*, New Delhi (Roli Books) 2008

Rothfarb, Edward Leland, *Orchha and Beyond: Design at the Court of Raja Bir Singh Dev Bundela*, Mumbai (The Marg Foundation) 2012

Rowland, Benjamin, *The Art and Architecture of India: Buddhist, Hindu, Jain* (The Pelican History of Art), London and Baltimore (Penguin) 1953

Tillotson, Giles, *Nagaur: A Garden Palace in Rajasthan*, Jodhpur (Mehrangarh Museum Trust) 2010

— (ed.), *Stones in the Sand: The Architecture of Rajasthan*, Mumbai (The Marg Foundation) 2001

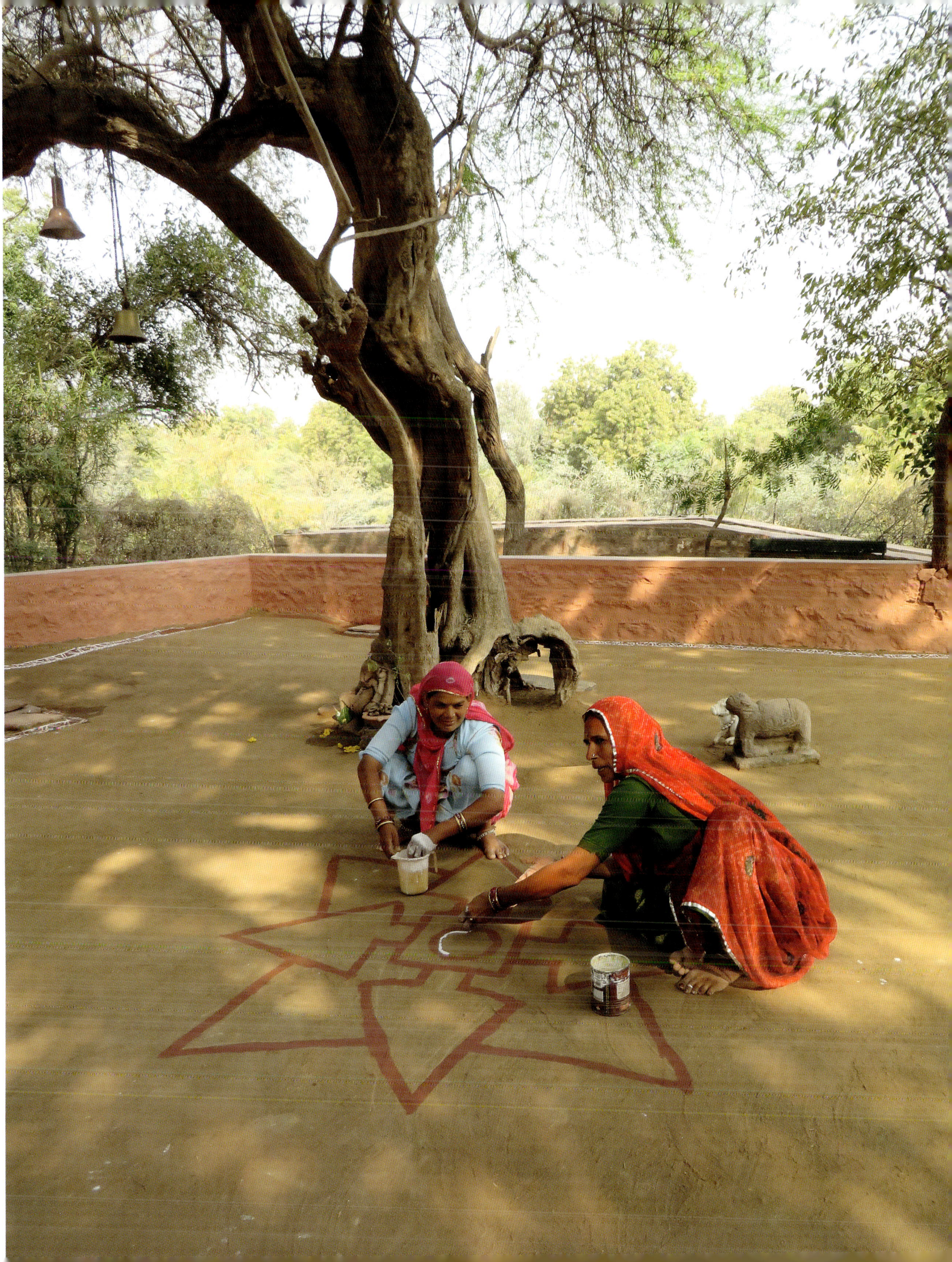

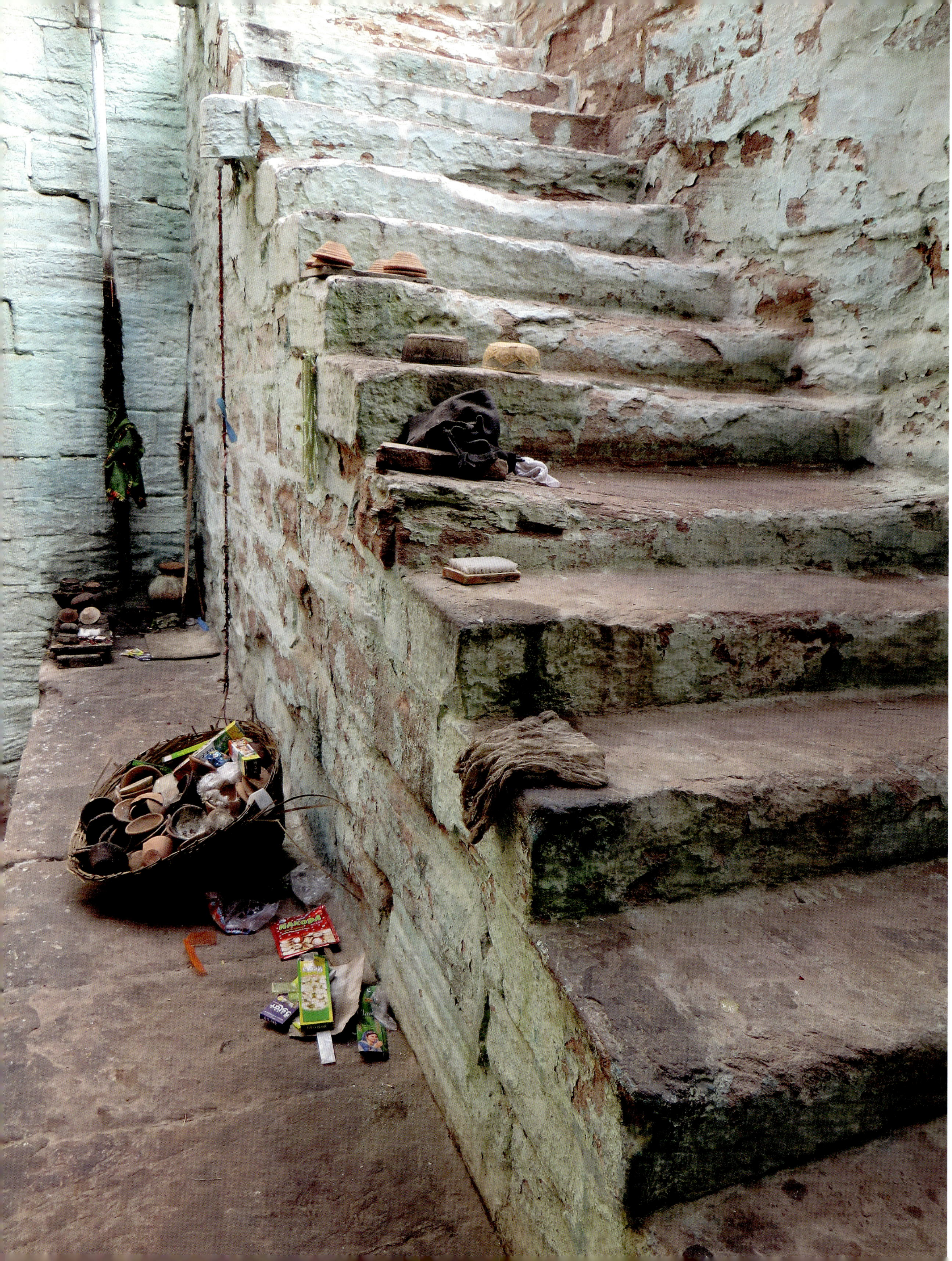

ACKNOWLEDGEMENTS

I avoided writing a book about the stepwells of India because I was daunted by the factual inconsistencies and the lack of reliable information on so many of those that I had visited. Fortunately, right from the start of my obsession I was given help and encouragement, without which I would have got nowhere.

It was the groundbreaking books and research by the scholars Jutta Jain-Neubauer, Julia Hegewald and Morna Livingston that inspired and informed me throughout this process. I pestered all three authors mercilessly, and cannot thank them adequately for their patience with me. Professor Kirit Mankodi was also generous with his knowledge in our correspondence.

Madhuvanti Ghose, curator at the Art Institute of Chicago, gave me priceless advice around the clock and has been unfailingly supportive. I'm grateful for wonderful support from my extraordinary companions and guides in Ahmedabad, Nirav and Urvashi Panchal, who showed me treasures. The author and academic Yatin Pandya devoted hours of precious time to me. And Professor Shilpa Das at the National Institute of Design was a valuable source of information. My thanks go to each of them.

In Delhi, the Renaissance man Himanshu Verma, who was there from the beginning, squired me around local baolis. I am sincerely grateful to the ever-helpful Divay Gupta, of the Architectural Heritage Division of INTACH, for writing the foreword to this book. My thanks also go to Dr B.R. Mani, formerly of the Archaeological Survey of India (now Director General of the National Museum), who helped to remove obstacles when I became desperate, and to Dr Nandan Dimri, Director of Antiquities at the ASI, who also stepped in to assist me.

Dr Vandana Sinha of the celebrated American Institute of Indian Studies was exceedingly accommodating and informative; thanks to the historian Atul Dev for connecting us. The digital resources of the Indira Gandhi National Centre for the Arts were tremendously useful, as were the perceptive reading and comments of the historian Mayank Kumar. The enthusiastic film-maker Hemant Gaba joined me on several baoli hunts; I am delighted that he reached out to me. Shikha Jain of the Development and Research Organisation for Nature, Arts and Heritage (DRONAH) offered valuable assistance, as did the art historian Mitchell Crites, who has dubbed me the 'Begum of Baolis'.

I am extremely grateful to the Jaipur-based conservation architects Manas Sharma and Yash Pratap Singh Shekhawat, who were both unstinting with their time and indispensable information. Particular thanks to Manas for taking me round two cities, and to the conservator Shalin Sharma for the introduction. In Haryana, the cultural historian Ranbir S. Phaugat's detailed advice was profoundly valuable, and I also thank Rattan Lal Saini, Samrat Narula and Yashpal Gulia for their insights. The environmental activist Rajesh Joshi – a redeemer of baolis in Jodhpur – was especially dedicated to this project, and I received other significant input from the scholars Malvika Bajaj Saini, H.B. Maheshwari and Ritu Joshi.

So many far-flung aficionados of stepwells contributed substantial information and much-needed support, in particular Vipin Gaur, Fiona Foster Darcy and Vishwanath Srikantaiah, along with Philip Earis, whose burgeoning online Stepwell Atlas is an important resource. The architectural preservationist Vincent Michael shared his expertise and contacts, while key technical input came from the engineer Bob Magruder and Professor James Wescoat.

Were it not for the peaceful retreat generously bestowed on me by Jill Ingrassia-Zingales and Luigi Zingales, there would simply be no book, and if Douglas Dawson had not invited me to lecture at his gallery, I would have kept these photographs to myself. Christopher Jobson rescued me with his internationally popular blog, Colossal, when I was at my wits' end, and my trusted mentor Gere Kavanaugh was a tireless cheerleader and haranguer. I am indebted to my exceptionally loyal friends and family, who listened (or pretended to) as I talked endlessly about stepwells. I am fortunate to have these people in my life.

It was the vision and enthusiasm of the publisher Hugh Merrell that brought this book to life; Claire Chandler's skilful editing and Nicola Bailey's elegant design turned a fantasy into reality. My gratitude to you is boundless.

Finally, I wish to thank my son, Finnian, whose encouragement and love sustain me.

INDEX

Page numbers in *italic* refer to the illustrations.

Abhaneri, Rajasthan 36, 40, *40-43*
Adalaj, Gujarat 103, *103-105*, 108
Adi Kadi Vav, Junagadh, Gujarat *17*, 26, 78, *78-81*
Aga Khan Trust for Culture 23
Agarwal community 85
Agra, Rajasthan 82, 101, 142, *142-43*
Agrasen, Emperor 84-85
Agrasen ki Baoli, Delhi 40, 84-85, *84-85*, 91
Ahhichatragarh Fort, Nagaur, Rajasthan 128
Ahmedabad, Gujarat 20, 48, 53, 102, 182, *182-83*, 208
Akbar, Emperor 17, 131, 132, 137, 142
Akbarnama 17
Akbar's Baoli, Agra, Rajasthan 101, 120, 142, *142-43*
Ali Ghaus Khan Baoli, Farrukhnagar, Haryana 186, *186-87*
Ali Jaan, Mirza 131, 170
Ambapur Vav, Gujarat 108, *108-109*
Amer, Rajasthan *15*, 82, *82-83*, *114-17*, 115, 164, *164-67*, 184, 190, *190-93*
American Institute of Indian Studies 22
Amritvarshini Vav, Ahmedabad, Gujarat 182, *182-83*
Andhra Pradesh 7
Anirudh Singh, Rao Raja 148, 153
Archaeological Survey of India (ASI) 18, 23, 40, 49, 53, 64, 74, 85, 118, 122, 125, 176
Asarwa, Gujarat 20, 48-49, *48-49*, 96, 106, *106-107*
Asi River 46
Assi Khambha Baori, Gwalior, Madhya Pradesh 120, *120-21*

Babero 62
Badshahpur Baoli, Haryana 214, *214-15*
Bahadur Singh Barot ki Vav, Patan, Gujarat 53, 204, *204-207*
Bahuchara Mata *14*, 94
Bakhtiar Kaki 64
Bal Samand Lake Palace, Jodhpur, Rajasthan 126
Barda Hills, Gujarat 69
Batris Kotha Vav, Kapadvanj, Gujarat 58, *58-59*, 60
Begada, Sultan Mahmud 101, 102, 103, 108, 118
Bhadla, Gujarat 62, *62-63*
Bhairavi 49
Bhamaria Vav, Mehmedabad, Gujarat *100-101*, 101, 120
Bhao Singh, Rao Raja 150
Bhavani 48
Bhawalde, Rani 150
Bhawaldi Baoli, Bundi, Rajasthan 148, 150, *150-51*, 153
Bhimdev, King 53
Bhora-ji-ka Kund, Bundi, Rajasthan 156
Bhuj, Gujarat 188, *188-89*
Bir Singh Dev, Raja 168

Birkha Bawari rainwater-harvesting system, Jodhpur, Rajasthan 23
Bishan Singh, Raja 115
Bochavdi Vav, Dhank, Gujarat 34, *34-35*
British East India Company 20
Budh Singh, Rao Raja 148
Bundelkhand region, Madhya Pradesh 168, 178
Bundi, Rajasthan 13, 148-62, *149-63*

Champaner, Gujarat *22*, 118, *118-19*
Chand, Raja 40
Chand Baori, Abhaneri, Rajasthan 13, 36, 40, *40-43*, 115, 161
Chhardwari Baoli, Orchha, Madhya Pradesh 178, *178-79*
Chittorgarh, Rajasthan *124-25*, 125
Correa, Charles *22*, 23

Dabhai Kund, Bundi, Rajasthan 115, *160-61*, 161, 162
Dada Harir Vav, Asarwa, Gujarat 20, 48, 106, *106-107*, 182, 208
Das, Rai Bal Mukund 170
Datia, Madhya Pradesh 168
Dedadara, Gujarat *44-45*, 45
Dehgam, Gujarat 94, *94-95*
Delhi 7, 18, 23
 Agrasen ki Baoli 40, 84-85, *84-85*, 91
 Feroz Shah Kotla Baoli 76, *76-77*, 137
 Gandhak ki Baoli 64, *64-65*
 Mehrauli 64, 122
 Rajon ki Baoli 91, 122, *122-23*
 Red Fort Baoli 13, 74, *74-75*, 91
 Wazirpur Baoli *90-93*, 91
Delhi Sultanate 64, 91
Development and Research Organisation for Nature, Arts and Heritage (DRONAH) 17
Devi 14, 156, 190
Dhandhalpur Vav, Gujarat 60, *60-61*, 96
Dhank, Gujarat 18, 26, 30, *30-35*, 32, 34, 145
Dholavira, Gujarat 17
Durga 62

Farrukhnagar, Haryana 186, *186-87*
Farrukhsiyar, Emperor 186
Fatehpur Sikri, Uttar Pradesh 17, 132, *132-39*, 137, 176
Feroz Shah Kotla Baoli, Delhi 76, *76-77*, 137
Feroz Shah Tughluk, Sultan 76
Ferozabad 76

Gandhak ki Baoli, Delhi 64, *64-65*
Ganesh *16*, 17, 49, 96, 156, 180
Ganges River 45, 46
Gangvo Kund, Dedadara, Gujarat *44-45*, 45, 153
Gelmata ni Vav, Bhadla, Gujarat 14, 62, *62-63*, 70
Ghanerao, Rajasthan *16*
Ghumli, Gujarat 68-69, 69

Global Heritage Fund 23
Gram Bharati Samiti (Society for Rural Development) 23
Gujarat 7, 13, 14, 17-18, 30
Gulab Rai 194
Gwalior, Madhya Pradesh 120, *120-21*

Hampur Vav, Gujarat *144-47*, 145
Harappan civilization 7, 17
Harbola ki Baori, Jodhpur, Rajasthan 126, *126-27*
Harir, Dada 106
Harshat Mata Temple, Abhaneri, Rajasthan 40
Haryana 13
Hegewald, Julia 66, 142
Helical Vav, Champaner, Gujarat *22*, 118, *118-19*
Hindu stepwells 7, 14-17, 20, 102
Hindustan Coca-Cola 184

Iltutmish, Sultan 64
Indaravali Baoli, Fatehpur Sikri, Uttar Pradesh 14, 66, *136-39*, 137
Indian Army 74
Indian National Trust for Art and Cultural Heritage (INTACH) 23, 148, 150, 161, 162
Indira Gandhi National Centre for the Arts 22, 180
Inter-University Centre for Astronomy and Astrophysics, Pune 22
Isanpur, Gujarat 208, *208-209*
Islamic stepwells 7, 14, 17, 20, 102

Jai Singh II, Maharaja Sawai 115, 164, 184, 190
Jain, Shikha 17
Jain-Neubauer, Jutta 66
Jains 20, 36, 186
Jaipur, Rajasthan 82, 115, 148, 164, 184, *184-85*, 190
Jaipuriya Kund, Bundi, Rajasthan 158, *158-59*
Jaivanta Bai, Maharani 125
Jali Vav, Chittorgarh, Rajasthan *124-25*, 125
Jayasimha, Siddharaja 56, 58, 60
Jefar ji ka Kund, Bundi, Rajasthan 158, *158-59*
Jethabhai Vav, Isanpur, Gujarat 204, 208, *208-209*
Jhilani Vav, Dhank, Gujarat 30, 32, *32-33*, 34
Jhunjhunu, Rajasthan *198-201*, 199
Jiyani Chor ki Baoli, Meham, Haryana *174-75*, 175
Jodhpur, Rajasthan *21*, 22-23, 126, *126-27*, 148, 176, *176-77*, 194, *194-97*
Joshi, Rajesh 22-23, 194
Junagadh, Gujarat 26, *26-29*, 78, *78-81*
Junagadh Agricultural University 66

Kalal, Saidu 175
Kale Hanuman Baoli, Jaipur, Rajasthan 82, 184, *184-85*
Kapadvanj, Gujarat 56, *56-59*, 58
Karnataka 7
Katan Baoli, Osian, Rajasthan 36, *36-39*, 40, 115

Khan, Aamir 84
Khan, Adham 132
Khan, Ali Ghaus 186
Khan, Daulat 122
Khan, Faujdar 186
Khan, Zafar 86
kunds 14
Kundvav, Kapadvanj, Gujarat 56, *56-57*, 58, 60, 180
Kutch district, Gujarat 188

Laxmi Vilas Palace, Vadodara, Gujarat 86
Livingston, Morna 102
Lodi dynasty 91
Lolark Kund, Varanasi, Uttar Pradesh 46, *46-47*
Lutyens, Sir Edwin 168

Maaji ki Bawadi, Amer, Rajasthan 14, 164, 190, *190-93*
Madha Vav, Wadhwan, Gujarat 60, 70, *70-73*, 96
Madhava 70
Maham Anga 132
Mahendragarh, Haryana 202, *202-203*
Mahila Baag Jhalra, Jodhpur, Rajasthan *22-23*, 194, *194-97*
Maldeo, Rao 128
Man Singh, Maharaja 120
Man Singh I, Raja 164
Mandu, Madhya Pradesh 110, *110-13*
Manjushri Vav, Dhank, Gujarat 30, *30-31*, 34
Mankodi, Kirit 53
    The Queen's Stepwell at Patan 17
Manohari Baoli, Bundi, Rajasthan 149, *149*
Mata Bhavani ni Vav, Asarwa, Gujarat 14, 20, 48-49, *48-49*, 96
Meham, Haryana *174-75*, 175
Mehmedabad, Gujarat *100-101*, 101
Mehrauli, Delhi 64, 122
Mertani, Queen 20, 199
Mertaniji ki Bawari, Jhunjhunu, Rajasthan 20, *198-201*, 199
Mirza Ali Jaan ka Takht Baoli, Narnaul, Haryana *130-31*, 131, 170, 211
Mohenjo Daro, Pakistan 7, 17
Mridul, Anu 23
Mughal Empire 20, 132, 175, 182
Mukundpura Baoli, Haryana 170, *170-73*
Muslim stepwells *see* Islamic stepwells

Nadol, Rajasthan 50, *50-51*
Nagar Sagar Kund, Bundi, Rajasthan 162, *162-63*
Nagaur Fort Baoli, Rajasthan 128, *128-29*, 204
Naghpuria Baoli, Narnaul, Haryana 202, *210-13*, 211
Nagjibhai, Jivanlal 208
Narnaul, Haryana *130-31*, 131, 170, 202, *210-13*, 211
NASA 22
Nathawati-ji, Rani 20, 153
Navghan Kuvo, Junagadh, Gujarat 26, *26-29*, 78

Navlakha Temple, Ghumli, Gujarat 69
Navlakhi Vav, Vadodara, Gujarat 86, *86-89*, 94
Nawabi Baoli, Mahendragarh, Haryana 202, *202-203*
Nawlakhi Baoli, Jodhpur, Rajasthan 176, *176-77*
Neemrana Baori, Rajasthan *12*, 140, *140-41*, 175, 199

Orchha, Madhya Pradesh 178, *178-79*
Osian, Rajasthan 36, *36-39*

Pali district, Rajasthan 50
Panna Meena ka Kund, Amer, Rajasthan *114-17*, 115, 190
Patan, Gujarat 7, 48, *52-55*, 53, 204, *204-207*
Pavagadh, Gujarat 118
Phaugat, Ranbir 131, 170, 186, 202
Pogson, Major C.A. 17
Porbandar, Gujarat 69
Pradhanji ka Kund, Bundi, Rajasthan *154-55*, 155
Pratap Singh, Maharana 125
Prince Claus Fund 23
The Prince's Charities, London 148, 150
Puri, Sanjay 23

Quli Khan, Haider 182
Quli Khan, Mohammed 132

Ra Khengar Vav, Vanthali, Gujarat 66, *66-67*, 137
Ragunhathdas 182
Rai, Raghu 85
Raja Bir Singh Dev Baoli, Sirol, Madhya Pradesh 168, *168-69*, 178
Rajasthan 13, 14, 23
Rajkot district, Gujarat 62
Rajon ki Baoli, Delhi 91, 122, *122-23*, 190
Rajput kingdom 164
Rajputana 7
Rama Krishna Puram, Delhi 91
Ramayana 188
Ramkund, Bhuj, Gujarat 188, *188-89*
Rampura, Gujarat 96, *96-99*
Rani Baoli, Nadol, Rajasthan 50, *50-51*
Rani ki Vav, Patan, Gujarat 7, 17, 18, *19*, 20, 23, 40, 48, *52-55*, 53, 118, 204, 208
Raniji ki Baori, Bundi, Rajasthan 20, 150, *152-53*, 153, 155, 162
Rataba Vav, Rampura, Gujarat 60, 96, *96-99*
Rawla Narlai hotel and baoli, Rajasthan 23, 164
Red Fort, Agra, Rajasthan 101, 142
Red Fort Baoli, Delhi 13, 74, *74-75*, 91
Ruda, Queen 103, 106, 153
Rudabai Vav, Adalaj, Gujarat 9, 20, 94, 103, *103-105*, 106, 108, 153, 182

Saidhu Kalal ki Baoli, Meham, Haryana *174-75*, 175
Sampa Vav, Dehgam, Gujarat *14*, 94, *94-95*, 96, 103
Sarai Bawadi, Amer, Rajasthan 82, *82-83*, 184

Saraswati 156
Saraswati River 18, 53
Sardul Singh Shekhawat, Maharao 199
Sasu ni Vav, Lavana, Gujarat 162
Shah Jahan, Emperor 170, 175
Shah Jahan ki Baoli, Meham, Haryana *174-75*, 175
Shah Quli Baoli, Fatehpur Sikri, Uttar Pradesh 132, *132-35*, 137
Sharma, Manas 82, 180
Shekhawat, Yash Pratap Singh 164, 190
Shiva 17, 96, 108, 126, 145, 158, 178, 180, 182
Shree Abhaynath Mahadev ki Baoli, Bundi, Rajasthan 156, *156-57*
Sikhs 202
Silk Route 36
Singh Barot, Bahadur 204, 208
Singh Saheb ki Baoli, Mahendragarh, Haryana 202, *202-203*
Sirol, Madhya Pradesh 168, *168-69*, 178
Solanki dynasty 48, 56, 60
Sufism 64
Surya 17, 46

Tamil Nadu 7
Telangana 7
Thar Desert 194
Toorji ka Jhalra, Jodhpur, Rajasthan 21, 22, 164
Toran Baori, Udaipur, Rajasthan 180, *180-81*
Trikambarot Vav, Patan, Gujarat 204, *204-207*

Udai Singh II, Maharana 125, 126
Udaipur, Rajasthan 125, 180, *180-81*
Udayamati, Queen 20, 53
Ujala Baoli, Mandu, Madhya Pradesh 110, *110-13*
UNESCO World Heritage sites 7, 18, 50, 53, 118, 125, 132
Uparkot Fort, Junagadh, Gujarat 78

Vadodara, Gujarat 86, *86-89*
Vaghela, Sarangdev 70
Vahu ni Vav, Lavana, Gujarat 162
Van Talab Baoli, Amer, Rajasthan 164, *164-67*
Vanthali, Gujarat 66, *66-67*
Varanasi, Uttar Pradesh 7, 46, *46-47*
Vayadi ni Vav, Dhank, Gujarat 34, *34-35*
Vijay Bagh ki Bawadi, Amer, Rajasthan *15*
Vijay Singh, Maharaja 194
Vikia Vav, Ghumli, Gujarat *68-69*, 69
Vishnu 17, 96

Wadhwan, Gujarat 70, *70-73*, 96
Wankaner, Gujarat 20
War of Independence, First (1857) 175, 202
Wazirpur Baoli, Delhi *90-93*, 91

Yamuna River 76

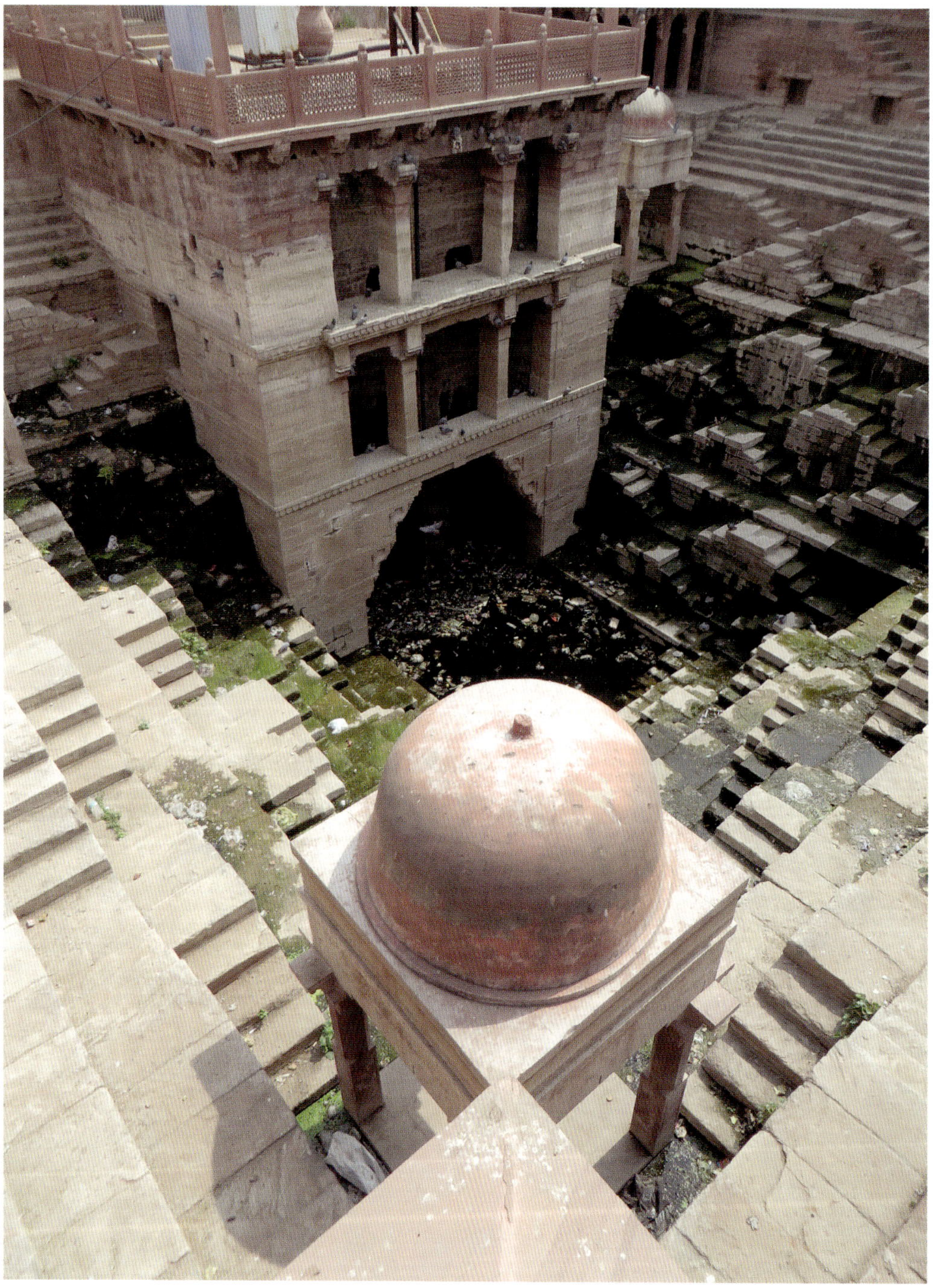